Eccentricity in Anthropology

Princeton Theological Monograph Series

K. C. Hanson, Charles M. Collier, D. Christopher Spinks,
and Robin A. Parry, Series Editors

Recent volumes in the series:

Nico Vorster
*The Brightest Mirror of God's Works:
John Calvin's Theological Anthropology*

Silje Kvamme Bjørndal
*The Church in a Secular Age: A Pneumatological
Reconstruction of Stanley Hauerwas's Ecclesiology*

Jeff McSwain
*Simul Sanctification: Barth's Hidden Vision
for Human Transformation*

Steven Underdown
*Living in the Eighth Day: The Christian Week
and the Paschal Mystery*

Jeffery L. Hamm
*Turning the Tables on Apologetics: Helmut Thielicke's
Reformation of Christian Conversation*

Riyako Cecilia Hikota
*And Still We Wait: Hans Urs von Balthasar's Theology
of Holy Saturday and Christian Discipleship*

Guillaume Bignon
*Excusing Sinners and Blaming God: A Calvinist Assessment of
Determinism, Moral Responsibility, and Divine Involvement in Evil*

Jeff McDonald
*John Gerstner and the Renewal of Presbyterian and
Reformed Evangelicalism in Modern America*

Eccentricity in Anthropology

David H. Kelsey's Anthropological Formula as a Way Out of the Substantive-Relational Imago Dei *Debate*

STEPHEN R. MILFORD

☙PICKWICK *Publications* • Eugene, Oregon

ECCENTRICITY IN ANTHROPOLOGY
David H. Kelsey's Anthropological Formula as a Way Out of the Substantive-Relational *Imago Dei* Debate

Princeton Theological Monograph Series 238

Copyright © 2019 Stephen R. Milford. All rights reserved. Except for brief quotations in critical publications or reviews, no part of this book may be reproduced in any manner without prior written permission from the publisher. Write: Permissions, Wipf and Stock Publishers, 199 W. 8th Ave., Suite 3, Eugene, OR 97401.

Pickwick Publications
An Imprint of Wipf and Stock Publishers
199 W. 8th Ave., Suite 3
Eugene, OR 97401

www.wipfandstock.com

PAPERBACK ISBN: 978-1-5326-6090-0
HARDCOVER ISBN: 978-1-5326-6091-7
EBOOK ISBN: 978-1-5326-6092-4

Cataloguing-in-Publication data:

Names: Milford, Stephen R., author.

Title: Eccentricity in anthropology : David H. Kelsey's anthropological formula as a way out of the substantive-relational *imago dei* debate / by Stephen R. Milford.

Description: Eugene, OR : Pickwick Publications, 2019 | Princeton Theological Monograph Series 238 | Includes bibliographical references.

Identifiers: ISBN 978-1-5326-6090-0 (paperback) | ISBN 978-1-5326-6091-7 (hardcover) | ISBN 978-1-5326-6092-4 (ebook)

Subjects: LCSH: Theological anthropology—Christianity. | Kelsey, David H.,—1937–. | Kelsey, David H.—Eccentric existence.

Classification: BT701.3 .M55 2019 (print) | BT701.3 .M55 (ebook)

Manufactured in the U.S.A.   06/06/19

For Aoife

Contents

Acknowledgments | xi

Introduction | 1

1. A Genuine Choice? | 7
   The Substantive Scheme 9
   The Relational Scheme 12
   Common Limitations 15
   One Question, One Answer 21

2. Kelsey's Postliberal Heritage | 27
   Three Postliberal Giants 28
       Paul Holmer (1916–2003) 30
       Hans Frei (1922–1988) 33
       George Lindbeck (1923–2018) 35
   A Postliberal Family Resemblance 41
       Preference for Narrative Theology 42
       Community-Orientated Hermeneutical Framework 45
       Pragmatic Epistemology 47
   Postliberalism, Truth, and Kelsey's Project 49

3. Buoys for Eccentric Existence | 53
   Sketching the Landscape 55
       EE: A Bird's-eye View 57
       Creedal Trinitarian Formulations in *EE* 60
   Eccentric Existence and the *Imago Dei* 67
       Against the Tradition: A Triple Helix *Imago Dei* 68

Eccentric Existence and the *Imago Dei* (continued)
    From General to Concrete: The Content of
    the *Imago Dei*   69
    Jesus: Image of God   71
    Human Being: Image of the Image of God   72
    Putting it All Together   75

4   An Anthropological Formula | 76
    Defining 'Formula'   76
    The Formulaic Elements   77
    The Structure of the Formula   80
    The Application of the Formula   82
    Strategy for Analyzing the Formula   85

5   Basic and Quotidian Identity | 89
    Identity: Enduring and Dynamic   91
    Identity and Eccentric Existence   94
        What Kelsey Is Not Asking   94
        The 'Who?' Question   96
        Identity: Basic and Quotidian   99
    Narrative Identity?   104
    The Gift and Vocation of Human Identity   109

6   Personal Identity | 112
    The Challenge of Persons   113
    Personal Identities, Not Identities of Persons   119
    A Trinitarian Anthropological Influence   122
    Creating Personal Identities in *EE*   128
    The Personal *Imago Dei*   131

7   Unsubstitutable Identity | 135
    The Challenge of Particularity   137
    Unsubstitutable Individuality   142
        Descriptive Dead Ends   143
        Limited Substitutability   146

      Concrete Singularity   147
      Unsubstitutable Individuality   149
   Imago Dei as God's Beloved   156
   Basic Unsubstitutable Personal Identities   157

8   Human Actuality | 160
   Possible, Potential, and Actual Human Beings   160
   Aristotle and Actuality   168
      The Priority of Actuality   168
      Actuality as *Energeia* and *Entelecheia*   170
      Two Important Connotations   175
   Elaborating on Human Actuality   178

9   Living Human Body | 183
   The Driving Force   184
   The Challenge to Human Embodiment:
   Resurrected Persons   192
      Embodied Resurrection   193
      Disembodied Resurrection   196
   A Third Proposal   199
   The Eschatological Continuity Question   204
   The *Imago Dei* as Non-dualistic Non-materialistic
   Living Human Body   207

Conclusion | 213
   What Is Offered   214
   Kelsey and the Limitations of the
   Substantive-Relational Debate   218
   A New Approach to the *Imago Dei*?   222

Bibliography | 229

Acknowledgments

It is true that the completion of a project of this nature is a long, lonely task defined by many hours of sitting in dusty libraries or in isolated contemplation. Nevertheless, the task cannot be completed without a great deal of support. As such, while the award may be individual, the accomplishment is corporate. I would therefore like to thank all those who have provided this much needed support over many years. Beyond the obvious divine intervention, the fact being so blatantly obvious it requires little mention, I wish to acknowledge the human. Credit must be given to the numerous people who have helped and encouraged me along the way: friends and fellow congregants. For example, Chris Brown for the PhD cover design. Even complete strangers were kind enough to help wherever possible. In particular Dr. Ariaan Baan, who freely gave his time for the Dutch translation of the summary.

Unsurprisingly, my family has been incredibly supportive. First and foremost, I note my parents who believed it was in me before I could see it in myself. Not only did they constantly encourage me to pursue this dream, but they often provided the financial means necessary. Their generosity has not gone unnoticed. Alongside my parents has been the constant, steadfast support of my wife. Although I had many moments of doubt, never for an instant did she display misgivings that I was capable of finishing this marathon. Often, I would wonder if she truly understood my limitations. On completion it is I who wonders whether I truly understood them myself.

Finally, I must thank my supervisors. The encouragement of Prof. dr. Benno van den Toren to join him at the Protestant Theological University is a key reason for the completion of this project. Although initially I had questions about studying in another country at a little-known institution (I confess my own ignorance here), my trust in Prof van den Toren was well placed and he has been an exceptional supervisor. His skill and dedication have been matched by Prof. dr. Rinse Reeling Brouwer who has provided invaluable insight. I cannot thank them both enough. They have supported me most excellently through every aspect of this project. As such, whatever failings exist this work are mine entirely.

Introduction

'Who am I?,' 'What am I?,' and 'How ought I to be?' are anthropological questions burning in the heart of every human being. For the Christian, the answer is often given in the form of two seemingly simple words: *imago Dei*. Over the last 2,000 years, numerous answers have been suggested as to what this enigmatic phrase actually means. Yet, as Douglas Hall eloquently states:

> Not everything that could be said about this symbol has been said . . . this "startling expression of the first chapter of Genesis" defies and transcends all of its historic explanations. It points toward a mystery of human identity that must be rediscovered by each generation of the believing community and worked out with regard to the specific problems and possibilities confronting that generation.[1]

In 2009, the Yale theologian David Kelsey offered this generation profound answers to anthropological questions raised by the Christian doctrine of the *imago Dei*. His proposals appear in a mammoth 1,051-page, two-volume project entitled *Eccentric Existence* (*EE*), a project that has been met with critical acclaim:

> This book will (or could and should) re-define theological anthropology for the next generation.[2]

> Without doubt, David Kelsey's *Eccentric Existence: A Theological Anthropology* (henceforth, *EE*) is one of the most significant and important contributions to the field of theology from this generation of theologians. . . . It is difficult to think of any comparable work in any area of theology in terms of both depth and scope in recent years; it is also difficult to think of any single work on theological anthropology throughout the history of Christian thought which engages with the singular topic so thoroughly and comprehensively. I cannot imagine any subsequent book on

---

1. Hall, *Imaging God*, 20; the internal quote is from Paul Ricoeur.
2. Buckley, "Buoys for Eccentric Existence," 15.

> this topic which would not engage in detail with Kelsey's work, and this is surely testimony to its significance. . . . It is surely now *the* standard primary text on theological anthropology.[3]

> David Kelsey's Eccentric Existence: A Theological Anthropology is an astonishing achievement. It is a feast of high quality thinking that requires a good deal of chewing but rewards with theological nourishment that is hard to equal in recent Christian thought. . . . [It] deserves to become a benchmark by which to assess contributions to theological anthropology for many years to come.[4]

The comments made in the quotations directly above are proving to be accurate as theologians take their time to digest *EE*. Indeed, we are starting to see secondary works that engage extensively with *EE*. For example, Gene Outka has recently edited a collection of responses to Kelsey's work.[5] These responses engage with Kelsey on topics as broad as ecclesiology, hamartiology, theological education and ecumenical dialogues. This is unsurprising considering that *EE* is immense in length and scope, so much so that John Thiel has termed it "a theological tour de force that defies categorization,"[6] while Charles Wood notes it is "at times a challenge to the reader's powers of endurance."[7] It is highly complex, multifaceted, intricate and idiosyncratic. Consider, for example, C. A. Morgan's experience of it:

> I find it difficult to engage Kelsey's argument on a single proposal. Each proposal is inseparable from the tightly woven fabric of the whole. The strength of this, of course, is that Kelsey shows the real complexity of the logic of Christian belief. However, his language is so precise and the distinctions so idiosyncratic to his own thinking (e.g., his typologies) that it is difficult to paraphrase him without misrepresenting him, or to adopt a proposed revision without engaging the entire work.[8]

So important do theologians deem *EE*, that the peer-reviewed journal *Modern Theology* devoted its entire January 2011 edition to a symposium

---

3. Greggs, "David Kelsey, Eccentric Existence," 449.

4. Ford, "What, How, and Who," 41. Also published with slight amendments as Ford, "Humanity Before God," 31.

5. Outka, *Theological Anthropology of David Kelsey*. Consider also McAnnally-Linz, "Extrinsic Grace and Eccentric Existence."

6. Thiel, "Methodological Choices," 1; cf. Craigo-Snell, "From Narrative to Performance," 147.

7. Wood, "Response to Eccentric Existence," 16.

8. Moran, "Review of Eccentric Existence," 53.

in its honor. This is only fitting considering the significance of Kelsey's project. He completed *EE* in his retirement, marking the culmination of a long and distinguished career by a leading theologian. It offers creative, unique and intriguing proposals that often go beyond binary debates such as conservative/liberal or pre-modern/modern (12).[9] Throughout our project, we see that *EE* presents us with a new way of doing theology; it is systematic and yet unsystematic (108–9), methodologically rich and yet free flowing,[10] focused and yet making allowances for extended in-depth discussions. An argument can be made that it is an important example of what a postliberal theology offers to the field of theological anthropology, going beyond mere discussions of the distinctiveness of postliberal methodology to its actual theologizing.[11]

These factors—its wide critical acclaim, its creativity, and its sophistication—justify our project, one that engages primarily with the proposals put forward by *EE*. This is not the first project to do so[12] and, in all likelihood, not the last.

Before we begin our discussions, some preliminary remarks must be made regarding our aims and methodology. Morgan's experience attunes us to two possible dangers when reading *EE*. The first is to take a single, or limited set of proposals out of the context of the whole. The second is the highly idiosyncratic nature of Kelsey's proposals that encourages in-depth critical evaluation which risks becoming very complex and lengthy in itself. To avoid both dangers, we must be specific with our objectives so as to select an appropriate topic within *EE* that takes cognizance of Kelsey's broader proposals but at the same time is manageable within a single thesis.

We can look to *EE* itself to identify just such a topic. Kelsey contends (in his final coda) that his proposals may be held together in a Christological interpretation of the image of God so as to "make a whole-in-complexity out of a set of unsystematically related anthropological proposals by providing a framework within which they can be ordered to one another in a single,

---

9. During the course of this project, we will follow Tom Greggs's referencing of *EE*. As such, all in-text citations of page numbers are to *EE*. See Greggs, "David Kelsey, Eccentric Existence."

10. Kelsey uses A and B chapters to distinguish the two.

11. Lindbeck, in *Nature of Doctrine*, concludes by questioning whether the postliberal project will be pursued. He states that there is much talk but "little actual performance" (Lindbeck, *Nature of Doctrine*, 135). It is arguable that his Yale colleague has here performed, although one wonders if Kelsey is included in the "younger theologians" about whom Lindbeck longingly exclaims, "May their tribe increase." See Lindbeck, *Nature of Doctrine*, 135.

12. Marais, "Eccentric Existence?" The focus of Marais's thesis, being that of ecotheology, is entirely different from the project at hand.

coherent theocentric picture of human being" (896). Focusing our attention on Kelsey's understanding of a theocentric picture of human beings in the image of God enables us to draw out some key anthropological themes that are on the one hand intertwined with his broader project and on the other hand focused enough to engage with in the space allotted us here.

The *imago Dei* cannot be taken without due cognizance of wider Christian discussions. As chapter 1 demonstrates, that wider debate is often presented in the form of two mutually exclusive schemes: the substantive or relational. We see that this debate presents us with a counterfeit choice between these two proposals. Although at first they appear distinct, on closer inspection we see that they make use of a similar approach to the questions surrounding the *imago Dei*. As a result, they present answers that are similarly shaped and subject to the same limitations. Is it possible that the unique, creative and postliberal approach offered by *EE* might help us get past these schemes, reshaping not only the answers but the questions themselves?

If Kelsey is to do this, we need to pay attention to *EE*'s particular "tone of voice" (9–10). Kelsey argues that *EE* "seeks to promote and provoke further exploration of the issues and further discussion, rather than assert conversation-stopper pronouncements of what Christians must say on a given topic" (10). He goes on to argue that his project is "in the hypothetical mode" (9). As such, he urges us not to take his proposals uncritically, but to take them as a springboard for further discussion and debate. He encourages us to be active participants in this conversation. Therefore, it is only right that we are both critical and constructive in our engagement with *EE*. That is, we should be critical in the sense of questioning his proposals in terms of their relation to the biblical witness, other Christian thinkers and their internal coherence and constructive in terms of interpreting and reinterpreting his proposals in light of broader debates on relevant topics.

When all this is considered, our aim is to constructively and critically evaluate Kelsey's description of the human being as the image of God in order to take the conversations surrounding the *imago Dei* beyond the substantive-relational debate. With this in mind, one may read our project in two ways. On the one hand, it can be read as a discussion of systematic theology, that is to say, as part of the debates surrounding the *imago Dei* and theological anthropology more broadly. On the other hand, it may be read as a work in contemporary historical theology. Its primary dialogue partner is an important theologian of the twentieth and twenty-first centuries, whose career has culminated in one of the most significant works of theological anthropology for a generation. Our project is, in many respects, a critical commentary on an important aspect of this theologian's life work.

We begin our discussions by critically evaluating the current state of debate within theological anthropology and, in particular, within the doctrine of the *imago Dei*. Here we demonstrate that the current state involves two opposing mutually exclusive dialogue partners that are so ingrained in our thinking that it is almost impossible to conceive of the *imago Dei* without appealing to one or the other. Yet, we also demonstrate that their views are based on a common approach and as such open to serious common limitations. Therefore, there arises a need to move past this debate. It is against this backdrop, set out in chapter 1 of our project, that critical comparative conversations between *EE* and wider sources are played out so as to find a path beyond the substantive-relational schemes.

Since *EE* is relatively new to the debate (less than a decade old) and, as has been noted, is highly complex, it is necessary to gain a firm grasp of both its author and its overall content. We dedicate three chapters to this task so as to lay the foundation upon which Kelsey's description of human beings as the image of God can be evaluated in our project. The first of these three chapters is chapter 2 which evaluates Kelsey's postliberal heritage, offering insight into the landscape in which *EE* is orientated. Chapter 3, on the other hand, provides an overview of *EE* itself so as to familiarize the reader with the broad framework on which Kelsey's construction of the image of God sits. Here the reader is attuned to *EE*'s central claim: human beings have their entire being extrinsically rooted. This is the reason our project is entitled *Eccentricity in Anthropology*.

In chapter 4, we turn our focus to the core theme of our thesis. In this chapter we demonstrate that Kelsey describes human beings as images of the image of God by making use of an anthropological formula. His argument is that human beings image God simply by being what they are: *basic unsubstitutable identities of actual living human personal bodies*. Our methodological approach in critically analyzing this formula is to divide it into five sub-terms and dedicate extensive discussions to each term so as to consider its relation to Kelsey's doctrine of the *imago Dei* against the backdrop of the substantive-relational debate.[13]

Chapters 5 to 9 critically and constructively consider each of the sub-terms individually. In these chapters, whenever possible, we focus on one or two important questions or issues applicable to the relevant sub-term. This requires a comparative discussion of theological and philosophical issues raised by the sub-term in question. Following this discussion, we engage in a critical comparative conversation about Kelsey and these

---

13. The relation between each of these terms are expounded on in chapter 4 of our project.

broader discussions. In order to treat Kelsey's proposals properly, we need to engage in detailed analysis of his construction, specific interests, idiosyncrasies and the sources he relies on. This critical comparative conversation between Kelsey and wider theological debates enables us to provide a constructive interpretation of *EE*'s proposals. As such, chapters 5 to 9 each conclude by bringing our constructive interpretation into dialogue with the substantive-relational debate. In particular, we consider how it is that Kelsey's proposals offer ways of conceiving of the *imago Dei* that are hospitable to both substantive and relational concerns and at the same time steer the conversation in new directions.

We conclude our project by considering the overall implications of our discussions. In that section, we reflect on Kelsey's eccentric approach in light of the substantive-relational debate, how it addresses concerns held by both sides, how it differs from their constructions and, ultimately, how it refuels and steers the debate toward new understandings of the *imago Dei*. It is for this reason that we have chosen the subtitle *Kelsey's Anthropological Formula as a Way Out of the Substantive-Relational Imago Dei Debate*.

I

A Genuine Choice?

THROUGHOUT CHRISTIAN THEOLOGY'S LONG history, the answer to the question 'What is the human being?' has often been given, consciously or unconsciously, within the context of the doctrine of the *imago Dei*. This phrase has been used as a categorical marker, that is to say, as "some essential structural feature of human beings that constitutes them as distinctively human and distinguishes them from animals who do not exhibit God's image" (895).[1] The term has been taken to speak to the very essence of humanity:[2] the *humanum*[3] or *vere Homo*.[4] Ray Anderson goes so far as to say that the bestowal of the image of God bestows humanity itself.[5] As such, the doctrine's importance cannot be overemphasized. To many, the position taken on the *imago Dei* has ramifications for every other area of Christian belief[6] and for the very meaning and value of humanity itself. In the words of Pope John Paul II:

> Man[7] has meaning in this world only as the image and likeness of God. Otherwise, he has no meaning and we might be led to say, as some people have done, that man is nothing but 'useless suffering.'[8]

1. Greggs, "David Kelsey, Eccentric Existence," 45.
2. Hughes, *True Image*, 4.
3. Anderson, *On Being Human*, 70.
4. Hall, *Imaging God*, 61.
5. Anderson, *On Being Human*, 70.
6. Many theologians are in agreement here. For just some examples, see Anderson, *On Being Human*, 70; Feinberg, "Image of God," 236; Clines, "Image of God in Man," 53; Hoekema, *Created in God's Image*, 1; Hughes, *True Image*, 4.
7. During the course of this work, when referring to the 'doctrine of man,' we do so with the gender-neutral interpretation of 'man' in mind. Along with Hoekema, we lament that the English language has no English word that corresponds to the German '*mensch*.' See Hoekema, *Created in God's Image*, 1. Since a great deal of the writing refers to the 'doctrine of man' and to 'man' in general (irrespective of gender), it would be cumbersome to adjust this traditional terminology. We do, however, use inclusive language wherever possible.
8. John Paul II, "Homily for the Mass at Bourget," 585. See also Schönborn, *Man*, 42.

It is no surprise, then, that the doctrine of the image of God has been widely debated with numerous proposals put forward regarding the exact meaning of the term '*imago Dei.*' Suggestions range from humanity's rationality to free will,[9] from the physical body[10] to human dominion over creation.[11] The sheer volume of work makes it almost impossible to produce even a summary of these varying proposals.[12] In fact, there is no agreement as to how many unique proposals exist and their individual historical and contextual developments.[13]

The reader will be relieved to learn that this chapter makes no attempt to produce this elusive definitive summary. As David Cairns laments, such a summary would "be in danger of confusing the reader, who would find the account disjointed."[14] Yet it is the task of the theologian to make sense of this doctrine, for to fail to do so would be to fail, as Pope John Paul II has suggested, to find meaning and purpose for the human condition. Such a failure, in the words of J. Edward Barrett, would be "an act of theological irresponsibility."[15]

With this in mind, this chapter concerns itself with what are widely considered to be the two broad categories into which most (if not all) theological positions regarding this doctrine fall: the substantive and relational.[16]

9. Berkhof, *Systematic Theology*, 202.

10. See, for example, Berkouwer, who calls on van Rad and Bavinck for support (Berkouwer, *Man*, 74–81).

11. This is Cline's ultimate contention. See Clines, "Image of God in Man," 250. It is also the contention of Middleton, *Liberating Image*, 15–90. Van den Toren understands this to be a misinterpretation of the biblical understanding based on a modernist, and subsequent postmodernist, subject-object dualism. Rather, he refers to the "cultural mandate" to make the world "liveable" and in this way fill and subdue it within clear limitations. See van den Toren, *Christian Apologetics*, 96–100.

12. An analysis of the summaries produced over the last 50 years clearly demonstrates this point. See Berkhof, *Systematic Theology*, 202–5; Culver, *Systematic Theology*, 248–57; Hoekema, *Created in God's Image*, 33–65; Overstreet, "Man in the Image," 44–58.

13. Grenz, *Social God*, 141–42. See also Cairns, *Image of God in Man*, 71; Towner, "Clones of God," 343–44.

14. Cairns, *Image of God in Man*, 71.

15. Barrett, "Theology of the Meaning," 172.

16. This categorical approach is well established, first proposed by Ramsey in Ramsey, *Basic Christian Ethics*, 249–84. It is used by numerous theologians such as Berkouwer, *Man*, 70–71; Bridger, "Humanity," 21–27; Cairns, *Image of God in Man*, 20; Clines, "Image of God in Man," 55; Fergusson, "Humans Created," 440–45; Grenz, *Social God*, 142; Hall, *Imaging God*, 88–112. As we have noted, there have been innumerable theories put forward, but most of these are assimilated into either the substantive or relational. For example, Grenz includes a telic category and yet is adamant that such a conception is but "one aspect of a constellation of themes that focus on a communal

These two categories are often presented as two mutually exclusive choices[17] in answer to the questions surrounding the *imago Dei*. The question this chapter considers is whether or not the substantive-relational debate does indeed present us with two viable yet conflicting alternatives to the anthropological 'What?' question, or if in fact this debate presents a counterfeit choice between two positions which, while being approached from different "mindsets,"[18] represent similar answers in different theological garb.

The Substantive Scheme

The substantive view, held by the majority of historical thinkers (895–97),[19] is perhaps the best known.[20] Hall argues that it is impossible to think of the *imago Dei* without referring to this view, if only subconsciously.[21] It remains deeply entrenched in protestant evangelical theology and is still very much current.[22] The central tenet of this view is that the image of God is found within the very essence of *anthropos*. The very substance[23] of the species known as *Homo sapiens* contains, in some form or another, the image of

---

understanding of relationality" (Grenz, *Social God*, 182). In recent years, a functionalist view has been proposed. Included as a third category in Erickson (which he ultimately rejects), the functionalist approach connects the *imago Dei* with the notion of humanity's dominion over creation. Human beings image God as they perform this function. See Erickson, *Christian Theology*, 527–29, 530–31; *Introducing Christian Theology*, 172–78. Fergusson is unconvinced the functionalist view offers a viable alternative. Although it may help to make sense of the context of Genesis 1:26–27, it invariably "shifts the problems rather than resolve them. The issue of which functions are exclusively performed by human beings is not readily discerned in Genesis" (Fergusson, "Humans Created," 445). Hall's work demonstrates that the functional view is very much within the relational category. See Hall, *Imaging God*, 106–7.

17. See, as examples, Grenz, *Social God*, 141–82; Hall, *Imaging God*, 89–108. Berkouwer makes direct reference to this choice and yet urges us not to make it. See Berkouwer, *Man*, 100–101.

18. A term used by Hall. See Hall, *Imaging God*, 98.

19. See also Hall, *Imaging God*, 89.

20. Grenz, *Social God*, 142.

21. Hall, *Imaging God*, 92.

22. Erickson, *Christian Theology*, 532; Grenz, "Jesus as the Imago Dei," 624; Grudem, *Systematic Theology*, 442–50. Grudem does acknowledge the relational aspects, albeit very briefly. See Grudem, *Systematic Theology*, 447–48; Visala, "Imago Dei."

23. The use of 'substance' is open to debate. In effect, authors of this view claim that the *imago Dei* is an inherent, integral part of the human being that cannot be removed from humanity, hence the term 'substantive.' Throughout our project, we understand substance in this vein, that is, an attribute/entity/thing that is capable of existing by itself without reference to relationality. See as an example of this use Harrison, "Embodiment of Mind," 35.

God. Thus, *Homo sapiens* possess certain "characteristics," "qualities," "capacities," "original excellences" or "endowments."[24] Since these attributes resemble corresponding qualities that one considers to be found in the Godhead, "their possession makes humans like God."[25]

The most widely held account puts forward human rationality as the cardinal characteristic. According to Stanley Grenz, the origin of this understanding may be found not in the biblical texts themselves but in the context of early Christianity. The early church fathers grappled with the Greek philosophical tradition and, following an Aristotelian structure of defining objects *per genius proximum et differentiam*, defined human beings as "the rational animal."[26] Human reason was considered the divine spark, which was later extended to include human will and volition (considered by many as two aspects of the single rationality with which God endowed human beings).[27] Grenz notes that this approach was so widely accepted in early church history that church fathers (both in the East and the West) took for granted that the human person was just such a rational animal.[28]

Edmund Hill argues that under Augustine's[29] teaching on the rational human soul, particularly as it images the Trinity in the three faculties of memory, intellect and will, the structural view flourished. Augustine's teaching became the standard interpretation in the theology of the medieval Western church, and it was this teaching that was adopted and adapted by Aquinas.[30] It is Grenz's contention that while Augustine was Aquinas' theological father, Aristotle was his philosophical mentor, and through a recasting of the Augustinian deposit in light of Aristotle's philosophy, Aquinas concluded that only intellectual creatures (specifically angels and humans) were made in God's image.[31]

24. Hall, *Imaging God*, 89.

25. Grenz, *Social God*, 142.

26. Grenz, *Social God*, 143. For a summary of Greek influence on patristic writers on the *imago Dei* see Hill, *Being Human*, 202.

27. Grenz, *Social God*, 144.

28. Grenz, *Social God*, 143–44.

29. At various times during the course of this project, we note authors who reference well-known thinkers (historical, contemporary, theological and philosophical). In this we are relying on others' interpretations of those original thinkers. We are aware of the dangers of this practice, in particular that these interpretations may be controversial. However, rather than risking the conversation slipping into debates about the interpretation of third-party thinkers, we keep our focus on the central points at hand, that is the points being made by the authors we reference directly, irrespective of their particular interpretation of third-party thinkers.

30. Hill, *Being Human*, 209–12. According to Grenz, this view became "the most influential anthropology" of the western church (Grenz, *Social God*, 158).

31. Grenz, *Social God*, 156–58.

Aquinas's theology developed a highly intellect-focused understanding of the divine image. Grenz argues that Aquinas believed God placed within the soul of every person the intellectual faculty as a natural capacity.[32] As a universally present structural quality of every human being, humans actually are the image of God. This image cannot be lost or destroyed, not even by the fall.[33]

It is this aspect—the universality of the image of God within every human being—that is the primary concern for substantive thinkers and offers the greatest lure for those eager to affirm universal human rights. If Christians are to assent to the concept of human rights—and there is much evidence that the vast majority of Christianity upholds this view[34]—then a universal human attribute must be identified as the basis for such an ontology, an ontology which ascribes to human creatures such a radical distinction from the rest of creation.

Since the doctrine of the *imago Dei* has acted as the "convergence of all Christian declarations about human rights,"[35] the implied universality of the substantive position is an attractive option. In affirming a universally present *imago Dei*, substantialistic thinkers attempt to establish and uphold the universal dignity and value of human beings everywhere, and in so doing establish the foundation upon which universal, inalienable human rights are built.

Yet the substantive concern to find this universally present distinctive human element is not always successful. It is a well-known fact that many human beings do not always display attributes such as rationality. Infants, those in comas and those with severe disabilities, to name but a few, display limited intellectual capabilities. In these cases, the universality of the substantive position is in question, and as a consequence the foundation of

---

32. Grenz, *Social God*, 161.

33. Much has been written about the relationship between the *imago Dei* and the Fall. For a good summary, see Anderson, *On Being Human*, 77; Berkouwer, *Man*, 119–48; Cairns, *Image of God in Man*, 20–23; Hoekema, *Created in God's Image*, 11–19. These authors argue convincingly against the loss of the image of God at the fall.

34. Some theologians have objected to the concept of human rights, with the most well-known being Hauerwas (see Hauerwas, "Politics of Justice," 45–68). Others maintain that the concept of human rights themselves is explicitly rooted in Christian beliefs. See Moltmann, *On Human Dignity*, 12. See also Tergel, "Human Rights and the Churches"; Cahill, "Toward a Christian Theory."

35. Moltmann, *On Human Dignity*, 12. Supported by Tergel, "Human Rights and the Churches"; Cahill, "Toward a Christian Theory." See also Scorer, *Life in Our Hands*, 158. Kelsey has pointed to the fact that Kant's secular approach verges on a doctrine of the *imago Dei* (Kelsey, *Eccentric Existence*, 277).

human dignity and value. We have more to say about this shortly, but for now let us consider the counter-scheme.

The Relational Scheme

The relational view may be considered relatively new to the debate.[36] Although some have argued that the origins of relational understandings lie in Augustine,[37] there is general acknowledgement that it is in Reformation thinkers where the relational view took root in earnest.[38] The reason for the move away from the medieval Aquinian substantive position is disputed. Cairns, for example, claims that Luther was afraid of the substantive view because it threatened his doctrine of *sola gratia*. If the image of God is to be found structurally within the human being, so Luther believed, it would imply that all human beings, at least in part, were universally valuable/worthy and therefore do not require grace for salvation.[39] Others have noted that while Luther did not openly stress the relational view, Calvin expressly taught it.[40] Cairns goes so far as to say that no other theologian since Augustine gave as much attention to the doctrine of the *imago Dei* as Calvin.[41] Building on what Augustine alludes to in *On the Trinity*, Calvin takes the metaphor of mirror and makes it central to his theology of the divine image. Using this metaphor, Calvin builds on a dynamic ontology of existence by expounding on the divine image as the act of mirroring God.[42] In this way, the image is not seen as something human beings possess, but something human beings have the potential to enact.[43]

---

36. Shults, *Reforming Theological Anthropology*, 124.

37. For different readings of Augustine in this regard, see Hall, *Imaging God*, 219n4, 219n22. Here Hall disagrees with Ramsey, who considers Augustine relational. Grenz has noted that, "The concept of the *imago Dei* that emerged from Augustine's reflections was sufficiently complex and many-sided so as to set the stage both for the triumph of the structural understanding in the Middle Ages and for its demise in the Reformation" (Grenz, *Social God*, 152).

38. Hall, *Imaging God*, 81, 101. Also see Pannenberg, *Anthropology in Theological Perspective*, 50. Calvin in particular is very influential in this regard, see Cairns, *Image of God in Man*, 128–45; Grenz, *Social God*, 166–70; Torrance, *Calvin's Doctrine of Man*.

39. Cairns, *Image of God in Man*, 121–27. For other opinions on Luther's relational view and his motives see Hall, *Imaging God*, 98–99. Grenz briefly documents Luther's move toward a relational position, see Grenz, *Social God*, 162–64.

40. Hall, *Imaging God*, 99. See also Grenz, *Social God*, 166–70.

41. Cairns, *Image of God in Man*, 144. See also Grenz, *Social God*, 166; Hall, *Imaging God*, 101.

42. Grenz, *Social God*, 166–67. Also see Augustine, *On the Trinity*, 15.8.4.

43. It should be noted here that Grenz contends that Calvin and the reformers were

What the reformers began so many years ago has, in recent times, begun to take root and flourish. The past century's emphasis on a social Trinitarian Theo-ontology[44] and the recent turn to relationality as a fundamental basis for ontology[45] have contributed greatly to the contemporary understanding of the *imago Dei* and Christian anthropology as a whole. Against the background of just such a turn in Christian theology, theologians such as Grenz are able to claim that there is a "near consensus that person is a relational concept"[46] and that, therefore, Christian anthropology should consider the *imago Dei* relationally rather than substantively.[47] In the West, a number of key thinkers have emerged in support of just such a claim. If one considers, for example, the work of Karl Barth,[48] G. C. Berkouwer,[49] Hall[50] and Grenz,[51] there is ample evidence to claim that, while the substantive view has hardly disappeared, the relational view has become very popular.

Rather than seeking the answers to the questions surrounding the *imago Dei* in endowments, gifts or capacities (which Hall believes are means to an end rather than ends themselves[52]), relational thinkers appeal to the inclination and proclivity in the human being toward relationality, particularly the relationship between God and mankind.[53] This is, according to the relational camp, the definitive feature that separates human beings from the rest of creation:

> Hence there is no point in asking in which of man's peculiar attributes and attitudes it [the image] consists. It does not consist in anything that man is. . . . He [God] willed the existence of a being which in all its non-deity and therefore its differentiation

---

unable to fully dislodge the substantive view from the doctrine of the image of God and subsequent centuries continued to display a preference for the rationally conceived Aquinian view. For a discussion on how and why this is so, see Grenz, *Social God*, 170–77.

44. See Grenz, *Social God*, 3–9. It should be noted, however, that not all relational thinkers affirm a social Trinitarianism.

45. For a discussion of this turn, see Shults, *Reforming Theological Anthropology*; cf. Kelsey, "Reforming Theological Anthropology."

46. Grenz, *Social God*, 9. We discuss the concept of person during the course of our project in its own chapter.

47. Grenz, *Social God*, 9.

48. Barth, *CD* 3/1:184–85.

49. See Berkouwer, *Man*.

50. See Hall, *Imaging God*.

51. See Grenz, *Social God*.

52. Hall, *Imaging God*, 107.

53. Hall, *Imaging God*, 98; van den Toren, *Christian Apologetics*, 106–18.

can be a real partner; which is capable of action and responsibility in relation to him; to which his own divine form of life is not alien; which in a creaturely repetition, as a copy and imitation, can be a bearer of this form of life.[54]

Using the metaphor of a mirror, relational thinkers consider the image of God not as something which is static (gifted to the human being) but which is dynamic (the vocation of the human being).[55] Such thinkers use the word 'image' as a verb[56] to indicate that which happens as the human being is orientated to God as a mirror is turned to an object.[57] The image of God is not that which the human being is, but that which the human being does and develops into as they turn to God (and particularly to Jesus) in responsive relationship.[58] The ultimate fulfilling of this image awaits eschatological consummation when the human being can reflect God unimpeded.[59]

The value of relational thinking lies in its dynamic ontology. Rather than viewing human existence from a static perspective, whereby the human being is simply gifted their essential nature, relational thinkers call on the human being as a responsible counterpart to God.[60] Human beings are human as they fulfil this role, hence the inclusion of the functionalist category within the relational.[61]

Relational thinkers argue that a dynamic ontology roots itself within Christology[62] better than a static ontology, which may refer to the *imago Dei* with very little reference to Christology. A Christian dynamic ontology conceives of Jesus Christ as the *imago Dei par excellence*[63] and, as such, the perfect model to imitate in relational engagement with God.[64] It is as the

54. Barth, CD 3/1:184–85.

55. See, as examples, Hoekema, *Created in God's Image*, 40; Torrance, *Persons in Communion*, 153, 189.

56. This is particularly evident in Hall. See, for example, Hall, *Imaging God*, 98.

57. Hall, *Imaging God*, 98–108.

58. This is one interpretation of Barth. See Barth, CD 3/1:184–206.

59. This is a central argument in Grenz's work. See Grenz, *Social God*, 224. For examples, see also Berkouwer, *Man*, 111; Hall, *Imaging God*, 82; Hoekema, *Created in God's Image*, 24–30; Jewett and Shuster, *God, Creation, and Revelation*, 492.

60. Barth, CD 3/1:185; Hall, *Imaging God*, 98; Torrance, *Persons in Communion*, 189–90.

61. See footnote 16 of this chapter.

62. See, for example, Grenz's contention that Christology is the central theological informing locus (Grenz, "Jesus as the Imago Dei," 627–28).

63. Hoekema, *Created in God's Image*, 73. See also Volf, *After Our Likeness*, 84.

64. Barth, CD 3/1:135–36; Berkouwer, *Man*, 107; Brunner, *Dogmatics*, 2:58–59; Grenz, "Jesus as the Imago Dei," 619–28; Hughes, *True Image*, 253; Pittenger, *Christian Understanding*, 31.

human being engages in responsible relationship with Christ (who is God) that they image God. Christ plays a dual role within this construction: as the *imago Dei par excellence* he is the perfect reflection of God, and at the same time, as God, he is the object being reflected.[65]

In Erickson's words, "The relational view has correctly seized upon the truth that the human alone, of all the creatures, knows and is consciously related to God."[66] Unlike a piece of art or statue that exists only to display the creator's creativity and wisdom, human beings have a vocation. This picture of humanity's value lying in God's special, relational vocation is, as Millard Erickson highlights, very attractive.[67]

However, as with the substantive, there are many instances within the human community of those who are unable either to attain the requisite relationality or to develop dynamically into such relationality. This is the case in numerous medical diagnoses such as autism, which partly indicates the inability of individuals to exhibit important aspects of human relationality but also in the case of those—who as a result of misfortune—are severely impaired. Instances such as these raise questions as to the viability of both the relational and substantive schemes. Indeed, on closer inspection it becomes apparent that these are not the only limitations.

Common Limitations

While the substantive and relational camps each offer value to the debate surrounding the image of God, they are both open to common limitations. In particular, their respective positions are open to five charges:

1) *Baptized in contemporary culture*. Relational theologians have argued that substantive positions tend to embrace values and attributes that are particular to their unique culture. Hall terms this phenomenon the "baptizing" of the doctrine of the *imago Dei* in "qualities lauded by the dominant culture of one's society."[68] The phenomenon is so widely acknowledged that Hendrikus Berkhof claims that "by studying how systematic theologies have poured meaning into Genesis 1:26, one could write a piece of Europe's cultural history."[69] According to relational thinkers, such 'bap-

---

65. Barth, *CD* 3/1:189. This mimics Barth's doctrine of election in which Christ is the elector and the elected. See Barth, *CD* 2/1:3–194.

66. Erickson, *Christian Theology*, 530. It should be noted, however, that Erickson remains very much substantive. See Erickson, *Christian Theology*, 532.

67. Erickson, *Christian Theology*, 529–30.

68. Hall, *Imaging God*, 91–92.

69. Berkhof, *Christian Faith*, 179. See also Hall, *Imaging God*, 91; Grenz, *Social God*, 143.

tizing' of the *imago Dei* in the host culture is problematic as it distorts the original meaning of the text. For example, those who speak of the rationality of the human being speak almost exclusively of Western rationality rooted in Greek philosophy. There is very little mention of the intellectual powers of alternate logic systems whose rationality may not always follow the classical Greco-Roman world view. Hall contends that it would not be difficult to demonstrate that Western rationality is far removed from anything the ancient author of Genesis 1:26 could have thought.[70]

Although relational thinkers slight the substantive camp for 'baptizing' notions of the *imago Dei* in their respective contemporary cultures, relational views unwittingly fall into the same trap. The past few centuries, and in particular the last few decades, have seen a "turn to relationality"[71] and a revival of the social Trinity.[72] It may be argued that relationality is a value held specifically by our contemporary culture. If such baptizing, according to relational thinkers, questions the authenticity of the tenets of the substantive position, are we not forced to question the tenets of the relational camp as well?

2) *A questionable universality.* Although the intention of substantive thinkers may be to establish a universality to the human condition, relational thinkers have argued that the effect of the substantive position is far from universal. The tendency of substantive thinkers to focus on a single, or limited, set of attributes often questions the ontological status of a large portion of the human population. For example, if one were to say that rationality is the defining characteristic of the image of God, what of those who are challenged in this respect? Put another way, if—as Christian theology has often proposed—the foundation of human dignity and value is the presence of the image of God,[73] and with it the definitive features of this image, then do those who fail to demonstrate such features have human dignity, value and the associated rights? The debates along these themes are well known.

Hall states it eloquently when he says:

---

70. Hall, *Imaging God*, 91. See also Schönborn, *Man*, 49. Clough has argued that problems with defining the exact type of necessary rationality has been so fraught with difficulty that some philosophers have gone so far as to define it in terms of humanity. For example, Jonathan Bennett defines 'rationality' to mean "whatever it is that humans possess which marks them off, in respect of intellectual capacity, sharply and importantly from all other known species." See Clough, "Not a Not-Animal," 13.

71. See Shults, *Reforming Theological Anthropology*.

72. See Grenz, *Social God*. This work speaks of a Theo-ontology in light of social Trinitarianism.

73. See, for example, Moltmann, *On Human Dignity*, 12. Backed up by Tergel, "Human Rights"; Cahill, "Toward a Christian Theory."

> If we look for the essence of the human in rationality, for instance, we automatically assume a hierarchical structuring of the world and must relegate all creations that do not possess the subtlety and skill of human reasoning to lower strata on the ladder of being.... One could speculate endlessly on how much damage has been done to children, to the mentally handicapped, and to the uneducated and illiterate in Western civilization on account of this avowedly 'Christian' practice of identifying the highest and best—the truly human!—with rationality.[74]

Relational thinkers such as Hall appear to make a stronger case for the universality of the image of God by appealing to relationality, and yet, on closer inspection, it becomes clear that they are appealing to the potential of such an image rather than the image itself. Relational insistence on the developmental features of the *imago Dei* results in the very same dichotomization of the human race as relational thinkers accuse substantive thinkers of making. The image of God, within this construction, is a "privilege of believers."[75] Individuals who fail to develop the necessary relationship with God fail to image God and, as a result, are dehumanized. Such individuals (and indeed entire societies) have, in the past, been referred to within relational literature as "subhuman," "inhuman,"[76] "dehuman"[77] and, in the case of Calvin, "double beasts."[78]

Although it is arguable that recent relational literature would shun such claims, there is evidence that even they are not entirely able to avoid the connotation of dividing the human community into those who image God and those who do not. Recent relational thinkers have pointed to the *eschaton* as the ultimate fulfilment of human relationality. This is an attempt within the relational scheme to point to a possible state in which all human beings will image God. Yet the result of such thinking does not solve the problem of human universality this side of the *eschaton*. Kelsey, speaking particularly about Grenz's eschatologically focused relational anthropology, finds the theological consequences of his position "very troubling" (904).[79] Kelsey's argument is that if human beings are only truly human at the *eschaton* (when the relationship between them and their creator finds absolute fulfilment[80]), then why treat human beings with respect here and now?

74. Hall, *Imaging God*, 108–9.
75. Berkouwer, *Man*, 106. See also Erickson, *Christian Theology*, 530.
76. Horst, "Face to Face," 267.
77. Hughes, *True Image*, 4.
78. Torrance, *Calvin's Doctrine of Man*, 73–81.
79. See also Kelsey, "Human Creature," 130; cf. Grenz, *Social God*, pt. 2.
80. Indeed, it does not solve the problem even at the eschaton. In a non-universalist scheme, presumably only some humans will image God.

3) *A non-holistic dualism*. The effect of selecting culturally relevant attributes as the basis of the *imago Dei* results in establishing a non-holistic form of dualism within the human being. The human being is treated as an object whose essential nature may be distilled and reduced to a single core feature that retains, in its own right, the image of God and, with it, the *humanum*.[81] Other features of human existence, the by-products of this distillation, are thrown by the wayside. We will refer to this approach as negative reductionism: the distillation of the human being into a single or limited set of features that is abstracted from the concrete human being and taken as the basis of the image of God. Such an approach has been common in substantively conceived body-soul dualism. Here, the non-physical soul is the root of the image of God and, as such, is the foundation upon which human dignity and value is built. The body is merely a temporary container that will ultimately wither and perish; its value is limited. Such an approach dichotomizes the human being into two co-existent yet unequal parts: those that are and are not incorporated in the *imago Dei*.

Although there are a few voices who affirm physical attributes as part of the *imago Dei*,[82] in general theologians have emphasized the non-physical. Aquinas,[83] Calvin,[84] Eichrodt[85] and Hodge,[86] to name a few, all deny that the physical body is part of the *imago Dei*. Hall clearly notes this limitation:

> As one reads the theology of the *imago Dei* in historical documents of this doctrine one gets the impression that there is a concerted polemic against the entire physical side of human reality almost as if one should be ashamed of being found 'in the body.' . . . It is certainly not the physical side of human being that most Christian commentators concentrate on in their

---

81. The insistence on rationality, for example, as the definitive attribute of the *imago Dei* has led some theologians to claim that other creatures were created in the image of God, namely angels. See, for example, Aquinas, *ST* 1.93.2.

82. For a good discussion on those who affirm the physical body as integral to the *imago Dei* (such as van Rad and Bavinck), see Berkouwer, *Man*, 74–81. Visala has attempted to incorporate the physical body into the substantive view. However, he ultimately concludes that the image of God is to be found in non-physical mental properties. Here he argues for property dualism rather than substantive dualism. Although he attempts to establish the physical as important to the non-physical, one is unconvinced that his appeal solely to the non-physical as the *imago Dei* does not, even if only unconsciously or slightly, diminish the physical. See Visala, "Imago Dei."

83. Aquinas, *ST* 1.93.6.

84. See Cairns, *Image of God in Man*, 75. See also Calvin, "Psychopannychia," 422–23.

85. See Berkouwer, *Man*, 74–75.

86. Hodge, *Systematic Theology*, 96.

interpretations of the image of God. Both in Catholic and in Protestant (especially neo-Protestant) doctrine, the obvious associations with the *imago Dei* are what would normally be identified as 'spiritual' characteristics.[87]

Hall's contention seems to be valid, especially when one reads theologians such as Hodge, who claims:

> God is Spirit, the human soul is a spirit. The essential attributes of a spirit are reason, conscience and will. A spirit is a rational, moral, and therefore also, a free agent. In making man after his own image, therefore, God endowed him with those attributes which belong to his own nature as a spirit.[88]

The non-physical is often seen as "higher," "nobler," "loftier" or "better"[89] than the physical, thereby being elevated at the expense of the physical. The consequences of such elevations are far reaching. It is well-known that within Christianity the body has, at times, been viewed with about as much respect as the cardboard packaging of cheap takeaway.

Yet the relational camp does not appear to solve the problem. Although objecting to the classical metaphysical view of body-soul dualism, by appealing to the relationality of the human being as the definitive feature of the image of God, the relational camp distils the essential feature of humanity to a single non-physical property within the human being. Although not substantively dualistic, this view represents a non-holistic property dualism.[90] The consequence is yet again an appeal to a single non-physical aspect of human being that epitomizes the image of God with other human features implicitly devalued.[91] At its extremes, such an approach defines humanity by the vague connections between relational beings who themselves are similarly defined. This construction of reality has recently come under

---

87. Hall, *Imaging God*, 90.
88. Hodge, *Systematic Theology*, 97.
89. Hall, *Imaging God*, 90.
90. For a very brief but clear distinction between substantive dualism and property dualism see Visala, "Imago Dei," 105.
91. Within the Roman Catholic Church, there have been moves after Vatican II to speak of a unity between the body and the soul. This is evidenced in the official catechisms. In dealing with the question of 'Man,' the catechism expressly affirms the unity between body and soul. However, the catechism also expresses that "'soul' also refers to the innermost aspect of man, that which is of greatest value in him, that by which he is most especially in God's image: 'soul' signifies the spiritual principle in man" (John Paul II, "CCC").

severe criticism by those who question the contemporary relational understandings of personhood.[92]

4) *A 'value anthropocentrism.'* Not only do certain human attributes suffer at the hands of negative reductionism, but in many cases all of physical creation can be viewed as secondary to the non-physical aspects of humanity. The physical attributes of human existence are, as Hall laments, the tangible link between human essence and the rest of creation.[93] Thus, some theologians claim that it is the *imago Dei* that "separates [the human being] from the vulgar herd,"[94] or "the brutes."[95] Lynn White has sharply criticized Christianity (particularly Western Christianity in the post-scientific revolution era) on this point: "Christianity is the most anthropocentric religion the world has seen . . . [it] not only established a dualism of man and nature but also insisted that it is God's will that man exploit nature for his proper ends."[96] Physical creation becomes nothing more than a servant to the non-physical *imago Dei*. Kelsey terms this notion "value anthropocentrism" (29–31, 116–18).[97]

Although Hall may protest,[98] it can be argued that both relational and substantive theologians' appeals to the non-physical as the seat of the *imago Dei* demonstrate a devaluation of nature. Even Hall has to admit that the relational character of the human being bestows upon them the "special" status and "specific function" as "steward"[99] of the created order.

5) *A vestigium Dei*. As theologians attempt to elevate the non-physical properties of the human being to such lofty heights—and in so doing distinguish the human being from the rest of creation—they create within the human being a *vestigium Dei*. Barth (a strong proponent of the relational *imago Dei*) raises this as a major dispute against the *analogia entis*. His argument is as follows: Should the substantive contention be valid, one could gain knowledge of the divine substance without relying on revelation. This is to

---

92. As examples, see Harris, "Should We Say"; Hill, "Divine Persons"; McFadyen, *Call to Personhood*; Kelsey, "Human Creature," 137.

93. Hall, *Imaging God*, 90.

94. Calvin quoted in Hall, *Imaging God*, 103.

95. Hall, *Imaging God*, 90; cf. Calvin, "Psychopannychia," 423.

96. White, "Historical Roots," 335. See also Rogers, *Ecological Theology*. Rogers surveys a number of published works which call for an ecologically responsible model of Christian theology.

97. There are a few exceptions to this view. We think, for example, of Buber, who speaks of an I-thou relationship between humans and the animal world, and in particular with his cat. See Buber, *I and Thou*, 144–48.

98. Hall, *Imaging God*, 106–7.

99. Such is the central theme of Hall's work. See especially Hall, *Imaging God*, 106–8.

say: By seeking knowledge of the human being itself, one could expound on the doctrine of God out of the created order—interpreted in its own light by the created mind—without the need for revelation or the intricate workings of the Holy Spirit. Thus, the created mind need only look to itself to come to an independent understanding of the divine essence.[100]

Such an approach offers the human being an "additional 'light' of natural reason"[101] apart from the light of revelation. The questions, however, are: Which light, revelation or natural reason is true and primary? Is biblical doctrine simply the confirmation of the knowledge of God, which can be gleaned independently in creation? If so, why rely on revelation at all? The result of such a *vestigium Dei* is the elevation of the human principle at the expense of revelation and the Holy Spirit.

While Barth may attempt to lay this charge against the use of the *analogia entis,* the consequence of his use of the *analogia relationis* is very similar. According to Barth, human beings image God as they analogously imitate the relationality of the three counterparts of the Trinity. They do this by engaging in responsible relationality with each other, epitomized by the relationship between male and female.[102] Kelsey summarizes this as follows: "[Barth's] focus on human bisexuality can be read as a focus on a relational feature of human life that is one heuristically useful analogue (possibly one of many) for the I-thou relationality of covenant fellowship between God and humankind" (927).

If this is the case, then is it not possible to look to the relationship that exists within the human community (most especially between men and women) and in so doing gain knowledge of the interior life of the Trinitarian community? As a relational community, is humanity not a *vestigium Dei*?

One Question, One Answer

Why is it that these two positions, approaching the topic of the *imago Dei* as they do from different mindsets, both develop conceptual constructions that are open to common limitations? Is it possible that these two positions are not as different as they claim to be? If we look closely at the underlying structures of their arguments, it becomes apparent that their respective approaches are similar. First, it can be noted that they both focus on the anthropological 'What?' question in the context of the doctrine of creation. They seek to address the question 'What is the human being?' or perhaps

100. Torrance, *Persons in Communion*, 125.
101. Torrance, *Persons in Communion*, 125.
102. Barth, *CD* 3/1:186. See also van den Toren, *Christian Apologetics*, 100–103.

more accurately 'What are human beings as created in the image of God?' Other anthropological questions such as the 'Who?' and the 'How?' questions, while present, are not the primary focus.

Second, in their attempt to answer the primary question 'What is the *imago Dei*?' or perhaps 'What are human beings as created in the image of God?' both substantive and relational thinkers seek an answer that a) is shaped by a single or very limited set of features (e.g., rationality or relationality), b) is rooted in the human being (as part of their essence or inclination toward relationality) and c) sets the human being apart from the rest of creation. This is partly what David Clough calls 'not-animal' methodologies. That is to say, such anthropologies seek to understand what it is about human beings that makes them "not-animals."[103] To achieve an answer of this shape, theologians pose a secondary question that is similarly shaped: What single feature within the human being sets humanity apart from the rest of creation? This 'shaping' forces both views to seek an answer that inevitably leads to the appeal for a non-physical property within humanity that sets humanity apart from the rest of physical creation.[104]

It may be argued that the instinctive desire to elevate the human being above the "brutes"[105] of creation has led to this non-holistic duality. According to Hall, it can be shown that "the whole enterprise of defining the *imago Dei* in our Christian conventions centers on the apparent need to show that human beings are different from all other creatures."[106] The result of this desire is an unhealthy emphasis on the non-physical. Take for example William Baker's approach:

> The view that identifies the image as an internal quality, such as psychological make-up, reason, some spiritual quality, personality, or moral awareness has prevailed for most of Christian history . . . since the thing that makes humanity truly unique and different from the animal realm—and Genesis 1 and 2 seem to be stressing this point—is its spiritual, rational, and moral

---

103. Clough's argument is that such methodologies invariably fail to consider the context of humanity as an animal creature and in so doing elevate certain attributes at the expense of others. The consequence is the marginalisation of those humans who do not exhibit these features, and at the same time this methodology enables human beings to exploit seemingly lesser creatures. See Clough, "Not a Not-Animal," 4–5.

104. This mutual approach and secondary question is noted by Kelsey who argues that the first *desideratum* of his project is that theological anthropology proposals should not rely on comparisons and contrasts between human beings and other creatures (Kelsey, *Eccentric Existence*, 29–31).

105. Hall, *Imaging God*, 90.

106. Hall, *Imaging God*, 90.

capability, the view that equates the image of God with the inner quality of humanity is most likely.[107]

The elevation of the non-physical leads to a range of dichotomizations rooted in the construction of a categorical hierarchy of being. That which is non-physical is considered categorically a better way of being than that which is physical. Human experience is constructed as a contradistinction,[108] set against itself and nature. It is set against itself on two accounts. Firstly, the human being itself is dichotomized into non-physical (soul) and physical (body). Humanity becomes a contradiction in terms, one part pitted against the other: The non-physical aspect of the human being has unqualified dignity and value, while the physical body is degraded. The spirit or soul becomes all that is worth preserving, while the body is seen as the servant of the non-physical, to be used and abused as the spirit sees fit. Church history has shown the harmful consequences of this thinking.

Second, humanity is dichotomized into those who image God and those who do not. The few human beings who are able to display or develop, to a greater or lesser extent, the non-physical properties associated with each camp (rationality or relationality) image God to a greater or lesser extent. Individual human beings may thus be placed on a spectrum. At one end, the image of God is fully developed, and at the other human beings fail to develop either the substantive attributes or the required relationship to have any trace of the *imago Dei*. Most human beings find themselves somewhere along this spectrum. This is problematic on a number of grounds, not least of which is the question of human dignity and value.

At the same time, the human being is set against the rest of quotidian creation. Being cardinally non-physical in its true essence, the human being cannot be on par with the physical creation into which it is set. The human being becomes the *dominus* of creation. Even in Hall's attempted ecologically friendly construction, the created order becomes something that needs a steward. At first glance, the move away from 'dominion' to 'stewardship' in recent theology appears to nuance theology in eco-friendly ways. Yet on closer inspection, it soon becomes apparent that creation is no less degraded as it is subjected to the whims of its human regent, particularly those who image God. It cannot look after itself. Like a helpless child, creation needs the assistance of a wiser parent who knows what is best for

---

107. Baker, *In the Image of God*, 36–38.

108. By this we mean a distinction that is made through negative contrast and comparison often leading to a distinction of opposition rather than merely simple and natural difference.

it. Hall states that human beings "are set by their creation in the society of creatures as first among equals."[109]

With such lofty elevations for the privileged and lucky few who are able to image God comes the inevitable creation of the human being (at least parts of the human being) as a *vestigium Dei*. Looking to these few human beings who are able to image God, provides a route apart from revelation that leads to knowledge of the inner nature of the Godhead.

When all this is considered, is it fair to say that the substantive-relational debate presents us with a viable choice? Is it not, on closer inspection, a counterfeit choice? Are we not presented with similar approaches wrapped up in different theological garb? Recognizing the limitations of the substantive-relational debate as it currently stands, there is evidence in the literature of an alternate view that seeks to amalgamate the best of both categories.[110]

Hall, for example, claims that it is impossible to have an act of will (vital to relationship) without some cognition.[111] He claims that "there are obvious points of overlap between the two conceptions of the *imago*," but he immediately goes on to say that, in his opinion, "[the two views] are so fundamentally different that communication between theological schools influenced by them becomes virtually impossible."[112]

Doner attempts to join the substantive and relational views together by claiming that the *imago Dei* ought "to be viewed partly as original endowment, partly as destination." However, he goes on to say that "capacities are not God's actual image, but merely its possibility."[113] Bridger, who is very relational in his thinking, claims that while the relational understanding of the image of God should be primary, the substantive understanding can be linked to relational understandings, "provided that the language of attributes is cast within a relational framework."[114] Yet I. Howard Marshall claims that Bridger has the balance wrong. To Marshall, it seems that "the fact that humanity has a nature which is capable of relationships [is] much more important."[115]

109. Hall, *Imaging God*, 287.
110. Van den Toren is one such example. See van den Toren, *Christian Apologetics*, 113–17. See also Gunton, *One*, 188–209.
111. Hall, *Imaging God*, 94.
112. Hall, *Imaging God*, 105.
113. Grenz, *Social God*, 181.
114. Marshall, "Being Human," 54.
115. Marshall, "Being Human," 54. See also Volf, *Exclusion and Embrace*, 179–80.

These arguments are very much current. A recent work by Aku Visala attempts to defend the substantive view by countering some of the challenges alluded to above. In the process, Visala argues for a modified substantive position that incorporates relational features such as the importance of relationality and the developmental aspect of human beings. Nevertheless, in his appeal to a substantively conceived soul—perceived here as the non-physical seat of mental capacities that is physically dependent—he relies on a limited set of distinctive features distilled from the human being as a whole that distinguishes humans from the rest of creation. He, too, is firmly established in one camp: the substantive.[116]

Considering these problems, it is no wonder some have questioned the role of the *imago Dei* altogether. David Fergusson, for example, has highlighted the issues with both the substantive and relational categories. As a consequence, he argues: "What the imago concept does not enable is some shortcut to identifying a single property or function that differentiates us from the other animals and which may be considered godlike in some privileged sense."[117] As such, "to understand its meaning involves recourse to a more holistic description that includes functional, relational, and practical elements."[118] However, Fergusson is wary of "overloading"[119] the image of God, which might struggle under the theological weight it has traditionally carried. His ultimate conclusion is that the image of God designates the name of the human being rather than some innate quality. *Imago Dei* "names us as God's creatures"[120] and does so "as a signifier of the human condition before God rather than the specification of some elusive ontological or ethical ingredient."[121] The result of Fergusson's analysis is his undertaking of "some repair work."[122]

All these authors have proved unsatisfactory in resolving the substantive-relational debate. Their arguments are not developed in any clear and coherent manner. There is little elaboration as to what it means to have a nature that is capable of relationship or how humanity's substance and nature can support and make possible humanity's relationship with the triune God. In almost all cases they make use of negative reductionism in order to establish that which distinguishes the human being from the rest of creation.

116. Visala, "Imago Dei."
117. Fergusson, "Humans Created," 449.
118. Fergusson, "Humans Created," 440.
119. Fergusson, "Humans Created," 449.
120. Fergusson, "Humans Created," 451.
121. Fergusson, "Humans Created," 451–52.
122. Fergusson, "Humans Created," 451.

Those who point to a possible alternate view almost always side firmly with one camp or the other. If we are to have any hope of reaching a satisfactory answer to the questions surrounding the image of God, a completely different approach is in order.

It is against this backdrop that our discussion of *EE* takes place. What contribution does Kelsey's construction offer? Is it that his contribution fits neatly into one or the other of these two camps? Or is it perhaps possible that his anthropology offers a way of conceiving the image of God in ways that are open to both substantive and relational thinkers yet drives the debate forward in new directions? With these questions in mind we now turn our attention to a discussion of Kelsey's theological heritage.

Kelsey's Postliberal Heritage

KELSEY CONTENDS THAT THE application of conventional categories used to identify overall theological methods such as liberal, postliberal or narrative "seems to [him] to be utterly unilluminating and unhelpful" (12). He claims that *EE* was not worked out as a project in any *a priori* method such as postliberalism (12). Indeed, James Buckley (speaking on *EE*) notes that "those accustomed to sorting theologians, traditional or modern, in groups or movements or schools rather than engaging them on particular theological claims will have a difficult time placing this theological anthropology."[1] Nevertheless, Kelsey admits that "it is possible after the fact to identify contestable choices about procedure, mostly made implicitly in the course of developing material theological proposals" (12).

Effectively, what Kelsey is saying is that—while it may be that he did not set out to write works that utilize a postliberal theological methodology—in hindsight it is possible to identify the use of such methodological choices in his project. Yet it is arguable that this very assertion is postliberal. Kelsey seeks to counter "today's methodologically hyper-self-conscious world of technical academic theology" (12) by claiming that the "craft" (12) of theology is "too much of an art form to be regulated in that way" (12). This contention is—as this chapter demonstrates—postliberal. In one sense, Kelsey is stating that just as the practice of the Christian faith is prior to theologizing, theologizing is prior to methodology. As such, the very notion that theological methodologies may be identified in hindsight demonstrates and underlying postliberal theological methodology.

It is no wonder, therefore, that David Ford contends that *EE* "might be seen as the theological culmination of the Yale school."[2] There is further justification for Ford's contention. Kelsey is a Yale graduate and spent 40 years lecturing at Yale Divinity School. This chapter considers Ford's assertion by tracing Kelsey's theological heritage. We focus on the impact this theological context has on *EE*. Our approach is to consider three

---

1. Buckley, "Buoys for Eccentric Existence," 15.
2. Ford, "What, How, and Who," 42.

important theological figures, each of whom Kelsey spent years working alongside. From this discussion, we draw out the distinctive ways theology is conducted in this school of thought and its relationship to Kelsey's theological corpus.

Three Postliberal Giants

Postliberal theology[3] understands itself as a reaction to liberalism, which it sees as rooted in the Enlightenment and modernist agendas that—through the use of foundationalism[4]—resulted in the demythologization and demystification of the Christian faith.[5] For the postliberal, modernism is profoundly individualistic, rooted in Descartes, who placed the individual rational self at the center of thought. In contrast, pre-modernism—and to a certain extent post-modernism—construes the individual as belonging to a community[6] in which shared beliefs, practices, conventions and traditions shape the individual.[7] Postliberals value this latter view and, as such, call for a return to what they consider to be pre-modern Christianity, that is, a faith rooted first and foremost in the Christian community.[8] At the same time, postliberals recognize the formative and lasting impact of modernism and

---

3. For a discussion on the rise and decline of postliberalism, see DeHart, *Trial of the Witnesses*, 1–32, 41–53. It should be noted that Wright, convincingly, questions the decline of postliberalism (Wright, *Postliberal Theology*, 3n5).

4. Postliberalism does not work with a precise or even consistent understanding of foundationalism, even though the term is used widely throughout the literature. For more on postliberalism's understanding of and active aversion to foundationalism, see Goh, *Christian Tradition Today*, 173–76; Holmer, *Grammar of Faith*, 81–109; Lindbeck, *Nature of Doctrine*, 15–19; Phillips, *Faith After Foundationalism*; Vidu, *Postliberal Theological Method*, 117–56; Wallace, *Second Naiveté*, 88–96. Also consider Gunton, *One*, 129–35; Stout, *Flight from Authority*, 25–41 (cf. 64–76); van den Toren, *Christian Apologetics*, 41–44, 138–42. For a discussion on those who question the anti-foundationalist approach, see Gunton, *One*, 134–35; Kamitsuka, *Theology and Contemporary Culture*, 50–53, 77–80; Vidu, *Postliberal Theological Method*, chap. 4.

5. Michener, *Postliberal Theology*, 2–3.

6. The notion of community is fraught with difficulty. Blackshaw, recognizing the difficulty of defining community, contends that it is most often used as either an appropriating or orientating *device*. Reading much postliberal thought, one could argue that postliberals make use of community as an orientating device that understands community as a relational term (orientating its members). See Blackshaw, *Key Concepts in Community Studies*, 7–10. Within *EE*, Kelsey refers to the 'Community of faith' by which he means a group of individuals who are related through shared practices, even across time and space (Kelsey, *Eccentric Existence*, 13–15, Chp. 1B; cf. Ford, "What, How, and Who," 47).

7. Thiselton, *New Horizons in Hermeneutics*, 142–47.

8. More is said on this during the course of this chapter.

liberalism. Therefore, they understand that it is impossible to return to their view of pre-modern Christianity.[9]

To achieve their distinctive theology, postliberal theologians draw on a range of sources from theology, philosophy and anthropology to sociology.[10] Important influential thinkers include Augustine, Aquinas, Barth and Wittgenstein. It is for this reason that John Wright has termed postliberalism a "contemporary retrieval of Augustinian Thomism through interaction with twentieth-century linguistic philosophy"[11] and describes the postliberal method as "analytic Augustinian Thomism."[12] It is not possible, or necessary, in the space allotted here to engage in an intricate discussion on the accuracy of Wright's postliberal methodological description. For that discussion, we point the interested reader to the relevant literature.[13] What is valuable to our purposes here is to consider three significant postliberal theologians, 'giants' of this school of thought: Paul Holmer, Hans Frei and George Lindbeck. Is it arguable that these three theologians are pioneers of the postliberal movement and that their theologies epitomize characteristic features of postliberalism.[14] Of key importance to us is that Kelsey spent

9. Michener, *Postliberal Theology*, 2. See also Lindbeck, *Nature of Doctrine*, 7; Wallace, *Second Naiveté*, 92; Wright, *Postliberal Theology*, 4. Postliberalism's understanding of and relation to pre-modern and modern Christianity and liberalism is highly complex. For discussions on their diverse understandings consider Lindbeck, *Nature of Doctrine*, chap. 2 (cf. 126n1, 127); "Search for Habitable Texts"; Goh, *Christian Tradition Today*, 174–75, 209–11, 373–76. For *EE*'s discussion of the distinction between pre-modern and modern theological anthropology see Kelsey, *Eccentric Existence*, 27–41; cf. Marais, "Eccentric Existence?," 35–36. It should be noted that Pecknold, Dehart, and, to a certain extent, Michener argue that postliberalism is a "critical conversation" with liberal theology rather than being anti-modern/anti-liberal: DeHart, *Trial of the Witnesses*, chaps. 4, 5; Michener, *Postliberal Theology*, 2–3; Pecknold, *Transforming Postliberal Theology*, 1.

10. For a good overview of some of the key sources, see Michener, *Postliberal Theology*, 19–47.

11. Wright, *Postliberal Theology*, 7–8. Wright argues that his justification for this claim comes from Incandela. See Wright, *Postliberal Theology*, 8n11.

12. Wright, *Postliberal Theology*, 9. By this he means that postliberals read Aquinas and Augustine through the lens of linguistic philosophy, and in particular through their understanding of Wittgenstein's linguistic philosophy. For more on how Wright understands this particular description of postliberalism see Wright, *Postliberal Theology*, 6–9, 43–52.

13. Much of the literature surrounding postliberalism refers to and discusses how postliberals draw on a particular interpretation of these authors. See as examples Goh, *Christian Tradition Today*, 145–56; Michener, *Postliberal Theology*, 41–46; Pecknold, *Transforming Postliberal Theology*, 34–60; Placher, *Triune God*, 14–17, 35–39; Wright, *Postliberal Theology*, 6–9, 45–52; Wallace, *Second Naiveté*, 104–8.

14. It is commonplace in the literature surrounding postliberalism to reference these authors, in particular Frei and Lindbeck. As examples, see Goh, *Christian*

decades working closely with these theologians. Drawing out distinctive aspects of postliberalism from their theologies provides a good basis for better understanding Kelsey's theological heritage.

Paul Holmer (1916–2003)

Although *EE* makes little reference to Holmer,[15] Holmer is an important contributor to the rise of postliberal theology. Holmer received his PhD from Yale and from 1960 to 1987 lectured at Yale Divinity School alongside Kelsey. Michener notes that Holmer is not one of the most well-known figures associated with postliberal theology, but his book, *The Grammar of Faith* (1978), is significant in the field for its integration of Wittgenstein's philosophy with theology. As such, Michener claims that "at the very least, Holmer should be considered a 'forerunner of postliberal theology.'"[16]

Holmer begins *The Grammar of Faith* by considering what theology is. He claims that "the subject itself has lost its substance; and its own logic has become blunted by misuse and confused by the learned themselves."[17] His argument is that all theology is interpretive. He provides a caveat to this statement. He does not contend that "everybody must interpret always, or that all understanding involves interpretation, or even that each person is entitled to his own interpretation."[18] Rather, theology as interpretation must be understood within the framework of the Bible that addresses sinners, "not the curious."[19] Scripture, according to Holmer, is addressed to "those

---

Tradition Today; Harink, *Paul Among the Postliberals*, 18–20; Kamitsuka, *Theology and Contemporary Culture*, 15–26; Michener, *Postliberal Theology*, 49–72; Pecknold, *Transforming Postliberal Theology*, 1–12; Vidu, *Postliberal Theological Method*. Wallace includes Kelsey as one of four theologians "driving" this movement. See Wallace, *Second Naiveté*, 87.

15. It is notable that he does not feature in the bibliography of *EE*, but Kelsey is aware of Holmer's work. See Kelsey, "Bible and Christian Theology," 392.

16. Long quoted in Michener, *Postliberal Theology*, 23. Holmer's influence has gone almost entirely unnoticed. He receives very little mention in the literature about postliberalism. For example, he receives no bibliographic reference in either DeHart, *Trial of the Witnesses*, or Pecknold, *Transforming Postliberal Theology*. It is interesting to note that in the latter work he is referred to as "a young colleague" of Lindbeck even though he predates Lindbeck (Pecknold, *Transforming Postliberal Theology*, 17). There are exceptions to this. For example, Vidu, *Postliberal Theological Method*. However, even this work only pays Holmer minor tribute.

17. Holmer, *Grammar of Faith*, 3.

18. Holmer, *Grammar of Faith*, 4.

19. Holmer, *Grammar of Faith*, 9.

who want to redeem their lives, not to the idlers who are looking for exciting ways to spend them."[20]

What Holmer is saying is that theology and biblical interpretation are best done within the context of the Christian community of faithful believers and not in the context of academic scholarship. Holmer maintains that the different approaches to theology (historical-critical or theology proper) are "like games in one respect—namely, that therein we can play the field according to the rules."[21] Playing these games does not mean that we are any closer to understanding scriptures themselves. Critiquing modernity and the historical-critical hermeneutic, Holmer claims that while such 'games' do yield certain understandings, yet these understandings are "historical understandings and usually nothing more."[22]

Holmer's reference to 'games' in this context draws upon his understanding of the linguistic philosophy of Wittgenstein. Referencing Wittgenstein, he proposes that "theology is the grammar of faith."[23] Holmer interprets Wittgenstein as postulating that the function of language depends not on external rules or regulations, but on the context in which the language is employed. Children, for example, learn *Reigenspielen* (dance games such as *Ring a Ring o' Roses*), in which words and actions are learned in the context of a game without knowing the meaning of the words in other contexts. To Wittgenstein, there are countless language games:

> How many kinds of sentences are there? Say assertion, question, and command?—There are *countless* kinds: countless different kinds of uses of what we call 'symbols,' 'words,' 'sentences.' And this multiplicity is not something fixed, given once for all; but new types of language, new language-games, as we may say, come into existence, and others become obsolete and get forgotten.... Here the term 'language-*game*' is meant to bring into prominence the fact that the *speaking* of language is part of an activity, or of a form of life.[24]

---

20. Holmer, *Grammar of Faith*, 9.

21. A very Wittgenstein approach. See Holmer, *Grammar of Faith*, 6.

22. Holmer, *Grammar of Faith*, 8. Kelsey displays a similar understanding in his description of 'Bible,' 'scripture,' and 'holy scripture,' yet he claims that the study of biblical texts can be subject to literary, historical, and social criticism. It is evidenced in his discussions that such studies cannot produce *the* meaning of the text (Kelsey, *Eccentric Existence*, 136–47).

23. Holmer, *Grammar of Faith*, 17. See also King, *Meaning of God*, 13–20, 157–61; Lindbeck, *Nature of Doctrine*, 33.

24. Wittgenstein, *Philosophical Investigations*, 110.

Holmer incorporates Wittgenstein's theory into theology. He argues that theology is like the rules and structures for the language of the Christian faith. When someone learns a new language, they often attempt to learn the grammar. However, learning the grammar does not equate to speaking the language. Rather, one learns the grammar not so that one may speak of the grammar, but that one may speak to everything else in accordance with the grammar. The more one becomes skilled in the grammar, the more one speaks grammatically. Ultimately, the aim of the grammar is to speak "grammatically without ostentatiously remembering the grammar at all."[25]

It should be noted that Holmer's understanding of how the grammar of language (and faith) is learned is not by rote or even through classes and courses extracted from the practice. Rather, one primarily learns a language and its grammar through exposure to everyday practice, where the rules and grammar are already in place. It is the correct practice of the language that comes first, and only then can one analyze the grammar and structure of that language. The same is true for the Christian faith. Theology may describe the grammar of the faith, but it is the practice of this faith (the speaking of the language of faith) that is the object of theology (the grammar). The ultimate aim of theology is not to learn theology but to practice the Christian faith, or in Holmer's words, to "become Godly in all things."[26]

Holmer's contention that theology is a "language game" (*Sprachspiel*)[27] questions the veracity of theological statements for those who are not part of the Christian game. He understands modernity as being characterized by foundationalism, which sought to establish Christian authenticity (or lack thereof) through extra-biblical foundational claims. Holmer, however, objects to any attempt at conceiving of Christianity as an "edifice that is built upon extra-religious foundations."[28] This includes philosophical attempts as well as attempts in systematic theology to formulate schemes to establish the foundations of Christianity upon "facts."[29] To Holmer, there are no non-theological facts that are "indisputable, definitive, [or] religiously neutral."[30] What counts as 'fact' in one field does not necessarily transpose to another. He claims, "it turns out that historical facts are just historical,

---

25. Holmer, *Grammar of Faith*, 18.
26. Holmer, *Grammar of Faith*, 19.
27. Wittgenstein, *Philosophical Investigations*, 50.
28. Holmer, *Grammar of Faith*, 81–82.
29. Holmer, *Grammar of Faith*, 85–108.
30. Holmer, *Grammar of Faith*, 98.

and little else,"[31] while "theological statements, finally, if reducible at all, are reducible only to theological facts."[32]

We must be careful to interpret Holmer properly on this point. He is not claiming that there are no foundations or 'facts' altogether. Rather, he is claiming that the foundations for each discipline are different. Within Christian theology, it is not false to say that Christians have a foundation for their religious 'facts' but it may not be that these foundations or 'facts' have an exact correspondence with foundations or 'facts' in other disciplines. To understand what counts as a 'truth statement,' one must understand the relevant statement within a particular community.[33] It is arguable, therefore, that Holmer best epitomizes postliberalism's 'pragmatic'[34] epistemological approach. We say more on this later in this chapter.

Hans Frei (1922–1988)

Hans Frei was one of Kelsey's closest Yale companions. A cursory reading of Kelsey's broader work quickly demonstrates how much his theological career was intertwined with Frei's.[35] It is noteworthy that Frei thanks Kelsey for his help "through numerous conversations and readings"[36] in his "landmark"[37] book, *The Eclipse of Biblical Narrative* (1974). According to Ronald Michener, this book, along with Lindbeck's *The Nature of Doctrine* (1984), "set the stage for any theologian associated with or advocating a postliberal theology."[38]

---

31. Holmer, *Grammar of Faith*, 101.
32. Holmer, *Grammar of Faith*, 102.
33. Holmer, *Grammar of Faith*, 108–9.

34. The word 'pragmatic' is taken from the secondary literature and should not be confused with other, non-postliberal notions of pragmatism. For more, see footnote 140 of this chapter.

35. Kelsey dedicates *To Understand God Truly* to Frei (see Kelsey, *To Understand God Truly*). He thanks Frei for his assistance in *Uses of Scripture* (Kelsey, *Uses of Scripture*, ix). He writes an article heavily dependent on Frei's narrative methodology in *Scriptural Authority and Narrative Interpretation*, which is a project dedicated to Frei (Kelsey, "Biblical Narrative and Theological Anthropology"). Wells, speaking on *EE*, notes that, "If there is one theologian who had more influence on these pages than any other, it would seem to be Kelsey's erstwhile Yale colleague Hans Frei. . . . It is as if Frei's central insights were the leaping off point for a 30-year investigation that led finally to the publication of this grand work" (Wells, "Review of Eccentric Existence," 36).

36. Frei, *Eclipse of Biblical Narrative*.
37. Michener, *Postliberal Theology*, 50.
38. Michener, *Postliberal Theology*, 50.

In *The Eclipse of Biblical Narrative*,[39] Frei traces the hermeneutic turn in modernity from a realistic or literal[40] reading of scripture to a factual, historical-critical analysis. His argument is that in pre-modern times,[41] Western Christian readings of the Bible, through tools such as figuration and typology, were highly literal.[42] The direction of biblical interpretation was from internal to external. That is to say, extra-biblical thought was incorporated into the "one real world detailed by the Bible story."[43]

In Frei's argument, the rise of modern rationalism led to the breakdown of the literal mode of biblical interpretation. In the seventeenth century, authors such as Cocceius and Bengel, who attempted to locate contemporary events within the narrative framework of the biblical story and in so doing predict future stages of history, brought about a new way of conceiving of biblical narratives. Such an approach encouraged a logical distinction between the stories the Bible told and the 'reality' they depicted. There arose an intense interest in the factual truth (or falsehood) of biblical stories. The failure of this enterprise—along with the rise of modernity in the eighteenth century[44] in the form of empirical, positivistic thinking with a focus on historical-critical hermeneutics—led to the breakup of the cohesion between the literal meaning of biblical narratives and their reference to actual events.[45] The direction of biblical interpretation began to change. Biblical narratives were interpreted in light of extra-biblical 'facts' and typology or figuration as legitimate explanations of scripture. Literal and realistic interpretations were no longer considered valid.[46]

Historical-criticism "became standard scholarly practice."[47] Biblical stories were "tested against specific factual occurrences,"[48] and their reliability as 'history,' and consequently 'truth,' was established by comparing their intratextual features with extra-textual knowledge. The literal reading of the text came to mean two things: 1) grammatical and lexical exactness and

---

39. This work should be read alongside Frei, "'Literal Reading' of Biblical Narrative." For the abridged version, see Frei, "Does It Stretch or Will It Break?"

40. This is to say realistic or literal within the narrative itself, rather than referencing extratextual realities. We have more to say on this later in this section.

41. Frei, *Eclipse of Biblical Narrative*, 17–51.

42. Frei, *Eclipse of Biblical Narrative*, 1–4.

43. Frei, *Eclipse of Biblical Narrative*, 3. This approach is very similar to Lindbeck's intratextuality. See Lindbeck, *Nature of Doctrine*, 113–24.

44. Frei, *Eclipse of Biblical Narrative*, 51–65.

45. Frei, *Eclipse of Biblical Narrative*, 4–5.

46. Frei, *Eclipse of Biblical Narrative*, 5–8.

47. Frei, *Eclipse of Biblical Narrative*, 9.

48. Frei, *Eclipse of Biblical Narrative*, 9.

2) the relationship between the text and "how the facts really occurred."[49] As a consequence, the meaning of the text was associated with the 'truth,' 'factuality' and historical accuracy of the narrative.[50]

For Frei, the situation resulted in the confusion between what he calls history-likeness (literal meaning) and history (ostensive reference). Let us expound further. Frei contends that there is a difference between the historical character of biblical narratives and their 'history-like' or 'realistic' elements.[51] A narrative's 'realistic character' refers to the indispensability of the narrative shape (including chronology, meaning, theme, subject matter, etc.) and to the characters who are agents and sufferers of actions in the cultural and social context of the narrative. The 'meaning' of the narrative is not to be deduced by subjecting it to historical-critical analysis. Rather, it has meaning as it functions as a coherent whole:

> 'Meaning' in this view is logically distinct from 'truth,' even where the two bear so strong a family resemblance as the designations 'history-like' and 'historical' imply. The factuality or non-factuality of at least some of these narratives . . . involves a separate argument from that concerning their meaning.[52]

Much of Frei's work has subsequently focused on the role narratives play in theology and, in particular, as they are employed and used by Christian communities in their search for meaning and truth.[53] It is arguable that Frei epitomizes postliberalism's narrative preference, something we shortly come to discuss.

George Lindbeck (1923–2018)

Lindbeck was appointed to the faculty of Yale in 1952 before the completion of his PhD in 1955 and remained until his retirement in 1993. His work is intertwined with both Frei[54] and Kelsey. Kelsey, for example, thanks him for

---

49. Frei, *Eclipse of Biblical Narrative*, 7.
50. Frei, "Literal Reading," 62.
51. Frei, *Eclipse of Biblical Narrative*, 10–14.
52. Frei, "Literal Reading," 63.
53. Consider for example: Frei, "Literal Reading"; Frei, *Eclipse of Biblical Narrative*; Frei, *Identity of Jesus Christ*; Frei, "Theological Reflections," 1993; Green, *Scriptural Authority and Narrative Interpretation*.
54. See Lindbeck, "Toward a Postliberal Theology," 88 (cf. Frei, "Literal Reading" 70); Lindbeck, "Toward a Postliberal Theology," 91 (cf. Frei, *Eclipse of Biblical Narrative*, 2–3); Lindbeck, "Bible as Realistic Narrative," 85 (cf. Frei, *Eclipse of Biblical Narrative*, 10–12); Frei, "Does It Stretch or Will It Break?," 72.

his help in *The Uses of Scripture in Recent Theology* (1975),[55] while Lindbeck's article "The Bible as Realistic Narrative" (1980)[56] is heavily reliant on that same work. Lindbeck's book *The Nature of Doctrine* (1984) has been called "a programmatic statement"[57] of the Yale school's thought and is, in the words of van den Toren, an "important and . . . paradigmatic, example of the implications of the linguistic turn from modernism to postmodernism."[58]

In *The Nature of Doctrine*, Lindbeck considers the role doctrines play within Christian ecumenical discussions. He describes two[59] prevailing "theological theories of religion and doctrine."[60] The first, known as the cognitive-propositional approach, emphasizes the cognitive aspects of religions and "stresses the way in which church doctrines function as informative propositions or truth claims about objective realities."[61] For proponents of this approach, a doctrine is either always true or always false, due to its propositional character. Such an approach offers challenges for ecumenical discussions. For cognitive-propositional proponents, agreement can only be reached if one or both sides abandon their earlier positions.[62]

In contrast, the experiential-expressive approach emphasizes the resemblance of religions to aesthetic enterprises and, as a consequence, "interprets doctrines as non-informative and non-discursive symbols of inner feelings, attitudes, or existential orientations."[63] For proponents of this approach, "the general principle is that insofar as doctrines function as non-discursive symbols, they are polyvalent in import and therefore subject to

---

55. Kelsey, *Uses of Scripture*, ix.

56. Lindbeck, "Bible as Realistic Narrative."

57. van den Toren, *Christian Apologetics*, 47. See also Wallace, *Second Naiveté*, 154.

58. van den Toren, *Christian Apologetics*, 47. Buckley claims that there has been more debate about this book than any of Lindbeck's other writings. See Lindbeck, *Church in a Post Liberal Age*, 170. Moor claims that "it must count as one of the most provocative theological books to have been published in recent decades" (Moor, *Realism and Christian Faith*, 92).

59. To be accurate, Lindbeck notes a third theory that attempts to combine the first two. However, although in some respects better able to account for the variable and invariable aspects of religious traditions, he argues that this third approach has difficulty coherently combining the concerns of the first two. Indeed, he states that "even at their best . . . they resort to complicated intellectual gymnastics and to that extent are unpersuasive." As such, within his work, this third approach is "subsumed under the earlier [two] approaches" (Lindbeck, *Nature of Doctrine*, 16–17).

60. Lindbeck, *Nature of Doctrine*, 16.

61. Lindbeck, *Nature of Doctrine*, 16.

62. Lindbeck, *Nature of Doctrine*, 16.

63. Lindbeck, *Nature of Doctrine*, 16.

changes of meaning."[64] As such, religiously significant meanings may vary even though doctrines may remain the same and vice versa.[65] Ultimately, such an approach must concede that "there is thus at least the logical possibility that a Buddhist and a Christian might have basically the same faith, although expressed very differently."[66]

Lindbeck argues that neither of these approaches is adequate. On the one hand, there is the experiential-expressive approach under the influence of Enlightenment thinkers such as Kant, whose "revolutionary Copernican 'turn to the subject'"[67] deconstructed metaphysical and epistemological foundations of earlier cognitive-propositional views. Such a deconstruction was later exacerbated by scientific and historical developments that made it difficult to accept the literalistic propositional interpretations of certain biblical doctrines, such as the doctrine of creation. The consequence was the implied relativity of all doctrines and the desolation of truth.[68] On the other hand, the cognitive-propositional approach, while "intellectually brilliant and empirically impressive,"[69] no longer fits into the "deobjectification"[70] that is characteristic of individualistic and religiously pluralistic modern societies. Within such a context, "fewer and fewer contemporary people are deeply embedded in particular religious traditions or thoroughly involved in particular religious communities."[71] As such, they find it difficult to accept a set of objective truth propositions.[72]

Rather than accepting an amalgamation[73] of the two approaches, which would require "complicated intellectual gymnastics,"[74] Lindbeck proposes an alternate model to understanding religions: the cultural-linguistic

64. Lindbeck, *Nature of Doctrine*, 17.
65. Lindbeck, *Nature of Doctrine*, 17.
66. Lindbeck, *Nature of Doctrine*, 17.
67. Lindbeck, *Nature of Doctrine*, 21.
68. Lindbeck, *Nature of Doctrine*, 20–21.
69. Lindbeck, *Nature of Doctrine*, 21.
70. Lindbeck, *Nature of Doctrine*, 21.

71. Lindbeck, *Nature of Doctrine*, 21. Lindbeck does not indicate whether he is referring to concepts of religious plurality or multiple religious belongings.

72. It should be noted that Lindbeck goes on to explain that these same factors, that is the deobjectification of religions and doctrines, "also create difficulties for thinking of the process of becoming religious as similar to that of acquiring a culture or learning a language" (Lindbeck, *Nature of Doctrine*, 21–22).

73. However, Buckley argues that in some respects this is exactly what Lindbeck is doing in his cultural-linguistic approach (Lindbeck, *Church in a Post Liberal Age*, 171–72).

74. Lindbeck, *Nature of Doctrine*, 17. This is an accusation he lays against those who have attempted just such an amalgamation.

approach.⁷⁵ Building very much on the work of Holmer and Wittgenstein, Lindbeck's proposed approach draws on elements of anthropology, sociology and philosophy that emphasize the aspects of religion that resemble languages, together with their correlative forms of life and thus their similarities to cultures. In the cultural-linguistic model, religious membership is akin to competency in language. That is to say, "to become religious involves becoming skilled in the language, the symbol system of a given religion . . . to interiorize a set of skills by practice and training."⁷⁶

This particular approach to understanding religions construes doctrine as "communally authoritative teachings regarding beliefs and practices that are considered essential to the identity or welfare of the group in question."⁷⁷ Drawing on the explicit linguistic analogy, Lindbeck distinguishes between the vocabulary and grammar of the Christian faith. The vocabulary consists of the symbols, concepts, rites, injunctions and stories of a religion, while doctrines are chiefly concerned with the grammar or rules of the religion.⁷⁸

To clarify the point, we can draw attention to distinctions in Lindbeck's work. This includes distinguishing between religion, doctrine and theology, but also distinguishing between first-order religious language and practice and second-order reflection.⁷⁹ Lindbeck does not explain exactly what he means by this latter distinction. One deduces from the sparse references that

---

75. It is interesting to note that Lindbeck states his approach has not been inspired by Christian theology but by anthropology, sociology and philosophy. He therefore engages in a "pretheological inquiry" into the suitability of his approach over others. See Lindbeck, chap. 2.

76. Lindbeck, *Nature of Doctrine*, 34. For a critical discussions of Lindbeck and postliberal use of Wittgenstein, see Vidu, *Postliberal Theological Method*, 30–32, 93–95, 165–67, 171–74.

77. Lindbeck, *Nature of Doctrine*, 75. Here he distinguishes between doctrine and theology, arguing that—while often correlative—theology is a variety of theological explanations, communications and defences of the faith that generally deal with what is desirable to teach rather than what "functions as communally essential." In this sense, theological theories are "optional" rather than communally normative. See Lindbeck, *Nature of Doctrine*, 76.

78. Lindbeck, *Nature of Doctrine*, 80–81.

79. Lindbeck, *Church in a Post Liberal Age*, 84. It is interesting to note that in a similar fashion, Frei references first-order theology (the language and practice of the faith) and second-order theology (theological reflection on the language and practice of the faith), although he adds third-order theology: statements that distinguish similar discourse in diverse contexts. See Frei, *Types of Christian Theology*, 48. Moor and Vidu are both critical of this distinction for reasons beyond the scope of our project, see Moor, *Realism and Christian Faith*, 98–99; Vidu, *Postliberal Theological Method*, 96–98, 157–91.

first-order practice (also known as "first-order propositions"[80]) refers to the vocabulary of the religion as referenced directly above.[81] On the other hand, doctrine and theology, while distinct, are both part of second-order reflection on first-order religious practice.[82] As second-order reflection, doctrines correspond to the rules of the Christian language. Let us elaborate.

Lindbeck argues for a "regulative" or "rule"[83] theory of doctrine that can help communities develop an understanding of doctrines that is "both firm and flexible, both abiding and adaptable."[84] "Rules," argues Lindbeck, "retain an invariant meaning under changing conditions of compatibility and conflict."[85] Doctrines, as rules, are not propositional statements or expressive symbols, rather, they instantiate syntactical rules that guide the use of the respective community's vocabulary.[86] They acquire their force not on the basis of their underlying objective propositional truth claims, but as the grammar of a religion.

According to Lindbeck, the best way to sum up the practical difference between propositional and regulative approaches is akin to considering the contrast between interpreting a truth and obeying a rule.[87] For example, one may claim in one instance that Jesus is the Messiah while in another the incarnate Logos. Propositional approaches seek to interpret the truth of both these statements with the possibility of alternative, perhaps even conflicting, views. A regulative approach seeks to obey the rule by understanding what

80. Lindbeck, *Nature of Doctrine*, 69.

81. Lindbeck, "Toward a Postliberal Theology," 84; Lindbeck, *Nature of Doctrine*, 10, 80–81. It is possible that doctrinal formulations may be part of this first order. For example, when one recites the Apostle's Creed, one recites doctrinal formulations as part of the first-order language and practice of the religion. See Lindbeck, *Nature of Doctrine*, 80–81. Furthermore, there is confusion as to the role of language within this distinction. Language usually includes both vocabulary and grammar, yet in Lindbeck's construction language and vocabulary are part of the first order while grammar is firmly in the second. See Lindbeck, *Nature of Doctrine*, 79–84; "Toward a Postliberal Theology," 84.

82. Here Lindbeck refers to technical theology and doctrine qua doctrine as opposed to operational theology or doctrinal statements. See Lindbeck, *Nature of Doctrine*, 10, 69, 80–81; "Toward a Postliberal Theology," 84. For Lindbeck's distinction between theology and doctrine see Lindbeck, *Nature of Doctrine*, 76.

83. Lindbeck, *Nature of Doctrine*, 18, 79–88.

84. Lindbeck, *Nature of Doctrine*, 79.

85. Lindbeck, *Nature of Doctrine*, 18.

86. It is important to note that Lindbeck is speaking about doctrines qua doctrines. Although doctrinal sentences may function symbolically or have practical application as part of the vocabulary of a religion, Lindbeck is primarily concerned with the role doctrine plays as doctrine. See Lindbeck, *Nature of Doctrine*, 80–81.

87. Lindbeck, *Nature of Doctrine*, 107.

is applicable in which circumstances. While the doctrinal formulations may differ, "the story of passion and resurrection as well as the basic rules for its use remain the same."[88]

Using this cultural-linguistic approach, Lindbeck concludes *The Nature of Doctrine* with an addendum[89] entitled "Toward a Postliberal Theology."[90] Until this point, the term 'postliberal' had yet to be coined.[91] In this addendum, Lindbeck argues that: "all the standard theological approaches are unhelpful. The difficulties cannot be solved by, for example, abandoning modern developments and returning to some form of preliberal orthodoxy. A third, postliberal, way of conceiving religion and religious doctrine is called for."[92]

Using the linguistic metaphor of 'text,' Lindbeck argues that cognitive-propositional and experiential-expressive approaches rely on an 'extratextual' method. In this method, religious meaning is established by referring to extratextual sources such as foundational propositions or individual experiences and expressions. In contrast, a cultural-linguistic approach explicates religious meaning by use of an 'intratextual' methodology that locates religious meaning within a religious system or text.[93]

Here Lindbeck incorporates aspects of both Holmer and Frei. The intratextual method considers the meaning of any vocabulary (word, symbol or action) as best understood within the system in which it is employed (the language). As such, Christian doctrines (akin to the rules or grammar of the system) obtain their authority communally in the manner they are employed by the community.

Due to its reliance on a set of texts, Christianity is more than metaphorically intratextual. The measure of faithfulness of Christian adherents in a cultural-linguistic approach is calculated based on the degree to which descriptions and practices correspond to the "semiotic universe paradigmatically encoded in holy writ."[94] The world of scripture is considered—by those who speak the Christian language—the real and authentic world:

---

88. Lindbeck, *Nature of Doctrine*, 83, 107.

89. Lindbeck, *Church in a Post Liberal Age*, 170.

90. Lindbeck, *Nature of Doctrine*, 112–38. This chapter is also published with a slight different introduction in Ochs, *Return to Scripture*; Lindbeck, *Church in a Post Liberal Age*.

91. Michener, *Postliberal Theology*, 62. See also Placher, *Triune God*, ix; Pecknold, *Transforming Postliberal Theology*, 1; Wright, *Postliberal Theology*, 6.

92. Lindbeck, *Nature of Doctrine*, 7.

93. See Lindbeck, *Nature of Doctrine*, 113–24. For more on Lindbeck's intratextual method see Goh, *Christian Tradition Today*, 184–202.

94. Lindbeck, "Toward a Postliberal Theology," 89.

"Intratextual theology redescribes reality within the scriptural framework rather than translating scripture into extrascriptrual categories. It is the text, so to speak, which absorbs the world, rather than the world the text."[95]

The quotation given directly above, along with our discussions of Holmer, Frei and Lindbeck, indicates that postliberalists argue for a particular understanding of the role of truth, scripture, doctrines and theology. Let us turn now to consider the influence their approach has had on David Kelsey's theological *corpus*.

A Postliberal Family Resemblance

David Kelsey's work spans four decades of writing. His *oeuvre* encapsulates topics as broad as a theological analysis of Paul Tillich's theology;[96] critical discussions on theological education;[97] teleology;[98] soteriology;[99] and numerous works on the uses of scripture in theology[100] and theological anthropology.[101] It is not possible in the space allotted to engage in an in-depth discussion of Kelsey's *corpus*. Many of these works are discussed elsewhere in this project. For now, we focus on the question of Kelsey's postliberal heritage and, in particular, how he synthesizes "some of the key themes of colleagues with whom he has been in conversation over decades."[102]

Mark Wallace suggests that postliberalism displays a number of "family resemblances,"[103] three of which are particularly pertinent to our project: a) a preference for narrative theology (epitomized by Frei), b) a comm-

---

95. Lindbeck, *Nature of Doctrine*, 92.

96. Kelsey, *Fabric of Paul Tillich's Theology*.

97. Kelsey has produced two books in this regard: Kelsey, *To Understand God Truly*; *Between Athens and Berlin*. While it may be argued that his analysis of *Paideia* within these works touches on a postliberal theology, space does not allow us the luxury of an in-depth analysis at this time. Moreover, the concept has little to do with our overall topic, and Kelsey's broader postliberal heritage, as we will see, is easily established through numerous other works. For a helpful discussion and comparison of these works, see Hütter, "Worth Discussing."

98. Kelsey, "God and Teleology."

99. Kelsey, "Redeeming Sam"; *Imagining Redemption*.

100. Kelsey, "Appeals to Scripture in Theology"; "Bible and Christian Theology"; Kelsey, *Uses of Scripture*.

101. Kelsey, "God's Power and Human Flourishing"; "Spiritual Machines"; "Two Theologies of Death"; "Biblical Narrative and Theological Anthropology"; "Human Being"; "Personal Bodies"; "Wisdom Theological Anthropology"; *Eccentric Existence*.

102. Ford is speaking here particularly of *EE*, but the argument applies to Kelsey's wider *corpus* as well. See Ford, "What, How, and Who," 50.

103. Wallace, *Second Naiveté*, 92. See also Michener, *Postliberal Theology*, 4–12.

unity-orientated hermeneutical framework (epitomized by Lindbeck) and c) a pragmatic epistemology (epitomized by Holmer). As we turn to discuss each of these facets of postliberalism, we note their influence on *EE*.[104]

Preference for Narrative Theology

Recall our discussions on Frei's narrative focus. There is much evidence for a postliberal preference for narrative theology.[105] A reading of primary sources within postliberalism very quickly establishes this point,[106] which is widely referenced in the secondary literature.[107] Indeed, C. C. Pecknold goes so far as to make postliberalism virtually synonymous with 'narrative theology.'[108]

Gabriel Fackre provides an explanation for the recent rise of interest in narrative theology.[109] He argues that the second half of the twentieth century was characterized by a cultural shift in the west, which resisted modernity's "tyranny of definitions and dogma."[110] In Fackre's explanation, countercultural movements of the sixties and seventies were particularly disenchanted with the rationalistic intellectualism of modernity that offered a dry linear logic, which failed to deliver on the promises of modernity. These counter-

---

104. It is important to keep in mind the complexity of a theological school such as postliberalism. We soon see that these 'family resemblances' do not exist as independent concepts within postliberalism nor do they systematically build on each other. It is not the case that either of the authors discussed above are responsible for a single aspect of postliberalism. Although it may be argued that one author epitomizes a particular aspect of postliberalism, they incorporate a wide range of postliberal features, drawing on their colleagues at different stages in their respective academic careers. It is not our purpose here to disentangle postliberalism, to demonstrate the exact author from which Kelsey draws a particular postliberal feature or even to critique Kelsey's postliberal methodology extensively.

105. What exactly counts as narrative theology and its particular methodology is a debate beyond the purposes of our project. The interested reader is pointed to numerous secondary sources on the topic. For example, Fackre, "Narrative Theology"; Goldberg, *Theology and Narrative*; Hauerwas and Jones, *Why Narrative?*; Jones, "Narrative Theology."

106. For some examples consider Frei, *Identity of Jesus Christ*; "Literal Reading"; *Eclipse of Biblical Narrative*; Lindbeck, "Bible as Realistic Narrative."

107. Comstock, "Two Types of Narrative Theology"; Goh, *Christian Tradition Today*, 222–47; Pickstock, "One Story," 26; Wallace, *Second Naiveté*, 89–96; Placher, *Triune God*, 43–81; Vidu, *Postliberal Theological Method*, 45–87, 193–245.

108. Pecknold, *Transforming Postliberal Theology*, 1; cf. Michener, *Postliberal Theology*, 4.

109. Fackre, "Narrative Theology"; cf. Frei, *Eclipse of Biblical Narrative*.

110. Doty quoted in Fackre, "Narrative Theology," 346.

cultural movements appealed to human imagination, right-brain thinking, spontaneity and poeticism as alternative, yet equally valid, forms of truth. Within this context, the part of narrative took on a prominent role: "Telling a tale suggests a perspectival stance and confessional commitment without the necessary entailment of universal truth claims."[111]

Postliberal theologians emerged in the second half of the twentieth century out of the countercultural movements Fackre references. They were part of what Gary Comstock terms the 'pure narrative' group:

> *Pure narrative* theologians are those tied to, or inspired by, what has gone on in New Haven [Yale]: the antifoundational, cultural-linguistic, Wittgensteinian inspired descriptivists. Frei, Lindbeck, Hauerwas, and David Kelsey believe narrative is an autonomous literary form particularly suited to the work of theology. They oppose the excessive use of discursive prose and abstract reason, insisting that Christian faith is best understood by grasping the grammatical rules and concepts of its texts and practices. Narrative is a privileged mode for doing this.[112]

Postliberals argue that narrative plays a number of key roles within the Christian community. For example, narrative acts as the primary source of Christian 'truth claims.' Speaking about the methodology of narrative theology, Fackre argues that Christian communities have long tended to derive the meanings of their regulations and doctrines directly from narratives, and in particular from the narrative of the life of Jesus Christ.[113] In this theological method, 'truth' is not established extratextually, but intratextually (recall our discussions on Lindbeck).[114] Although the narrative of Jesus of Nazareth may include reference to external realities such as historical facts, the narrative itself is to be read in light of a "transhistorical"[115] vision, whereby the narrator orders characters and events within a narrative plot so as to point to what is ultimately true.[116] Within this transhistorical vision, the biblical narrative is not objective history that tells of events as they happened, nor is it a myth that personifies abstract truth in an esoteric

---

111. Fackre, "Narrative Theology," 342.

112. Comstock, "Two Types of Narrative Theology," 688.

113. Fackre, "Narrative Theology," 350. See also Frei, "Literal Reading" 37–39.

114. Lindbeck, *Nature of Doctrine*, 113–24. At this point, one could mention the realistic nature of narrative that promotes a closeness between objects and signs.

115. Fackre, "Narrative Theology," 351.

116. Barr in Fackre, "Narrative Theology," 350.

form.[117] Rather, the narrative consists in and of itself as truth interpreted by the community of believers.[118]

Moreover, the narrative both creates and unifies the appropriating and interpreting community. As Christian communities reflect on biblical narratives, particularly the narrative of Jesus Christ, they interpret this narrative to have an authoritative role in their communities. As the narrative is told, retold and performed (such as in the sacraments), its authoritative role has the effect of forming and establishing a sense of communal identity.[119] This community then associates itself with others who assign this narrative a similar role, thereby uniting individuals across space and time.[120]

That Kelsey himself emphasizes the importance of narrative is undeniable. His broader *corpus* widely utilizes narrative theology,[121] and he has engaged extensively in discussions on narrative methodology (in particular as it applies to Frei and anthropology).[122] Narrative is central to his theology, not only beyond *EE* but within *EE*, so much so that some have criticized *EE*'s "extreme"[123] commitment to narrative theology. In *EE*, narrative is a primary driving force for much of Kelsey's anthropological proposal. He constantly refers to narratives as the basis of his arguments,[124] and there are numerous examples of discussions that are narrative driven. One could note, for example, his reliance on the narrative of Job 10[125] or his insistence that his anthropology is worked out against the backdrop of three narrative plots of God relating in creative blessing, reconciliation and eschatological consummation, which are considered the "overall formal structure of the picture of human existence" (897).[126] Of interest here is his extensive

---

117. Lindbeck, "Toward a Postliberal Theology," 94.

118. Michener's interpretation of Frei. See Michener, *Postliberal Theology*, 52–53; cf. Lindbeck, "Toward a Postliberal Theology," 94–95; Kelsey, *Uses of Scripture*, 45.

119. Kelsey, *Uses of Scripture*, 90–97.

120. For more, see Kelsey, *Eccentric Existence*, 13–155; Fackre, "Narrative Theology," 350; Jones, "Narrative Theology," 32; Frei, "Literal Reading," 37–39.

121. Kelsey, *Imagining Redemption*; "Redeeming Sam."

122. Kelsey, "Biblical Narrative and Theological Anthropology"; cf. Kelsey, *Uses of Scripture*, chaps. 3, 5.

123. Pickstock, "One Story," 27. See also Ford, "What, How, and Who," 46.

124. For example, see Kelsey, *Eccentric Existence*, 161–62; chapter 4B. For his discussion of Job's narrative of creation, see Kelsey, *Eccentric Existence*, 245–80.

125. Kelsey, *Eccentric Existence*, chaps. 6, 7.

126. Kelsey, *Eccentric Existence*, 897–900. We discuss his triple helix approach in further detail in the proceeding chapter. Consider also Kelsey, "Personal Bodies," 142–48; "Wisdom Theological Anthropology," 47–51.

reference to Frei, in particular Frei's narrative identity description tools.[127] We have much more to say on this in chapter 5.

Community-Orientated Hermeneutical Framework

As our discussions above have demonstrated, postliberalism understands all reality to be absorbed by the narratives of scripture as they are interpreted by the Christian community. While postliberals do take into account extratextual material, this material is interpreted in light of intratextual understandings.[128] Doctrines are not constructed on these extratextual experiences and then subsequently used to form communities that are willing to believe these doctrines. Rather—as Holmer emphasizes—within postliberalism, one learns and understands the doctrine and faith of Christianity in much the same way as one learns a language: not by poring over the rules and grammar, but by immersing oneself in the community that speaks the language and in this way learning the grammar so as to speak grammatically.[129] In a very real sense, one has to be a believer in order to believe, to be part of the community in order to interpret the community's language.[130]

Kelsey has drawn extensively on the notion of a community-orientated hermeneutic approach. There is much in Kelsey's wider theological corpus to support this claim. For brevity, we note two instances. First, his understanding of secondary theology as a Christian 'language game' makes similar use of Wittgenstein as both Holmer and Lindbeck do. In this regard, his understanding of secondary theology is that it is a particular function or activity of a particular community.[131] Second, his extensive work on the role of scripture within Christian theology emphasizes the communal role of biblical interpretation. For example, in his work *The Uses of Scripture in Recent Theology* (1975),[132] he argues that the manner in which scripture is used to authorize

---

127. Kelsey, "Biblical Narrative and Theological Anthropology"; cf. Kelsey, *Eccentric Existence*, 334–37, 385–87.

128. In this regard, postliberals engage with extratextual material on an *ad hoc* basis. We have more to say on this in chapter 9. For a discussion on opponents to this view, particularly Tracy's opposition, see Kamitsuka, *Theology and Contemporary Culture*, 46–73.

129. Holmer, *Grammar of Faith*, 19; Michener, *Postliberal Theology*, 6–7. For a critique of Lindbeck's intratextuality see Moor, *Realism and Christian Faith*, 103–7.

130. See van den Toren, *Christian Apologetics*, 51–56.

131. Kelsey, *Eccentric Existence*, chap. 1B; Kelsey, "Bible and Christian Theology," 390–93; Holmer, *Grammar of Faith*, 17–25; Lindbeck, *Nature of Doctrine*, 32–40.

132. Kelsey, *Uses of Scripture*. This should be read in conjunction with Kelsey, "Appeals to Scripture."

theological formulations is best understood through a functionalist methodology.[133] In chapter 5 of that work, he claims that part of what it means to call a text scripture is to affirm its use within the religious community in question. This is to claim that the community accepts the authority of the text for the community and further, that the community commits itself to activities in which the text plays an authoritative role.[134]

As such, Kelsey's understanding of scriptural authority is intimately linked to his understanding of Christian community. In his construction, there is a dialectic relationship whereby the one defines the other and *vice versa*.[135] Christianity is a community that is defined by the practice of accepting biblical text as authoritative, and the text is defined and accepted as authoritative by the Christian community. To claim that scripture has authority is not to claim that there is a particular attribute to the text akin to its date, age or authenticity. Rather, it is to claim that the text is used within the context of the Christian community in such a way as its authority is affirmed and established.[136]

> Biblical writings are scripture insofar as they are used in the activities comprising the common life of the Christian community, most basically, as those activities that serve to 'author' the identities of the community and of its members: it is for that reason that they also serve to 'authorize' theological proposals.[137]

The above quotation highlights clearly the role of the community in Kelsey's theology. Such a communal understanding of theology comes to the fore as Kelsey discusses his methodological approaches in chapter 1B of *EE*. His claim is that theology is an ecclesiastical practice and can only be understood properly as it pertains to the Christian community in which it is practiced (13–14). It is in utilizing these practices that the community gains its identity (14–15), and it is only within this context that primary and secondary theology is properly understood (17–45).

---

133. This is Henry's interpretation of Kelsey. See Henry, "Theology and Biblical Authority." See also Michener, *Postliberal Theology*, 78–81; Hasel, "Relationship," 123.

134. Kelsey, *Uses of Scripture*, 89–119. For Kelsey's understanding of the canonising role of scripture, see Kelsey, *Eccentric Existence*, chap. 3B.

135. Kelsey, *Uses of Scripture*, 90–97; *Eccentric Existence*, chap. 1B; Michener, *Postliberal Theology*, 80–81.

136. Kelsey, *Uses of Scripture*, 97–100; "Bible and Christian Theology," 394–95. See also Michener, *Postliberal Theology*, 78–79. This approach has attracted much criticism.For example, see Frame, "Uses of Scripture," 342–43; Hasel, "Relationship," 123. It should be noted that Kelsey later modified his proposal slightly by references to *de facto* and *de jur* authority. See Kelsey, "Bible and Christian Theology."

137. Kelsey, "Bible and Christian Theology," 394–95.

Pragmatic Epistemology

Postliberalists' community-orientated hermeneutical approach and their functionalist methodology understands all systems of knowledge to be rooted in a particular community and culture (hence Lindbeck's cultural-linguistic approach).[138] Rather than seeking a single overarching truth embraced by all cultures at all times, postliberals highlight the differences and particularities of knowledge systems. The postliberal interest is not so much in the content of 'truth claims' themselves or in their universal veracity. Rather, postliberals are interested in the manner in which truth functions within the Christian community.[139] To Michener, this is the "pragmatic approach to 'truth'"[140] that characterizes postliberalism.

As we have noted in our discussion on Holmer and Lindbeck, postliberals speak of Christian doctrine as the grammar of the Christian faith. As Lindbeck states, it is second-order reflection on first-order practice. Truth, therefore—within postliberalism—is not obtainable through appeals to external propositions. Rather, truth finds its ultimate meaning as it functions internally within the language and culture of the Christian community.[141] The notion of neutral objective 'facts' is, in the words of Holmer, "at best, a borrowed usage from historical and scientific contexts, and at worst, an inflated and ill-begotten posit, trading on some intellectual conventions but quite without substance."[142] The postliberal approach has led some to argue that postliberalism promotes a "relativist alethiology."[143] We have much more to say on this topic in the final sub-section of this chapter, but for now, let us remain focused on the way Kelsey utilizes 'truth claims' and Christian propositions.

In chapter 1B of *EE*, Kelsey outlines his understanding of the distinction between primary and secondary theology. This discussion is remarkably similar to Lindbeck's understanding of doctrine and theology as second-order reflection on first-order Christian practice and Frei's understanding

---

138. Lindbeck, *Nature of Doctrine*, 32–41. See also Vidu, *Postliberal Theological Method*, 90–101.

139. Michener, *Postliberal Theology*, 8–13. See also van den Toren, *Christian Apologetics*, chap. 2.

140. Michener, *Postliberal Theology*, 96; cf. Pickstock, "One Story," 26; Vidu, *Postliberal Theological Method*, xi, 241–46. Pecknold's work explores the strength of postliberalism particularly as it applies to Lindbeck's pragmatism. See Pecknold, *Transforming Postliberal Theology*.

141. Michener, *Postliberal Theology*, 8–13.

142. Holmer, *Grammar of Faith*, 98; cf. chp. 5. See also Frei, *Eclipse of Biblical Narrative*, 1–16, 51–65.

143. Wallace, *Second Naiveté*, 108. See also DeHart, *Trial of the Witnesses*, 41–52.

of first- and second-order theology.[144] Primary theology is defined, within *EE*, as "an informal, non-technical, often un-selfconscious [sic] engagement in the practice of theology" (19). It is the enacted practices of the community as they respond to God's relating. Kelsey is quite clear that *EE* is "not an enactment of the practice of primary theology" (19).

Secondary theology, in Kelsey's construction, is a unique practice within the Christian community. It emerges as a result of questions raised about the adequacy of Christian enactments in primary theology. As Christian communities attempt to ensure that their practices are appropriate within changing cultures and contexts, a need (or perhaps a desire) develops to engage in formal critical analysis of primary theological doctrines and formulations. Thus, within Kelsey's construction, "secondary theology is inherently an analytically descriptive, critical, and revisionary practice" (21). Kelsey claims that his secondary formulations rest on primary theological practices. As such, they are shaped by members of Christian communities and are therefore "epistemically fallible" (22). Let us explore this claim further.

Kelsey claims that "to do theology is to assess the truth of the community's speech, where appropriate and in regard to the appropriate senses of 'true.'"[145] Here he uses the notion of 'truth' in particularly postliberal ways. He urges us not to seek the 'truth' in scriptural texts in ways akin to asking the 'meaning' of the text, as if the texts have a certain property that needs to be drawn out through interpretation. Rather, interpretation itself is a function of the particular interpreter. Using Fowl, Kelsey argues that the focus of interpretation should not be on the objective meaning of the text itself but on the diverse interpretive aims, interests and practices used in interpreting texts. As interpreters approach texts with diverse interests, they bring different methods of study to obtain an "underdetermined interpretation" (134). The different aims, interests, methods and disciplines help determine the interpretation of the text in such a way as to leave the interpretation open for other interpreters with different aims, interests and methods (134–35). In effect, Kelsey is claiming that the authority and veracity of each 'truth claim' is established not by appealing to the authority or truthfulness of the canon itself, but to the practices of the community and, in particular, the practices of the relative interpretative secondary theology (153).

Our purposes here do not merit an in-depth critique of the methodological choices of *EE*. The proceeding chapters of this thesis pick up some

---

144. It should be noted that they each have a particular take on this distinction. See Lindbeck, "Toward a Postliberal Theology," 84; cf. Frei, *Types of Christian Theology*, 48. See also footnote 79 and 81 of this chapter.

145. Kelsey, "Bible and Christian Theology," 392.

of these discussions. All that we are doing at this juncture is highlighting to the reader that Kelsey makes extensive use of postliberal features and, in particular, a preference for narrative theology, a community-orientated hermeneutic and a pragmatic, functionalist epistemology. Considering the preceding discussion, we must conclude that however "implicitly" (12) Kelsey's methodological choices may be, it is arguable that his work should be read within the context of postliberalism. Since this is the case, let us turn now to briefly engage in a critical evaluation of postliberalism insofar as it has shaped Kelsey's theology.

Postliberalism, Truth and Kelsey's Project

Postliberalism presents a unique approach to theology that raises a number of questions. Some of these questions are picked up in subsequent parts of our project, for example, the narrative nature of *EE*. However, considering the substantive concern to establish a universality to human existence, as well as Kelsey's insistence that human existence is eccentrically rooted in God (arguably an objective reality), the suitability of *EE* to address questions of universal truth is of keen interest here. Postliberalism's use of a functionalist methodology and a pragmatic epistemology seemingly implies its non-suitability for questions of universal truth. Indeed, on this point it has received much criticism.[146]

Carl Henry, for example, speaking specifically about Kelsey's postliberal understanding of the authority of scripture, claims that the consequence of postliberalism is that theology is left without absolute truth. Henry's argument is that Kelsey displays an epistemological relativity and a functionalist view of scripture.[147] Wallace echoes a similar concern with what he terms postliberalism's "relativistic epistemology."[148] Their critique must be taken seriously:

> The epistemological relativity underlying this notion not only dissolves any fixed meaning for Kelsey's own proposals about 'normativity,' 'authority' and 'scripture,' but also whatever fixed meaning he would attach to meaning itself under any and all circumstances. It therefore reduces theology to an intricate exercise in futility and nonsense. . . . For all its utility, Kelsey's

---

146. Henry, "Theology and Biblical Authority," 321–23; Pecknold, *Transforming Postliberal Theology*, 7–8; Vidu, *Postliberal Theological Method*, xi, 241–46.

147. Henry, "Theology and Biblical Authority," 315–23. See also Hasel, "Relationship," 123; Michener, *Postliberal Theology*, 78–81.

148. Wallace, *Second Naiveté*, 108.

volume does not help us much with the overarching concern of the transcendent truth of the Christian religion.[149]

If Henry and Wallace's critique is justified, then there exists an "incommensurability"[150] between Christian propositions and different language games. With no "overarching conceptual scheme,"[151] the value, meaning and veracity of religious statements cannot be compared to, judge, or be judged by any external dialogue partner.[152] Ultimately, postliberalism is accused of being closed off to the wider world: any "discussion with external paradigms has been ruled out."[153] Wallace sums up the problem eloquently:

> Herein lies the basic contradiction in the Yale school's radical intratextualism vis-à-vis its relativist aletheiology: if we say that the bible is to absorb the world, then the Christian community does make truth-claims about reality; and yet if notions of truth are as 'incommensurable' as Lindbeck suggests, it is difficult to see what force, if any, such an intratextual claim would have other than as a private wish, a tribal outlook.[154]

If we are to read Kelsey (a postliberalist theologian) in this light, then the claims made by *EE* are of limited value, relative only to a particular community. Indeed, there is some support for this view. After all, our discussions in this chapter have placed Kelsey firmly within postliberalism, and

---

149. Henry, "Theology and Biblical Authority," 323. Moor and Phillips lay a similar claim against Lindbeck (see Moor, *Realism and Christian Faith*, 95; Phillips, *Faith After Foundationalism*, 202–5, 214).

150. Lindbeck, *Nature of Doctrine*, 49.

151. van den Toren, *Christian Apologetics*, 51.

152. This is contrary to a core Christian claim: that of universal truth. Christianity has always promoted an objective ontological epistemology. Its core claim is that God is *the* absolute reality and that its propositional claims are universally valid. There is much written on realism and whether there exists an independent, objective reality. For an introductory reading, see Gunton, *One*, 129–35; Kamitsuka, *Theology and Contemporary Culture*, 52–53; van den Toren, *Christian Apologetics*, 16–18, 120–153, Chp. 4; cf. Moor, *Realism and Christian Faith*.

153. Vidu, *Postliberal Theological Method*, 241 (cf. 242–246). There are those who would question this contention. For example, DeHart, *Trial of the Witnesses*, 278. Wright references how postliberal theologians engage in wider debates (Wright, *Postliberal Theology*, 5–6, 134–36). It is interesting to note that Frei, critiquing the theology of Phillips's radical way of doing theology that is almost exclusively internally focused, argues that such an approach is circular, akin to a snake eating its own tail (Frei, *Types of Christian Theology*, 46–55 [cf. 91–94]).

154. Wallace, *Second Naiveté*, 108.

he himself has argued that his work is secondary theology within Christian particularism and therefore "epistemically fallible" (22).[155]

Yet, the nuances of postliberalism must be taken into consideration before simply accepting this critique. Lindbeck himself claims that his understanding of postliberalism is not relativistic.[156] In his distinction between 'intrasystematic' and 'ontological' truth, he demonstrates that postliberal theologians do not deny the existence of an independent and objective reality. However, just as grammar alone affirms nothing either true or false, so theology and doctrine—to the extent that they are second-order discourse—assert nothing either true or false about ultimate reality. Their 'truth' is intrasystematic rather than ontological.[157] As theological discourse, postliberalism raises the question about how truth is obtained and used within the Christian community, and not necessarily about what is and is not true. To help clarify the point, Michener makes use of Marshall's distinction between alethiology and epistemology:[158] "Alethiology is about the meaning of claiming a proposition is truth and epistemology is about how humans know and justify that which is classified as 'truth.' George Lindbeck holds to a realist alethiology and a coherentist, pragmatic epistemology."[159]

What Michener argues here is echoed by Andrew Moor's contention that Lindbeck and other postliberal theologians distinguish between the realistic nature of first-order theology (which speaks to a universal reality) and the relativistic nature of second-order doctrinal statements, which are descriptions of first-order theology. In postliberalism, truth exists in first-order Christian practice, the community's response to the ultimate reality of God. Doctrinal statements, however, are descriptions of first-order practice, and, as such, their veracity is a measure of their grammatical function within the Christian language game.[160]

As we move now to speak directly about *EE*, we would do well to keep in mind this distinction. Although it is appropriate for postliberalism to speak to topics and doctrines that concern universal application, indeed Kelsey notes that there are 'nonnegotiable buoys' (the topic of our next chapter) to which his anthropological claims adhere, and *EE* itself is a postliberal work in secondary theology. As our introduction has indicated, *EE*

---

155. See also Kelsey, *Eccentric Existence*, 6–7.

156. Lindbeck, "Search for Habitable Texts," 154. Michener offers valuable insight in this regard. See Michener, *Postliberal Theology*, 96–98.

157. Lindbeck, *Nature of Doctrine*, 64–69.

158. Michener, *Postliberal Theology*, 98.

159. Goldberg, *Theology and Narrative*, 98.

160. Moor, *Realism and Christian Faith*, 94–98.

is not attempting to "assert conversation-stopper pronouncements" (10). Its claims are made within the context of Christian particularism, meant to be read by Christians who themselves are engaging in first-order theological practice. Kelsey does not entirely exclude non-Christian engagement. He is well aware that many anthropological questions and proposals set out in *EE* do not arise exclusively from/within Christian traditions (6–7) and that non-Christians may well be interested in what Christians have to say on questions raised in *EE* (3). However, should one wish to debate the universal veracity of *EE*'s claims, one would have to measure them against the respective first-order theology on which they are based (the practice of the Christian community) and whether they are grammatically correct within this particular language game. This debate is not what our project is about. Rather, while not necessarily accepting this argument, our project respects the postliberal premise with which Kelsey set out to write *EE*. As such, this project understands *EE* as narrative in nature and open to interpretation by the Christian community with particular interpretive aims and interests. Our project is worked out in that context, seeking to critically evaluate and interpret *EE* from within the Christian community. This project has particular interpretive aims and interests. We have set out some of our aims in the preceding chapter. As we progress, particularly in the next two chapters, our interpretive aims become clearer.

3

Buoys for Eccentric Existence

THE PREVIOUS CHAPTER EXPLORED the broader theological heritage of David Kelsey. We turn now to speak of *EE* itself. Our primary aim here is to provide an orientation for readers who have limited knowledge of *EE*. With this aim in mind, this chapter (along with chapter 4) is more descriptive than subsequent chapters and focusses almost entirely on *EE*.

Orientating the reader to *EE* is hardly an easy task. *EE* "eludes any easy summary."[1] Over the last few years, a number of authors have attempted to provide an overview. James Buckley, for example, provides a detailed summary of *EE* in just over a page.[2] It is, however, difficult to understand if one has not already read *EE*. Tom Greggs's, David Ford's and Charles Wood's summaries are longer, yet they are only marginally easier to comprehend and still require a theologically trained mind.[3] R. Carbine, Nathan Crawford, Charles Raynal and Sam Wells all provide humbler alternatives, yet they are in danger of simplifying *EE*'s proposals.[4]

The reason the task is challenging is twofold. On the one hand, *EE* is very long. As it is over 1,000 pages, "one cannot help but be impressed (perhaps even intimidated) by the sheer scale of the project."[5] On the other hand, the work is very complex. Stephen Plant compares the work to Michelangelo's painting of the Sistine Chapel.[6] Greggs concurs, stating "both are overwhelming feasts, which relate in different (but connected) ways the various narratives of God's ways with the world in complex unity."[7] Both

---

1. McFarland, "Review of Eccentric Existence," 423.

2. Buckley, "Buoys for Eccentric Existence," 19–20.

3. Greggs, "David Kelsey, Eccentric Existence," 450–56; Ford, "What, How, and Who," 46–56; Wood, "Response to Eccentric Existence," 16–27.

4. Carbine, "Review of Eccentric Existence"; Crawford, "Review of Eccentric Existence," 355–56; Raynal, "Review of Eccentric Existence"; Wells, "Review of Eccentric Existence," 35.

5. Greggs, "David Kelsey, Eccentric Existence," 456. For a reason for its scale, see Buckley, "Buoys for Eccentric Existence," 15–16.

6. Plant quoted in Greggs, "David Kelsey, Eccentric Existence," 458.

7. Greggs, "David Kelsey, Eccentric Existence," 458.

Greggs and Ford comment that the work is hardly an easy read and that "it is difficult to image those outside the professional world of theology having the [necessary] patience with the book."[8]

The length and complexity of the book are compounded by Kelsey's systematically unsystematic approach (44–45).[9] In *Imagining Redemption*, Kelsey argues that he does not "promote a systematic structure of technical philosophical doctrine as the intellectual framework that will explain the meaning of Christian beliefs most profoundly or demonstrate their truth most persuasively."[10] This same approach is picked up in *EE*.[11] Here, Kelsey exclaims in introductory chapter 1B that Kierkegaard's maxim, "existence is not a system," ought to be taken seriously (44–45).[12] This is particularly relevant when one considers that Kelsey roots his project not in abstract systematic theorizations of Christian beliefs, but in the "unsystematic, conceptually shaped practices that constitute the common life of ecclesial communities" (45). As such, Kelsey's project proceeds in postliberal fashion. Recall our discussions on Lindbeck who distinguished between first-order language and practice and second-order reflection.[13] Kelsey argues that *EE* is rooted first and foremost in the language of faith (primary theology as practiced by Christian communities) and proceeds to speak about the grammar (secondary systematic theorizations).[14] According to Kelsey, "when [*EE*] addresses anthropological questions, the practice of Christian secondary theology *has* to be systematically unsystematic" (897 [emphasis added]). This is the "methodological imperative" (897) that his project takes seriously, and *EE*'s claims are therefore "laid out in a systematically unsys-

---

8. Greggs, "David Kelsey, Eccentric Existence," 449; Ford, "What, How, and Who," 52. See also Crawford, "Review of Eccentric Existence," 356.

9. Cf. Marais, "Eccentric Existence?," 42.

10. Kelsey, *Imagining Redemption*, 88, 86–94.

11. Theil traces the origin of this approach to Kelsey's book *Imagining Redemption*. See Thiel, "Methodological Choices" [2011] 9; "Methodological Choices" [2016] 11–12.

12. In this respect, Kelsey is a disciple of Barth who contended for the non-systematic approach to theology based in the '*Geschichte*' of Jesus Christ. In Barth's construction, dogmatics is a science in that it is focused on the objective reality of the Word of God. Therefore, dogmatics, rather than conforming to a system, must always be freely obedient to the Word of God. As such it is "less a system than the report of an event" (Barth, *CD* 1/1:275–87; 1/2:861–79). See also Hunsinger, *How to Read Karl Barth*, 53; cf. Hasel, "Relationship," 120–21; Kelsey, *Uses of Scripture*, 39–50; Michener, *Postliberal Theology*, 43–46.

13. We have noted the slight variations among postliberals in their understanding of the first and second orders in chapter 2.

14. In chapter 1B of *EE*, Kelsey goes to great lengths to define and distinguish his project as a work in secondary theology that is nevertheless related to primary theology.

tematic fashion" (1009). While this approach offers some advantages, not least of which are those pointed out by Nadia Marias as "a greater suppleness, flexibility and adaptability,"[15] it does present the reader with an obstacle to a comprehensive survey of *EE*'s landscape.

It is, therefore, impractical for us to aspire to such a comprehensive survey within the space allotted to us in this chapter. Since our aim is to provide an orientation to *EE* within the context of a project on the *imago Dei*, this chapter focusses on that end. With this in mind, we provide a very brief discussion of *EE* as a whole. The aim of this discussion is to provide a very cursory overview orientating the reader to the different parts, key movements and propositions in *EE* and to some of the challenges Kelsey's construction proposes. It is not possible or necessary within this discussion to engage in constructive comparative and analytical debates of substantial theological positions such as Trinitarianism, Christology, soteriology, ecclesiology, etc. We leave these analytical discussions for subsequent chapters. The final section of this chapter focusses on Kelsey's construction and use of the *imago Dei* within *EE*. This is particularly pertinent to our project, and it is for this reason that this chapter is significantly weighted in that direction.

Sketching the Landscape

In Kelsey's introduction to *EE* he raises the question: "Does Christian faith bring with it any convictions about human being that are so rock bottom for it that they are, so to speak, nonnegotiable in intellectual exchange with anthropologies shaped by other traditions?" (7). The non-negotiable convictions are, to Kelsey, "like buoys that mark the channels of the deep" (1008). Within *EE*, Kelsey attempts to set out these non-negotiable buoys.[16]

> I suggest the claims about human beings that are nonnegotiable for Christian faith are claims about how God relates to human beings. These claims are as follows: (a) God actively relates to human beings to create them, (b) to drawn them to eschatological consummation, and (c) to reconcile them when they are alienated from God. (8)

---

15. Marais, "Eccentric Existence?," 42. There are those who would question the unsystematic nature of Kelsey's approach. Greggs, for example, has argued that Kelsey's "threeness [*sic*] is in some ways a 'single systematic structure.'" And yet even he has to admit that it does offer some advantages (Greggs, "David Kelsey, Eccentric Existence," 457).

16. We say 'attempts,' as his success is open to question. See Buckley, "Buoys for Eccentric Existence," 21–22.

As the title of *EE* suggests, Kelsey's main argument is that the human being is to be conceived eccentrically. By eccentric, he means that the human being finds the root—or basis—of their being externally: in God's triadic relating in creative blessing, eschatological consummation and reconciliation (893).[17] This understanding of humans provides the premise behind the structure of *EE*. Beginning with an in-depth introduction into the kind of project *EE* is and is not, Kelsey divides *EE* into three parts.

He contends that the three parts form "an interconnected, interdependent, and mutually reinforcing whole" (xi), and at the same time each "can be read on its own" (xi).[18] Each part deals with one of the triadic narrative relations between God and all that is not God and follows a comparable structure.[19] Beginning with the ultimate and proximate contexts implied by the narrative,[20] Kelsey proceeds to address the anthropological 'What?,' 'How?,' and 'Who?' questions and concludes each part with an exploration of sin and sins.[21] Kelsey argues that "all three parts are theologically necessary, logically different from each other, irreducible to one another, and yet

---

17. Questions can be raised as to the order of this triadic relation. It is interesting to note that Kelsey deviates from the creedal formulations that often place eschatology after reconciliation. Indeed, Kelsey considers this to be the "traditional" approach (Kelsey, *Eccentric Existence*, 896). Of further interest is that Barth, in one sense, places reconciliation before creation, since God created with a view to reconciliation. Barth, *CD* 3/1:74; 2/1:611–12. Kelsey lays out his understanding of this triadic relationality, including his logic for deviating from this order in a number of places. Since the order is not directly relevant to our project and does not substantially affect our objectives in this chapter, we refrain from commenting further. For the interested reader, see Kelsey, *Eccentric Existence*, 120–31, 895–900; "God's Power," 23–46; "Personal Bodies," 142–49.

18. Kelsey claims that parts 2 and 3 are each "starting over from the beginning" (Kelsey, *Eccentric Existence*, 441, 605).

19. For Kelsey's understanding of this structure see Kelsey, *Eccentric Existence*, 10–11.

20. We analyze what Kelsey means by ultimate and proximate context when we come to discuss Kelsey's understanding of our basic and quotidian identities in chapter 5. His argument is based on his understanding that God is relational both imminently in the perichoretic relations of the Trinity *in se* and economically in His relations to all that is not God *ad extra* (Kelsey, *Eccentric Existence*, 917–19). Both Buckley and Theil have highlighted this as one of the essential buoys of *EE*, see Buckley, "Buoys for Eccentric Existence," 23; Thiel, "Methodological Choices," 3. For Kelsey's understanding of God's imminence in relation to his economy see Kelsey, *Eccentric Existence*, 48–49.

21. Kelsey has a very distinct hamartiology which distinguishes between sin (in the singular), sins (in the plural) and evil. It is not possible within the space of this chapter or our overall project to engage with Kelsey on this. It is therefore purposely left for others to illuminate. For an overview see Kelsey, *Eccentric Existence*, 1034–44; cf. Kelsey, "Response to the Symposium," 83–86; Marais, "Eccentric Existence?," 61–66; McDougall, "Trinitarian Grammar." McDougall's article also appears in Outka, *Theological Anthropology*, 107–26.

inseparable from each other [but] it remains vague just how to take them together" (893). It is for this reason that Kelsey ends his work with three extended codas, which are designed to demonstrate the "wholeness-in-complexity" (893)[22] of his anthropological proposals.

Of particular interest to a discussion of the structure of *EE* is Kelsey's unique use of 11 'B' chapters, which expound on 'A' chapters. The reason for their inclusion is, according to Kelsey, "today's methodologically hyper-self-conscious world of technical academic theology" (12). These 'B' chapters, in Kelsey's words, are "as unavoidable as it is (often) tedious" (xii). They are included in *EE* to help the reader understand where Kelsey "stands on relevant methodological issues in academic theology" (xiii) and are distinguished from the rest of the work by use of a differently sized typeface.[23]

EE: A Bird's-eye View

Kelsey begins his work by stating that from the outset one is "entitled" to know the "ultimate concern" (1)[24] addressed by *EE*. With this in mind, he lays out what he considers are *the* three anthropological questions his project addresses. These are expressed as the 'What?,' 'How?,' and 'Who?'[25] of human existence. This is quickly followed by a discussion as to who is raising these questions. He argues that his project is to be understood within "Christian particularism" (6–7),[26] where his questions are asked within the context of self-described Christian communities.[27] Chapter 1B provides

22. Kelsey does not expand on what he means by "wholeness-in-complexity" and the reader is left to assume his meaning. We take it to mean that while his project is complex and systematically unsystematic, it nevertheless has some sort of unity/wholeness to it. One could compare this to his use of the term 'wholeness' in his deliberations on the wholeness of scripture; however, this discussion is left for another time. For more see Kelsey, *Eccentric Existence*, 152–56. See also Kelsey, *Uses of Scripture*, 100–108.

23. McFarland believes they "exert a corresponding drag on its rhetorical momentum without paying corresponding dividends" (McFarland, "Review of Eccentric Existence," 423). While we can appreciate McFarland's experience, Kelsey's B chapters are useful to our project as they offer insight into the technicalities of Kelsey's constructions. This is particularly relevant for chapter 9B of *EE*. See chapters 4 to 8 of our project.

24. Here, Kelsey is quoting Paul Tillich.

25. For more on the anthropological questions, see Kelsey, *Eccentric Existence*, 1–2; cf. Kelsey, "Human Creature," 121–30.

26. By this Kelsey means that it is to be read within the context of Christian anthropological discussions. For his understanding of how his project is Christian particularism, see Kelsey, *Eccentric Existence*, 3–9.

27. For Kelsey's understanding of these Christian communities see Kelsey, *Eccentric Existence*, 3–7. Kelsey does not exclude those from other communities being

an extended and in-depth discussion on the distinction between primary and secondary theology, with Kelsey attesting that *EE* is a work of the latter. In chapter 2A, he sets out the Trinitarian and Christocentric basis of his anthropology and in so doing justifies his triadic narrative approach, which is expounded on in chapter 3A (discussed shortly). Chapter 2B sets out the parameters of his anthropology. He argues against *EE* as a work of apologetics, limiting his discussions to the logic of Christian belief and not the logic of coming to believe. He ends his introductions with chapter 3B, which defines and defends his understanding of scripture as "Christian Canonical Holy Scripture."[28]

In part 1, referred to in *EE* as "Living on Borrowed Breath,"[29] Kelsey explores the narrative of creation. Using the Trinitarian *taxis*[30] "It is the Father who creates through the Son in the power of the Spirit" (122), this section primarily speaks to the anthropological 'What?' question. In Ford's words, Kelsey "shift[s] the scriptural centre of gravity in the doctrine of creation"[31] from Genesis 1–3 to Wisdom literature. Using Job 10 as his scriptural anchor, Kelsey expounds on what it means to be and to have a living body.[32] As Kelsey expands on what the human being is, much of the anthropological formula we discuss takes shape. It is for this reason that our project focusses on part 1 of *EE*. Kelsey goes on to speak of the "existential hows" of human flourishing[33] in terms of faith, that is, of the human call to be wise for the quotidian context and in so doing respond to God's relating in creative blessing through faithful loyalty, which is characterized by "reverent and awed doxological gratitude for [the] hospitable generosity of God's gift" (338).

---

able to follow his arguments, and he thus refers to his proposals as "conceptual bridge-building" between Christian communities and other communities (Kelsey, *Eccentric Existence*, 6–7).

28. Title of chapter 3B of Kelsey, *Eccentric Existence*.

29. The term is borrowed from Crenshaw (Kelsey, *Eccentric Existence*, 202).

30. Kelsey takes this term to be akin to an asymmetric pattern (Kelsey, *Eccentric Existence*, 121).

31. Ford, "What, How, and Who," 46.

32. It is arguable that he has drawn extensively on Ricoeur for this concept. He acknowledges that the phrase 'living body' is borrowed from Ricoeur, while the notions of having a body and being a body are very similar to Ricoeur's understanding of the link between the body as an object and the subjective experience of the body. See Kelsey, "Personal Bodies," 7, 155; Ricoeur, *Freedom and Nature*, 8–13; cf. Ricoeur, *Oneself as Other*, 33–35.

33. Kelsey writes much on this topic throughout his anthropology as well in other works, such as Kelsey, "God's Power."

Part 2, "Living on Borrowed Time," explores the narrative of eschatological consummation. Using the Trinitarian *taxis* "It is the Spirit, sent by the Father with the Son, who draws creatures to eschatological consummation" (122), part 2 speaks to the anthropological 'How?' question. In chapter 13, Kelsey elucidates how, in contrast to the narrative of creation, the narrative of consummation presupposes a telic element. Therefore, the context in which humans exist is one of promise that is given in the ambiguous context of the traditional 'now' and 'not yet' tension. Human beings are those "to whom the catastrophe of final judgment is happening" (527) and yet ultimately elected for eschatological consummation (527). The emphasis in this part is on the unique manner of the Spirit's relating. While the Father relates *to* us, and Jesus relates *among* us, Kelsey proposes that the relation of the spirit is best expressed by the adjective "circumambient."[34] In this manner, the Spirit is "the most embracing and necessary context" (443) of human existence. Such relation goes beyond the traditional binary constructs of 'within' and 'without' to highlight both the "environing context" and "intimately interior" (444) ways in which the Spirit relates. The existential hows are worked out in chapter 14 as human flourishing in hope, which is best characterized by glad (not gleeful) and happy (not euphoric) practices.

Part 3, "Living on Borrowed Death," expounds on the narrative of reconciliation and, using the Trinitarian *taxis* "It is the Son, sent by the Father in the power of the Spirit, who reconciles" (122), speaks primarily to the anthropological 'Who?' question. The narrative plot of reconciliation is enacted in the story of Jesus of Nazareth. Using this narrative, Kelsey draws attention to the many ways in which we are estranged from God. In describing Jesus' identity, Kelsey refers to Jesus' camaraderie with our proximate context. This highlights the complexity and ambiguity of a God who is one with those who are estranged from Him. As such, Jesus' narrative emphasizes how our proximate context is one of estrangement and yet reconciliation. We live, in Kelsey's words, in proximate contexts of "living deaths within which we nonetheless truly live and flourish by another's death" (626). The existential hows of living by another's death are explained in chapter 22 of *EE* by Kelsey's reading of the Sermon on the Mount, in which human flourishing is understood as "love to God" and "love as neighbour" (712–13).

From the above (very brief) overview, the reader begins to detect Kelsey's preference for triplets. This is typified in his focus on the three narratives, the three anthropological questions and the triplet of faith,

---

34. For a comprehensive understanding of his use of 'circumambient,' see Kelsey, *Eccentric Existence*, 443–46.

hope and love,[35] which characterizes the existential hows of human flourishing. The root of Kelsey's affiliation for triplets is his unique approach to understanding the Trinity.

Creedal Trinitarian Formulations in *EE*

Kelsey explicates the Trinitarian basis of *EE* in chapter 2A. These Trinitarian understandings of God "serve as theological 'buoys'"[36] for *EE*. Kelsey's use of the Trinity is uniquely postliberal. Rather than launching into a systematic discussion of the doctrine of the Trinity, Kelsey takes time to trace the origin of his Trinitarian understandings. Since, as Moran has noted, "his project is centered upon the God who is named and addressed in Christian liturgical and reflective practices,"[37] Kelsey highlights the ecclesiological, communal and liturgical use of the "triadic doxological formula" (47), repeated as "in the name of the Father, the Son, and the Holy Spirit" (47). This formula, used at important points in Christian practices (such as communion, baptism and marriage), is a specifically Christian description of God's identity and serves to shape Christian communal and personal identities:

> To use the formula is to say, among other things, that what and who we are and how we ought to be is constituted by God relating to us in this threefold way. Thus, the triadic formula serves to give an identity description, not only of God, but also of its users. (48)

Kelsey argues that each clause in the formula demonstrates a pattern, or in Greek *taxi*, of God's manner of relating. Although they always work together, the shape of their relating is expressed as the Father who creates, the Spirit who consummates and the Son who reconciles.[38]

---

35. The triplet of faith, hope and love plays an important part in Kelsey's theological anthropology. However, it speaks primarily to the anthropological 'How?' question: "Thus, Christian communities have long held that the basic dispositions appropriate to the presence of the kingdom of God are faith, hope, and love" (Kelsey, "Bible and Christian Theology," 388). Considering that our project is primarily concerned with the 'What?' and 'Who?' questions, this triplet is not a major feature of our deliberations.

36. Kelsey, "Response to the Symposium" 77.

37. Moran, "Review of Eccentric Existence," 458.

38. One can note the order of these relations. In many cases, theologians would refer to the Father, Son and Spirit, rather than Father, Spirit and Son. The logic of this order is found in Kelsey's description of the triple helix narrative plots. Of course, one should be careful about taking this order too seriously, as Kelsey is quite clear that each of the Trinitarian members is involved in each relation, although the shape/focus of their involvements is different. We have already alluded to the *Taxis* in our overview of the parts above. For more see Kelsey, *Eccentric Existence*, 47, 121–22, 915; cf. Grenz, *Social God*, 3–9.

It is Kelsey's contention that, in the history of Christian practice, the focus on God's threefold relating became a focus on God's relating in the single narrative of Jesus of Nazareth (Christology). This raised a number of questions as to the identity of Jesus and through conceptual contemplation led to the adoption of the Nicene Creed. To Kelsey, this creed is fundamental to a Trinitarian description of God:

> By a 'Trinitarian understanding' of God, I mean any understanding of God that is accountable to the Nicene Creed as summarized in the more recently conventional formula: God is one substance in three persons. (46)[39]

In this sense, Kelsey's emphasis on Trinity is not dogmatic or systematic, but rooted in primary theology's liturgical creedal formulations (47–66).[40] In postliberal fashion, Kelsey distinguishes between dogmatic and creedal formulations by claiming that his use of the creed emphasizes the practice of Christian communities while not committing that practice to any particularly limiting doctrine. Therefore, Kelsey refers to "Trinitarian understandings" (plural) rather than "*the* doctrine of the Trinity" (47 [emphasis added]).

Although Kelsey's project is Trinitarian, it is also Christocentric. Yet, as Buckley points out:

> It is important not to construe this proposal as univocally christocentric. That is, Kelsey says that Trinitarian understandings of God are "cognitively christocentric" (an understanding of Jesus Christ is decisively normative for knowledge of God as triune). They are not "ontologically christocentric" ("as though the very being of human persons is constituted by and revealed in the being of the Son of God incarnate") (65–66, 909–10). Instead "canonical narrative identity descriptions of Jesus as imager of God precisely in his humanity give him the status of 'grammatical paradigm' of human being" (1009)—grammatically christocentric, we might say. Kelsey leaves to another time or to other theologians the task of formulating "a fully developed Christology." (1011)[41]

---

39. He further states: "what I mean throughout by 'properly Trinitarian' understandings of God are understandings that arguably comport with this creed" (Kelsey, *Eccentric Existence*, 61).

40. In particular, consider the triadic role of the Nicene Creed as existential, which Marias refers to as "liturgical" (Marais, "Eccentric Existence?," 41), as well as rhetorical and methodological. Also see Moran, "Review of Eccentric Existence," 457.

41. Buckley, "Buoys for Eccentric Existence," 22.

The point raised by Buckley is pertinent to our discussions here. Kelsey does not develop either a dogmatically systematic Trinitarianism or Christology, and it would be difficult to compare and contrast his understanding with other major theologians. Consider, for example, Barth—a "major theological impetus behind postliberal theology"[42]—who wrestles with the problem of the two natures. The problem arises with the claim that every subsisting nature has to have a separate hypostasis. The Chalcedon formula identified the person of Jesus (both divine and human) with the second person of the Trinity. Yet in modern conceptions, it seems obvious that Jesus is fully human.[43] The two notions seem difficult to reconcile. Since Jesus has two natures, the implication is that he has/is two hypostases.

For Barth, a solution comes from distinguishing this claim from the principle that a nature requires an individuating hypostasis. Since Trinitarian hypostases are ontologically prior to the divine nature, they are not restricted by it. This entails freedom for the hypostatic *Logos* from the divine nature in such a way that it can obtain a human nature without losing the divine nature. Correspondingly, the fact that the human nature in Christ does not obtain a human hypostasis does not imply that there is no hypostatic instantiation. Barth contends that the human nature of Jesus has no substance apart from its union with the eternal *Logos*, or Second Person of the Trinity. The human nature subsists in the hypostasis of the divine *Logos*; therefore, it is *anhypostatic*. Its being is only to be found *in* the subsistence of the incarnate Son of God (*enhypostasis*).[44] Such discussions on the *anhypostatic/enhypostatic* union invariably lead do discussions on the *Logos asarkos/Logos ensarkos*.[45]

It is very difficult, however, to place Kelsey's Trinitarianism and Christology within such debates. On the one hand, he is clear that any interpretation of his Trinitarianism or Christology must be hospitable to both

---

42. Michener, *Postliberal Theology*, 43–46.

43. Tanner, *Jesus, Humanity, and the Trinity*, 25.

44. Barth, *CD* 1/2:132–71; 3/2:70; 4/2:49–50; Crisp, *Divinity and Humanity*, 72–89; Tanner, *Jesus, Humanity, and the Trinity*, 14–27; Waldrop, *Karl Barth's Christology*; McFarland, *Difference & Identity*, 40–42. Cyril's doctrine of *the anhypostasis* and the later adaptation of it by Leontius of Byzantium (*enhypostasis*) has been widely debated. It has been criticized for robbing Jesus of a humanity that is the same as the rest of humanity's. For a critique, see Berkouwer, *Person of Christ*, 305–26; Gunton, *Christ and Creation*, 47–58; Knox, *Humanity and Divinity of Christ*, 63–65; Pittenger, *Word Incarnate*, 100–102; Shults, "Dubious Christological Formula."

45. Barth's focus on the enhypostatic union invariably tends to focus on the Logos ensarkos rather than the Logos asarkos. See Barth, *CD* 3/1:154–56; 4/1:51–53; 4/2:32–34; 4/3:724; cf. McCormack, *Orthodox and Modern*, 183–91; Molnar, *Divine Freedom*, 61–81; Waldrop, *Karl Barth's Christology*, 46–47; Jenson, "Once More," 130–33.

Nicaean and Chalcedonian formulas. That is to say, God is one substance in three persons, and the person of Jesus of Nazareth is both fully divine and fully human (48-66).[46] On the other hand, Kelsey is quite clear that his claims, especially those made in chapters 18 and 19A, "can hardly count as an essay in Christology proper" (680) and that his project does not present a fully developed Christology (626).

Although Kelsey argues that his project is Christocentric, he contends that it is not Christocentric in ways that have been prominent in the practice of secondary theology, such as those whose Christocentricity relies on the cosmic Christ (909-10).[47] He argues that the task of Christology in secondary theology is primarily to explore the logic of Christian beliefs about who Jesus is. In this context, the "initial task is to offer a description of Jesus" (692) and only subsequently to explore the logical relations between the description of Jesus as given in the narratives and other theological proposals made in other theological loci (689-93).

Kelsey limits his proposals to this initial task, that is, to providing a narrative description of Jesus of Nazareth as given in the Gospels.[48] He insists that it is Jesus of Nazareth, in his humanity, who images God[49] and limits his proposals "to reflections on the implications for theological anthropology of the identification of Jesus Christ with the image of God in his created humanity" (1011). He does not develop in any real sense how Christ's humanity is rooted in the Trinity, let alone how this Jesus of Nazareth is the very self-same person as the Second Person of the Trinity. Although he does not deny that Jesus may be the image of God in his divinity, he leaves this for others to explore.[50]

---

46. It should be noted that he does not explore his understanding of the Chalcedonian formula as 'truly human' in any detail.

47. For more on his objection to 'traditional' Christology, especially as it is presented by Ogden, see Kelsey, *Eccentric Existence*, 680-83.

48. Kelsey, *Eccentric Existence*, chap. 18, 19A, 19B.

49. Kelsey, *Eccentric Existence*, 913, 915, 918, 920, 936-38, 985, 987, 1003, 1005-7, 1027, 1045. See also McFarland, "Review of Eccentric Existence," 434. McFarland very briefly considers the 'Christocentricness' of Kelsey's project. Kelsey here is not denying the Chalcedonian formula that the person of Jesus exists in two natures. He is simply turning his attention to the human nature, leaving discussion on the divine nature for others to pick up.

50. Kelsey affirms the cosmological Christ as the image of God, yet he does not explore the implications of this claim in any great detail. Instead, he prefers to focus on Jesus of Nazareth, as described in the gospel narratives as the image of God (Kelsey, *Eccentric Existence*, 956-1007, 1011). Since we provide a very broad orientation to *EE* as a whole, discussions on Kelsey's explicit or implicit doctrinal choices do not further our objectives in this chapter or the broader thesis. We therefore leave these discussions for another time.

This unique use of a Trinitarian and Christological basis for a triadic-shaped narrative anthropology has attracted some criticism. Greggs, while acknowledging that it would be unfair to demand detailed discussions of Trinitarianism in an anthropology, nevertheless claims that "it is not always entirely clear which conception of the doctrine of the Trinity it is that Kelsey works with."[51] He highlights how at times Kelsey refers to God as the "community-in-communion" (121)[52] of the three perichoretic hypostases (120, 168), thereby appearing to make use of social Trinitarianism. Yet when Kelsey discusses Grenz's model, he insists that this is not the case (1009–10). Furthermore, Kelsey seems to shift his Trinitarian focus to a Christological focus as he moves from part 1 to parts 2 and 3. To Greggs, Kelsey's use of Christology lacks real development on key issues such as the communication of idioms (1011) and Christ's humanity (1016).

Catherine Pickstock, who is arguably the fiercest critic of *EE* in recent years, contends that the problem with Kelsey's Trinity and Christology are based on Kelsey's use of narrative theology. Her critique, while passionately put, needs to be considered, as it revolves around the unconventional use of narrative in *EE*. Pickstock claims that "in the case of the narrative approach, so extreme is Kelsey's commitment to deriving the doctrine of the Trinity from a narrative basis, that he seems prepared to traduce the literary witness of the Bible itself."[53] Her objections to the narrative thesis of *EE* are numerous; the most serious is Pickstock's interpretation of Kelsey as arguing "that three distinct hypostases in God can only be discernible if it can be shown that God has revealed himself in three entirely distinct ways."[54] Furthermore, Pickstock sees in Kelsey's distinction between Jesus' "basic personal identity and his personal quotidian identity"[55] a distinction between who Jesus is and what Jesus does, thus departing from Frei's thesis.[56] She argues that this approach creates an "an ontological rupture combine[d] with a Christological heterodoxy."[57] The ultimate consequence of Pickstock's

---

51. Greggs, "David Kelsey, Eccentric Existence," 461.

52. It is interesting to note that Kelsey swaps this *taxis* without reason at different points in *EE* so that it reads "communion-in-community" (Kelsey, *Eccentric Existence*, 120; cf. 121, 1022, 1030–33, 1046).

53. Pickstock, "One Story," 27. Kelsey is adamant that he does not purport to establish Trinitarianism by a narrative approach. Kelsey, "Response to the Symposium," 78.

54. Pickstock, "One Story," 27.

55. Pickstock, "One Story," 32, referring to Kelsey, *Eccentric Existence*, 649–93.

56. See Frei, *Identity of Jesus Christ*, 136.

57. Pickstock, "One Story," 32. She is not exactly clear about how Kelsey distinguishes ontology from narrativity or how he distinguishes, within the Trinity, between what the three persons do and who they are.

reading of *EE* is her insistence "that Kelsey comes close to Nestorianism."[58] Who Jesus is is distinguished from what he does in his humanity, which, paradoxically, is just how he is the image of God in *EE*.[59] According to Pickstock, Kelsey's "account of Christology plays down the hypostatic union and the intimate association of Jesus' humanity with the second person of the Trinity in particular,"[60] and his "lowering of anthropology is matched by a lowering of Christology."[61]

To Pickstock, "the orthodox position, by contrast, sustains a narrative ontology whereby a character is continuous with what he does."[62] Pickstock calls the single-narrative approach the "more orthodox approach."[63] To her, "there is only one Christian story. In denying this, Kelsey denies the unity of the Trinity and the *communicatio idiomatum* in the God-Man."[64]

There are many questions about Pickstock's interpretation of *EE*. One could note, for example, the contention that there is only one Christian story. Although it is arguable that there is a common Christian thread (whatever this may be), the diversity and plurality of Christian communities separated by space and time seems to counter Pickstock's argument on this point. Indeed, there are four canonical stories. Furthermore, Kelsey is quite clear that who Jesus is and what he does are indeed one and the same. Kelsey's insistence is based on Frei (334–37, 385–87).[65]

Although we would be wise to take Pickstock's critique with a pinch of salt,[66] Kelsey's triadic narrative approach has received criticism from others.

58. Pickstock, "One Story," 33. Kelsey outright denies that *EE* proposes this view of Jesus. Yet he does go on to argue that "one cannot help wondering whether the proposed alternative's contention that 'the exemplary human person,' i.e., Jesus Christ, the Incarnate Son of God, 'was not a human person at all, but God 'impersonating' humanity' isn't well on its way to a quasi-docetic Christology. Heresy-spotting is so much fun!" (Kelsey, "Response to the Symposium," 79–80).

59. Pickstock, "One Story," 33. Also see Kelsey, *Eccentric Existence*, 915, 918, 936–38, 1005–7, 1045.

60. Pickstock, "One Story," 32.

61. Pickstock, "One Story," 34.

62. Pickstock, "One Story," 32.

63. Pickstock, "One Story," 29.

64. Pickstock, "One Story," 38.

65. See also chapter 5 of our project.

66. Her article in the symposium on *EE* has very little positive to say about *EE*. It should be noted that Kelsey responds by saying, "I hardly recognize *EE* in the picture of it given in her essay. . . . Far more troubling, a number of problematic ideas are attributed to *EE* that it simply does not advance. All of that makes the essay look as though much of its critique addresses some other book" (Kelsey, "Response to the Symposium," 77–78). In the same article Kelsey goes to great lengths to defend many of the critiques Pickstock levels against *EE*.

Greggs,[67] Buckley[68] and Ford[69] all question Kelsey on his triadic approach as opposed to the more 'traditional' single metanarrative. Kelsey insists that the 'traditional' single narrative presents an "all-too-easy harmonization of the canonical accounts" at the risk of "domesticating in dangerously misleading ways the complexity, ambiguity and fierceness of God" (468). This, to Ford, raises the question of "how so many could have got it so wrong for so long, and what their responses to the critique might be."[70] Kelsey, however, states that other theologians did not 'get it wrong,' but that many, if not all, the "traditional controversies in theology are marked by a misrepresentation of the ways in which God relates."[71] Nevertheless, when one considers the prevalence of the single narrative approach, Ford's question remains valid.

More than the narrative character of *EE*, there are questions about Kelsey's use of scripture and secondary sources. At key moments in his anthropology he relies heavily on a single, or limited, set of scriptures to the exclusion of others. At these times, he engages in lengthy and detailed exegesis into limited sets of scripture to affirm a point he wishes to make with little or no reference to alternate interpretations. For example, consider his discussions on Job 10 that take up most of chapters 7 and 8 and purposely exclude the Genesis texts (Chp. 4B); his discussions on the Pauline formula 'in Christ' (695–702); or his discussions on New Testament texts that speak of Jesus as the image of God (see his second coda). Reading *EE*, it is no surprise that Ford questions Kelsey's narrow focus on narrative to the exclusion of almost all other biblical genres and wonders if Kelsey's main argument may not have been better served by appealing to a wider range of biblical genres.[72]

In like fashion, it has not gone unnoticed that Kelsey's engagement with both scripture and other sources is "somewhat one-sided"[73] and *ad hoc*.[74] Examples are his uses of Westermann to support his preference for Wisdom literature at the expense of the Genesis account (Chp. 4B), his

---

67. Greggs, "David Kelsey, Eccentric Existence," 459–61.

68. Buckley, "Buoys for Eccentric Existence," 21–22.

69. Ford, "What, How, and Who," 43–46.

70. Ford, "What, How, and Who," 45.

71. Kelsey, "Response to the Symposium," 82–83. Ford appears to be 'convinced' by Kelsey's response. See Ford, "Humanity Before God," 36–37.

72. See Ford, "What, How, and Who," 45–46. Ford is unconvinced by Kelsey's response to him on this point. See Ford, "Humanity Before God," 39–40; cf. Kelsey, "Response to the Symposium," 81–82.

73. Greggs, "David Kelsey, Eccentric Existence," 462. It is noteworthy that chapter 4B of *EE* is entitled, "Why Wisdom? A One-Sided Conversation with Clause Westermann."

74. We have more to say about this in chapter 9 of our project.

use of Luz in his deliberations on the Sermon on the Mount (Chp. 22) or his use of Reid and Deissmann in his discussion on the formula 'in Christ' (Chp. 20B).[75] In all these instances there is little to no mention of other authors or interpretations.

There are other complications one could mention, for example, Kelsey's lack of discussions on particular issues[76] such as ecclesiology[77] or gender and sexuality,[78] or his lack of engagement with key theologians.[79] No doubt these and others will arise in the next few decades as Kelsey's work is read and re-read in light of its mammoth contribution to theological anthropology. Some of these subjects are raised in subsequent chapters of this thesis. However, our purposes here are not served by engaging in these discussions. Therefore, let us put these discussions aside for now and turn our attention to considering in detail Kelsey's doctrine of the *imago Dei*.

Eccentric Existence and the *Imago Dei*

Kelsey ends his project with three extended codas. The aim of these codas is to answer the "question of how to take [his proposals] together, how to construe their wholeness-in-complexity" (893). To do this, Kelsey demonstrates how his project goes "against the tradition" (897–900). Although there is a "notable absence of the phrase *imago Dei*" (896) throughout *EE*, the purpose of the coda "is to outline an alternative way in which the theme of the *imago Dei* can serve to exhibit how the three parts of [his] anthropology work together as a whole to render a single theocentric picture of human eccentric existence" (896). In this alternate view, it is Jesus of Nazareth, in his humanity,[80] who images God in the threefold relations of creation,

---

75. One should be cautious with one's critique here. Kelsey has subsequently explained that this is, "for better or worse," a methodological choice he has made not to engage in extensive discussions with secondary sources. See Kelsey, "Response to the Symposium," 80–81. Considering the aims of our project do not merit in-depth and lengthy critical analysis of Kelsey's use of scripture and secondary sources, during the course of this project we keep our focus on Kelsey's main arguments and respect his methodological choice where possible.

76. Moran, "Review of Eccentric Existence," 461.

77. See Wells, "Review of Eccentric Existence," 35; Greggs, "David Kelsey, Eccentric Existence," 462. For a counterview see Ford, "What, How, and Who," 52–53.

78. Ford, "What, How, and Who," 51; Greggs, "David Kelsey, Eccentric Existence," 459. See Kelsey's response in Kelsey, "Response to the Symposium," 80.

79. Greggs, "David Kelsey, Eccentric Existence," 462–63. See Kelsey's response in Kelsey, "Response to the Symposium," 80–81.

80. Kelsey does make allowance for Jesus to image God in his divinity, but he leaves it for others to expand (Kelsey, *Eccentric Existence*, 1010–11).

consummation and reconciliation. All other human beings "image the image of God."[81] Let us follow the contours of Kelsey's argument.

Against the Tradition: A Triple Helix *Imago Dei*

Kelsey notes that theological anthropology has in the past been organized around the concept of the *imago Dei*, which "was traditionally understood to be some essential structural feature of human beings that constitutes them as distinctively human and distinguishes them from animals who do not exhibit God's image" (895). This 'traditional' way of thinking was dominant in Christian theology right up to the middle of the twentieth century. Kelsey uses Dix's book, *The Image and Likeness of God* (1953), as an example of what he considers to be a common approach. His claim is that many authors construct their theological anthropology along similar lines to that of Dix: following a move from creation, through estrangement from God in sin to reconciliation with God and, ultimately eschatological glory (896).

This 'traditional' approach, however, is inappropriate to Kelsey as it is based on the single metanarrative plot of reconciliation. Kelsey's theological anthropology, in contrast, understands creation, reconciliation and eschatological consummation to be narrative plots in their own right and to move together as separate, yet inter-related, aspects of God's relating to all that is not God. Therefore, the 'traditional' use of the *imago Dei* "is not available to [his] project" (896). As a consequence, Kelsey proposes that "we may imagine the overall formal structure of the picture of human existence offered here as a triple helix" (897; cf. 897–900).

By 'triple helix,' Kelsey understands a complex structure whereby his three narratives are asymmetrically woven around each other in a fashion that mimics the double helix of human DNA. They do not converge at any point, they remain logically separate yet inter-related. They are asymmetrical in their priorities and presuppositions. Narratives of consummation presupposes creation yet do not presuppose reconciliation. Reconciliation, in contrast does presuppose both consummation and creation while the narrative of creation is both prior to and does not presuppose either consummation or reconciliation.[82] Consummation and reconciliation, in their interdependence on the story of Jesus and their mutual reliance on creation, together form a double helix around which the narrative of creation weaves (897–900). The triple helix is the underlying shape of the *imago Dei* which is

---

81. See Kelsey, *Eccentric Existence*, 1010, 1015–16, 1023, 1025, 1027, 1046.

82. For a discussion on the asymmetry of Kelsey's narratives, see Kelsey, *Eccentric Existence*, 121–22, 897–900.

to be understood as a relation to and an appropriate response to God's relating in creation, consummation and reconciliation. Let us turn to consider in more detail Kelsey's use of the *imago Dei*.

From General to Concrete: The Content of the *Imago Dei*

In order to identify exactly what the Bible has to say about the image of God, Kelsey engages in an in-depth discussion about the meanings of the words 'image' and 'made in God's image' in the Old Testament, particularly in Genesis 1:26. He considers the comments made by authors such as Westermann, Barth and van Rad (923-24). Ultimately, he concludes that no agreement may be reached (922-36):

> Interpretation of the key text (Gen 1:26-28) is so problematic and controversial that the most careful and influential exegeses seem to cancel out each other. Exegetical debates about Genesis 1:26-28 are simply too inconclusive to warrant giving 'image of God' the central, anchorlike role it has traditionally played in theological anthropology's accounts of what human being is. (900)

Based heavily on Westermann's commentary on the Genesis account as speaking to the narrative of reconciliation and not creation, Kelsey elaborates on his understanding of the role of 'image of God' in the Old Testament as follows:

> The *Adam* who is said in Genesis 1:26-28 to be created 'in' or 'according to' the 'image of God' is not an individual living human personal body. 'Image of God' is not an abstraction from humankind considered as the aggregate of human beings, each and all of whom are created in the image of God. Rather it is human as some sort of corporate whole that is created according to or after the image of God. Humankind as a whole exhibits the image of God in general. (922)

Although the Genesis use of the phrase 'image of God' is, according to Kelsey, reference to humanity in general and is put to "no theological use" (900) within the Old Testament, the term is used in more concrete and therefore "theologically richer ways in the New Testament texts" (901). He argues that that one may cluster New Testament texts that mention the image of God into three groups: 1) texts that speak of human beings as being the image of God, such as James 3:9 and 1 Corinthians 11:7, which speak of human beings as the image, and Colossians 3:10, which may also be interpreted as such; 2) texts that identify the image into which human beings are being transformed, such as 1 Corinthians 15:49, Romans 8:29 and Colossians 3:10; and 3) texts that identify Christ himself as the image, or the functional equivalent, such as Colossians 1:15, Hebrews 1:3a and 2 Corinthians 4:4 (938).

Kelsey dismisses the first two groups by claiming that they refer primarily to Christian behavior and God's relating in eschatological redemption, respectively. Therefore, they are not statements on the nature of human beings or on the content of the image of God (938–56). Having dealt briefly with the prior two categories, Kelsey turns his attention to those texts that speak of Jesus Christ as the image of God.

He engages in in-depth discussions on the texts of Colossians 1:15–20 (956–67), Hebrews 1:1–4 (967–88) and 2 Corinthians 4:4 (988–1002) to expound on his understanding of Jesus as the image of God. His discussions on these texts are very postliberal. Rather than contending that the phrase 'Jesus is the image of God' is a universally valid, doctrinal statement, or even an ontological statement about who Jesus is, Kelsey proposes a functional use of that statement. He argues that the use of this phrase in Christian communities is the driving force behind its use in the New Testament (906). These three texts speak of different ways Kelsey believes warrant the judgement that the story they assume, the story of Jesus' life, death and resurrection, is definitive of how Jesus images God (1007). To Kelsey, the image of God is none other than Christ, in his concrete particularity:

> Accordingly, in these three texts, 'Christ' is not the (religious?) name of a universal cosmological principle, one that somehow images incarnation of the divine . . . in these three texts 'Christ' is the name[83] of a concrete living human personal body in his distinctive relationship to God, in God's unique relationship to him, and in his distinctive relationships with fellow living human personal bodies in their proximate context. For these NT texts, the image of God just is Jesus Christ in his unsubstitutable human personal identity, as that is described by canonical narratives of the way in which God relates in and through all that Jesus does and undergoes in community with fellow human beings, to draw all that is not God to eschatological consummation and, when it is estranged from God, to reconcile it. (906)

In summary, while humanity in general may be said to image God in the Old Testament, it is in the New Testament that this general description

---

83. It is arguable whether 'Christ' is a name or a title.

is applied to the particular concrete human Jesus of Nazareth who is the content of the *imago Dei* (913). Let us explore this further.

Jesus: Image of God

First, it should be noted that Kelsey refers to Jesus *as* the image of God,[84] stating that Jesus *is* the image of God "simply by being a human creature" (1010).[85] Later in his work, while discussing the anthropological 'How?' question, Kelsey claims that Jesus is the image of God "whether he does anything or not, simply by being what he is" (1027). If one were to stop here, one could conclude that Kelsey's construction is very much substantive: Jesus is the image (noun). It is not a function of what Jesus does or engages in but simply a feature/characteristic of his very being. Yet there is more to Kelsey's construction that must be considered.

Not only does Kelsey use the phrase that Jesus 'is the image of God,' but also the term "images God."[86] Kelsey claims that Jesus' creaturely humanity "images God by the way he bodily acts, interacts with other creatures, and undergoes other's actions as a human creature" (1010). Furthermore, Kelsey frequently refers to Jesus as the "imager of God."[87] By speaking of Christ as the one who 'images God' and is the 'imager of God,' Kelsey takes 'image' as a verb: something Jesus does. On the one hand, Christ images God as he bodily acts, and on the other hand, he images God through what befalls him, as God (who is the active agent) relates to all that is not God through everything Jesus undergoes:

> NT uses of 'image of God' link the phrase to canonical New Testament narratives of God relating to all that is not God in and through what God does in and through what Jesus of Nazareth in his concrete particularity does and undergoes. (906)

To complicate matters even further, there are a few occasions where Kelsey claims that Jesus Christ both images and is the image of God at the same time.[88] The two statements may, on first impression, appear ambigu-

---

84. For example see Kelsey, *Eccentric Existence*, 896, 906, 915, 918, 920, 956, 1002, 1009, 1011, 1013 (cf. 912–15, 985), where it is claimed that Jesus is the content of the image of God.

85. It is noteworthy that in this text Kelsey also claims he 'images' God. We discuss this concept soon.

86. See for example Kelsey, *Eccentric Existence*, 1004, 1012, 1014–15, 1017, 1024, 1026, 1028, 1047.

87. See for example Kelsey, *Eccentric Existence*, 1009, 1023, 1026.

88. See for example Kelsey, *Eccentric Existence*, 1010, 1012, 1023, 1026.

ous. Ambiguity, however, is not a trait Kelsey is particularly averse to.[89] Kelsey holds this seemingly ambiguous construction together in two ways. First, he acknowledges the ambiguity and the distinction between the two ways Jesus is linked to the image of God. To Kelsey, the "enactment" (1027) of Jesus' response to God's relating to him in creative blessing signals the distinction between the way Jesus images God and the way he is the image of God (1027). Here, Kelsey references both a passive and active manner in which Jesus images God: passive in the sense of simply being created as the image of God[90] and active in his actions and responses to God for and on behalf of others. This distinction is rooted in Kelsey's understanding of the basic and quotidian identity, a topic we discuss in chapter 5. Second, in Kelsey's construction, the image is held together in the concept of personhood. The 'What?' (noun) and the 'How?' (verb) are held together by the 'Who?' The image of God is not a noun or a verb, which one either has or does. It is the very person of Jesus Christ. We have more to say on Kelsey's understanding of personhood in chapter 6 of our project.

Kelsey moves the concept of image beyond the notion of a characteristic or attribute of human beings (and specifically the characteristic of the human being Jesus of Nazareth) and defines it in terms of the person Jesus of Nazareth. Likewise, his construction moves the concept of *imago Dei* from an object to a subject:

> The significance of the notion of 'image of God' for theological anthropology emerges, I argue, when the question asked of the phrase 'image of God' is 'who is the 'image'?' rather than 'what is the 'image'?' and when the answer is, 'Jesus Christ.' (938)

Human Being: Image of the Image of God

This subject—the concrete image of God—Jesus Christ, has implications for the general image of God: humanity. In Kelsey's words, "Canonical narrative identity descriptions of Jesus as imager of God precisely in his humanity give him the status of grammatical paradigm of human beings" (1009); therefore, human beings "image the image of God" (1010).[91]

According to Kelsey, however, we do not image God insofar as our relations to one another image the relations between the Father, Son and Holy

---

89. Kelsey speaks on a number of occasions about the ambiguity of his construction of Jesus as the image of God. See for example Kelsey, *Eccentric Existence*, 1010, 906, 907, 908–10, 911, 920.

90. Here Kelsey is referring to Jesus of Nazareth and not the eternal Word of God.

91. Recall Buckley's observation of Kelsey being "grammatically christocentric" (Buckley, "Buoys for Eccentric Existence," 22).

Spirit. Kelsey believes that the triune relations constitute each of the distinct persons within the Trinity exhaustively,[92] but this cannot be said of human beings. Nor is it Kelsey's claim that human beings image God as their social relations among each other constitute their personhood, and they therefore image the social relations between the three persons of the Trinity, whose personhood is constituted by the relations of self-giving and receiving.[93]

More than this, human beings do not image God in the sense that their metaphysical dialectic constitutes them in the same way as the metaphysical dialectic of the persons of the Trinity.[94] In fact, Kelsey is suspicious of the concept of certain metaphysical responses in theological anthropology. He finds pre-modern anthropological proposals that ascribe to a metaphysical dualism,[95] primarily by linking the concept of 'soul' with the *imago Dei*, problematic (29–31, 39). Such dualism, to Kelsey, does not allow for the positive assessment of human bodies as God's creation. If the concept of the *imago Dei* is not to function, as it has done in the past (29–31), in non-holistic dualist ways, then Kelsey's understanding of the image of God must be rooted in some concrete reality. If it does not, it risks the unfortunate consequence of human beings, as eccentrically conceived, disappearing into the obscurities of pure relationality.[96]

In his attempt to avoid the negative consequences of past doctrines of the *imago Dei*, Kelsey offers an alternative approach. Given what canonical narratives claim about who and what Jesus is as he images God in his humanity, "we may assess other human beings as imaging God 'after the fashion' of Jesus' imaging God—that is, imaging the image of God" (1010).[97] All other human beings image this image, as they (like Jesus) are

92. Kelsey believes this is the position of Augustine (Kelsey, *Eccentric Existence*, 1009).

93. According to Kelsey, this is the position of Grenz (Kelsey, *Eccentric Existence*, 1009).

94. This, according to Kelsey, is the position of Zizioulas (Kelsey, *Eccentric Existence*, 1009).

95. Kelsey is cautious of non-holistic dualism. In his discussion on the second telling of Job's creation (Job 10), Kelsey claims that what is problematic about the narrative that Job has been given a living body is the grammatical equation of the relation between different actual entities. A distinction between 'mortal body' and 'immortal soul' has been a traditional way of analyzing this grammatical equation. Kelsey warns against this equation. His argument is that Job's telling of his having and being given an actual living body does not by itself entail a non-holistic dualist theological anthropology (Kelsey, *Eccentric Existence*, 272).

96. As is the warning of Hill and Harris to all who believe relationality alone offers a viable option to the definition of human existence (Harris, "Should We Say"; Hill, "Divine Persons"). Kelsey himself is aware of their warning (Kelsey, *Eccentric Existence*, 34).

97. Kelsey does claim, however, that there are boundaries to these remarks. He

related to by God in creative blessing, eschatological consummation and reconciliation (1010).

While Kelsey is not alone in linking the *imago Dei*, human beings and Jesus Christ,[98] his approach is unique. For example, Barth contends that "there can be no question, therefore, of a direct knowledge of the nature of man in general from that of the man Jesus"[99] because of the reality of sin and the mystery of the identification of Jesus with God.[100] Although there is no direct knowledge, Barth nevertheless contends that there is indirect knowledge as Jesus acts as both the "real man"[101] and the "royal man."[102] In this sense, Barth sees Jesus as being the 'real man' based on six defining characteristics, which he subsequently applies to human beings generally.[103] Yet this is not Kelsey's approach.

Rather than being an example that other human beings are to follow, or the prototype upon which others are based, or even the archetype which exemplifies other human beings, Jesus is the "grammatically paradigmatic human being" (1077), according to Kelsey.[104] Here Kelsey amalgamates the notions of prototype and archetype.[105] His construction should be read in light of postliberalism's emphasis on narrative theology and linguistic character. Jesus is grammatically—within the narrative and, at the same time, the Christian faith language—the paradigmatic human being. He simultaneously functions as both the prototype and the archetype in that context of the Christian faith language. We have more to say on this in the next chapter. For now, we simply note the unique nuance of Kelsey's construction of Jesus Christ as the *imago Dei*.

---

claims that "beyond anthropological oriented remarks about Jesus as the image of God in his humanity, a fully developed Christology would obviously also need to engage traditional proposals in Christian secondary theology about Jesus as the image of God in respect of his divinity as well" (Kelsey, *Eccentric Existence*, 1010).

98. For example, see Berkouwer, *Man*, 107; Brunner, *Dogmatics*, 2:58–59; Horst, "Face to Face," 270; Pittenger, *Christian Understanding*, 18–33.

99. Barth, *CD* 3/2:47, 71.

100. Barth, *CD* 3/2:71–72.

101. Barth, *CD* 3/2:132–202.

102. Barth, *CD* 4/2:154–264.

103. Barth, *CD* 3/2:68–71, 73–74.

104. One can compare such thinking to Barth's notion of Jesus Christ who, as the elected one, is both the prototype and the archetype in that he is the "original" and "essential" aspect of humanity. See Barth, *Christ and Adam*, 14–24, 74–82; Barth, *CD* 3/2:50. Consider also Barth, *CD* 3/1:183–207; 4/1:402; Gabriel, "Trinitarian Doctrine"; cf. Grenz, "Jesus as the Imago Dei."

105. Indeed, Kelsey uses the word 'prototype' himself (Kelsey, *Eccentric Existence*, 1023, 1027, 1029, 1047).

Putting it All Together

Kelsey's final coda draws together many of the key movements of *EE*, demonstrating how the three narratives speak to the three anthropological questions by appealing to Jesus as the paradigmatic human being who is the image of God. This final coda takes each anthropological question in turn and reveals its relation to the way Jesus images God in God's triple relations of creation, consummation and reconciliation. Each section culminates with the implications of humanity in general as images of the image of God.[106]

In summary, Kelsey argues that the three strands that weave around one another in canonical narrative identity descriptions of Jesus speak of the three ways in which Jesus images God. In being created, Jesus images God merely in being what he is. By virtue of God relating through all that he does and undergoes to reconcile estranged human creatures, Jesus images God in God's relating in reconciliation. He images God in his resurrected body that inaugurates God's eschatological consummation of human beings. Furthermore, Jesus images God as He enacts practices that express faith's attitude of reverent and awed doxological gratitude for the gift of God's creative blessing, along with practices that express hope's attitude of joy and love's attitude of a passionate desire for communion with God (who is constituted by the community-in-communion of the triune life) and with fellow estranged (and at the same time reconciled) human creatures.

In his created, resurrected and reconciling living body, Jesus is paradigmatic of what, who and how all other human beings are to be. As they are images of the imager of God, they, too, actively image the image of the triune God. They do so as they respond to God's relating in creative blessing, eschatological consummation and reconciliation and as they enact practices that mimic the appropriate responses of faith, hope and love.[107] In describing both Jesus Christ and human beings as images of the image of God, Kelsey makes use of an anthropological formula. A topic we now turn to.

---

106. For a summary of each section, see Kelsey, *Eccentric Existence*, 1026, 1033-34, 1050-51.

107. I have purposefully left out the concept of 'mystery', as it has little bearing on our overall discussions. It should be noted that this concept acts as a caveat to all of Kelsey's anthropological remarks, placing a limit on how far we can go to describe/identify both Jesus Christ and human beings who are both ultimately inexplicable. See Kelsey, *Eccentric Existence*, 919-21, 1015, 1026, 1033, 1050.

4

An Anthropological Formula

IN THE PREVIOUS CHAPTER we sketched the landscape of *EE*, drawing the readers' attention to some of the buoys for *EE* and, in particular, to Kelsey's construction of the *imago Dei*. This chapter follows closely from that discussion as we now turn our attention away from *EE* in general and to a specific aspect of Kelsey's project: his anthropological formula. The purpose of this chapter is to orientate the reader to this anthropological formula and, in particular, to its relation to Kelsey's understanding of the image of God. With this in mind we limit our discussions to the development, structure and application of the formula within *EE*, saving our constructive critical discussions for subsequent chapters.

Defining 'Formula'

It should be noted that *EE* does not set out to develop an anthropological formula. Kelsey gives no hint within his introductory chapters of either a primary or secondary objective that may result in such a description of human being. There is no chapter, sub-section or paragraph that deals directly with the concept of an anthropological formula. Indeed, any references to 'formula,' which are few and far between, seem almost incidental.[1] Rather, the formula develops naturally out of Kelsey's descriptions of human beings in part 1 of *EE*, which—as noted in the previous chapter—deals primarily with the 'What?' question and the doctrine of creation.

It is Kelsey himself who ascribes the description of 'formula' to his set of anthropological features. This is most evident in his definition and explanation of the use of the term *human* in the phrase *actual living human body*. Consider the following clause:

> The role of the word 'human' in the formula 'actual living human body' is to identify the subset of living bodies about which theological anthropological claims are made. (257)

---

1. For example, see Kelsey, *Eccentric Existence*, 257.

Here he describes the phrase 'actual living human body' as a formula. Let us pause briefly to consider how Kelsey uses the concept of a formula.

Kelsey makes use of the term 'formula' in a number of places throughout his theological *corpus*. Of note is his formulaic description of the Christian community.[2] Although the specific content of that description does not concern us here, the manner in which he makes use of a formulaic description assists us in clarifying his understanding of theological formulas in general. In that discussion, Kelsey's understanding is that a formula acts as a "placeholder" (333) that is "runic"[3] and can be "unpacked"[4] to yield a "fairly comprehensive systematic theology."[5] That is to say, Kelsey understands a theological formula to be a descriptive, shorthand placeholder for complex, often technical, theological ideas and doctrines. This notion of a theological 'formula' has parallels in both broader theological discussions and in *EE* itself.[6] As theology formulates an orderly, rational and coherent account of the Christian faith, its formulations are summarized into formulae. These formulae are then used as shorthand descriptions for the relevant more complex formulations. This usage is prevalent both within *EE* and throughout secondary theology. We think, for example, of the frequent reference to the Niceno-Constantinopolitan formula 'God is one substance in three persons' (46)[7] or the Pauline formula 'in Christ' (Chp. 20B).[8]

Therefore, when we speak of Kelsey's anthropological formula, we are speaking of a limited set of terms that are used within *EE* as descriptive placeholders for complex, often technical, theological theories. Without 'unpacking' this limited set of terms and critically analyzing the relevant concepts, the formula remains 'runic', that is to say, an obscure and unintelligible symbol. It is the labor of our project to do the necessary 'unpacking'.

The Formulaic Elements

The elements that make up Kelsey's anthropological formula emerge from Kelsey's discussions in part 1 as he seeks to answer the anthropological

2. Kelsey, "Bible and Christian Theology," 142–52.
3. Kelsey, "Human Being," 386.
4. Kelsey, "Bible and Christian Theology," 386.
5. Kelsey, *Eccentric Existence*, 386. Of course, 'systematic theology' needs to be understood here in terms of what we have said in the previous chapter.
6. Consider for example his discussions on the triadic liturgical Trinitarian formulas (Kelsey, *Eccentric Existence*, chapter 3A).
7. Cf. Spence, *Christology*, 48; Tanner, *Jesus, Humanity, and the Trinity*, 5–8; Zizioulas, "Human Capacity and Human Incapacity," 406.
8. Cf. Colijn, "Paul's Use"; Parsons, "'In Christ' in Paul."

'What?' question in the context of the doctrine of creation. In part 1, he begins with a description of the ultimate context of the human being as God's relating to all that is not God (Chp. 4A). In addition to this ultimate context, human beings live within the context of quotidian creation which forms their proximate context (Chp. 5A). Kelsey's understanding of our ultimate and proximate contexts underscores his entire anthropology, as the human being lives in the ambiguity of being given its identity as a gift (Chp. 6, 250–51, 270) yet having to enact a vocation in line with this identity (193–199). To Kelsey, this is represented by the terms *basic identity* and *quotidian identity* (Chp. 9B).[9]

Having established the broad framework in which human beings are set (our ultimate and proximate contexts), Kelsey progresses in chapters 6 and 7 of *EE* to describe important features of human being. In chapter 6, in the context of two ways Job describes his creation, as a) being a living body and b) having been given a living body, Kelsey develops his understanding of the term *living body* (248–50, 1019–23).[10] Within this discussion, Kelsey contends that human beings, as far as his anthropological proposals are concerned, have the ontological status of actualities (as opposed to potentialities or possibilities).[11] More than this, human living bodies, as Kelsey expounds on in chapter 7, are *personal actual human living bodies*. The inclusion of the concept *personal*[12] requires Kelsey to address issues surrounding individuality (391–401) and the unsubstitutability (387–91, 307–8) of individuals, which he does in chapter 9B.[13]

By the end of chapter 9B, Kelsey has formulated and discussed key anthropological concepts that are highly complex and technical. These formulations are summarized into formulae that are then used throughout *EE* as placeholders for the relevant complex ideas they represent. Take for example the following statement given in chapter 9B:

> Living human personal bodies' basic identity is God's gift. Their basic identity is not a potentiality whose realization is most desirable and into which human creatures may, or necessarily will, develop in time. Nor is it a logical possibility that human creatures may or may not appropriate in self-involving subjective

---

9. See also Kelsey, *Eccentric Existence*, chapters 12A, 13, 18, 19A, we have much more to say on this in the next chapter.

10. This is the central theme of chapter 9 of our project.

11. For Kelsey's understanding of actuality see Kelsey, *Eccentric Existence*, 251–55. This is the central theme of chapter 8 of our project.

12. This is the central topic of chapter 6 of our project.

13. This occupies chapter 7 of our project.

> acts that are existentially formative. Christian anthropological claims about human creatures' personal identity have the force of a claim that human creatures already actually have this identity by virtue of the triune God relating to them. Basic identity has the ontological status of actuality, not ideality. (384)

This quotation is just one example of Kelsey's use of formulaic placeholders that are persistently utilized throughout *EE* in answer to the anthropological 'What?' question. In no particular order, these formulaic elements may be listed as follows: *living bodies, personal, basic identity* and *actual*. When we consider that chapter 9B speaks in large part to the unsubstitutability of the human being, and that the quotation above is given in this context, we may add *unsubstitutable* to this list. The list now includes the following elements: *basic identity, living body, personal, actual,* and *unsubstitutable*.

The astute reader might notice that our list does not include the term *human*, yet the quotation above includes the phrase *actual living human bodies*. Kelsey's inclusion of the term *human* is a conundrum, seemingly using the term *human* to describe what 'human' means. The conundrum may be solved when one considers how the term *human* is employed within this formula. According to Kelsey, *human* is employed as a classification marker to identify which class of creature his anthropological claims refer to, namely those entities who have a specific DNA sequence (257–61).[14] The term serves to classify the biological class of beings to which his remarks are made in reference to the genetically identifiable species *Homo sapiens*. This term may be used to classify both living bodies (the human being itself) or substances that are human in their genetic make-up and yet are not *living bodies*, for example, dead skin or hair follicles. The term, therefore, acts within his formula to circumscribe its claims to a specific class of creature within the created order.

As such *human* (and its direct reference to human DNA) does not, within Kelsey's project, provide any anthropologically enlightening insight into the nature of human existence save to say that human beings, at some point in their history, have/had human DNA.[15] This is, of course, not to say that human DNA cannot shed very much light on theological anthropology. All we are saying is that in the context of Kelsey's anthro-

---

14. We take issue with Kelsey's use of human DNA in chapter 9 of our project.

15. We say 'have/had' because it is not particularly clear that Kelsey is contending that eschatologically consummated human beings have human DNA. As shown in chapter 9 of this project, Kelsey's construction of an eschatologically consumed humanity draws our attention away from material bodies while at the same time avoiding a purely non-physical glorified state.

pological formula, its significance is limited. Therefore, the term is not included in our list of terms to be critically evaluated in this project. We do, however, have some more to say about it later, in particular, about the role DNA plays in Kelsey's anthropology.

The Structure of the Formula

While it is relatively easy to justify the claim that *EE* makes frequent reference to the anthropological elements established in our previous sub-section, an overview of the manner in which Kelsey uses these elements draws our attention to their dynamic and complicated inter-related structure. As an example, let us consider the clause *living human personal bodies*, which is used throughout Kelsey's project.[16] This phrase is connected with *actuality* (as evidenced in the quotation above[17]) so as to read "actual living human personal bodies."[18] Sometimes the term *personal* is not included and it is given as "actual living human bodies" (e.g., 262, 264), while at other times the terms *actual* and *personal* are excluded and Kelsey simply refers to "human living bodies" (e.g., 251–55) or "living human body" (e.g., 1021–23).

As our quotation from chapter 9B demonstrates, the clause is closely associated with identity as *basic, personal* and *unsubstitutable*:

> The concept of personal identity was introduced in chapter 9A and reappears often in each of the parts of this theological anthropology, sometimes explicitly qualified as 'quotidian' personal identity, sometimes as 'basic' personal identity, sometimes as 'unsubstitutable' personal identity, sometimes as both of the latter two (257).[19]

This *basic unsubstitutable personal identity* is at times discussed in contrast to a distorted quotidian personal identity (e.g., 1046). Most intriguing of all is Kelsey's very close association of *personal identity* with *personal bodies*,[20] almost as if the two terms were synonyms. For example:

> Our personal identities as personal bodies drawn by the triune God to eschatological consummation can be described

---

16. See as examples Kelsey, *Eccentric Existence*, 384, 388–90, 423, 515, 536–42, 893, 1034, 1038, 1041, 1044.

17. Also see his discussions in Kelsey, *Eccentric Existence*, 536–42.

18. See as examples Kelsey, *Eccentric Existence*, 254, 314, 1015, 1020, 1026, 1046.

19. See also Kelsey, *Eccentric Existence*, 378–85.

20. Kelsey, *Eccentric Existence*, chapter 11, is particularly pertinent in this regard.

adequately only by telling stories about us that render us as ones at once chosen and rejected, affirmed and judged. (527–28)

The central point made here is that all the elements together, in varying orders, are used by Kelsey to answer the anthropological 'What?' question. The elements are inter-connected in a dynamic complexity that allows for a flexible construction rather than a rigid structure. For example, *personal* is connected with both *identity* and *living body*, while *living body* is closely related to *personal bodies*, *human bodies* and *actual bodies*. In this sense, one should not think of the formula as a linear equation with one term following from the other as if one plus another equals a third. Rather, the terms should be taken as a mesh that together describe human being.

More than this, while the elements may be used in varying orders to describe human beings, Kelsey also uses derivatives and abstractions as placeholders for his anthropological proposals. Consider the following statement:

> I promoted the phrase 'personal bodies' as a placeholder for the entire set of remarks about what we are. (333)

The term *personal bodies* is scattered throughout Kelsey's anthropology[21] and acts as a placeholder for his entire set of anthropological claims. By referring simply to *personal bodies*, Kelsey makes use of this formulaic derivative to avoid what would otherwise be a lengthy and repetitive anthropology.

The reason behind this complex approach may be rooted in Kelsey's postliberal heritage. As noted in the previous chapter, Kelsey presents an unsystematic systematic description of human beings. In this context, each formulaic term is a descriptive part of the anthropological formula that together gives a "wholeness-in-complexity" (893, 896). As a descriptive summary (a limited set of placeholders for complex ideas), the formula should not be taken as an independent sentence that obeys the rules of syntax and grammar. The terms are not always given in the same order, do not always appear together and, therefore, do not play a static grammatical function. It would be inappropriate, for example, to ask which term forms the subject, object or indirect object of the sentence.

Yet all this is not to say that Kelsey does not have a preferred order and structure to these elements, even if he allows for alternate presentations. Throughout his anthropology he frequently refers to the formula in a specific order. This is particularly evident when one reads his final coda

---

21 See as examples Kelsey, *Eccentric Existence*, 309–32, 354–55, 404, 407, 410, 412–13, 419, 443, 445, 480–81, 498, 501–29.

in which he often refers to "actual living human personal body."[22] As one reads *EE*, it is this order that is impressed upon one's mind. Therefore, one gets a sense that, even in the presence of various derivatives and abstractions, Kelsey prefers to describe the human being as a "basic unsubstitutable identity of an actual living human personal body."[23]

The Application of the Formula

As with Kelsey's doctrine of the *imago Dei*, his anthropological formula is applied first to humanity in general (part 1) and then to Jesus Christ in particular (parts 2 and 3). This is primarily evidenced in his use of formulaic derivatives in reference to Jesus. Kelsey argues that Jesus "is paradigmatic of what it is to be an actual living human personal body" (1011). He applies the derivatives *living human personal body*,[24] *actual living human body* (1023) and *human personal body* (1048) to Jesus as the paradigmatic human being. More than this, since his references to Jesus are to a specific human being, he includes the concept of identity far more frequently in his formulaic descriptions of Jesus of Nazareth than he does to humanity in general. This includes the derivative *human personal identity* (909), but more frequently *basic personal identity*,[25] which is often associated with the unsubstitutability of Jesus Christ.[26] Linking the formula to Jesus has implications for the doctrine of the *imago Dei*.

Recollect that our previous chapter discussed the relationship between Jesus of Nazareth, human beings in general and the image of God. That chapter noted that Kelsey understands Jesus to be the content of the image of God (1023) and simultaneously grammatically paradigmatic of human beings generally. Consequently, all human beings image the image of God who is Jesus. In applying the anthropological formula to a description of Jesus who is the content of the image of God, Kelsey closely associates the formula with the doctrine of the *imago Dei*.

Consider the following:

---

22. See the examples within his final coda Kelsey, *Eccentric Existence*, 1026, 1033–34, 1050.

23. Justification for this preference is particularly evident in Kelsey's application of the formula to Jesus Christ. See for example Kelsey's final coda, in particular Kelsey, *Eccentric Existence*, 906, 1009, 1010, 1012.

24. See as examples Kelsey, *Eccentric Existence*, 906, 1024, 1026, 1045, 1050.

25. See as examples Kelsey, *Eccentric Existence*, 1025, 1034, 1043, 1045–46.

26. Kelsey, *Eccentric Existence*, 626, 896–97, 905, 906, 912, 913, 915, 918, 920, 921, 102, 1012, 1045–50.

> The three lines of thought in this project that wind around each other in a triple helix yield three aspects of an answer to the perennial anthropological 'What?' question. The three are strands in canonical narrative identity descriptions of Jesus' unsubstitutable identity as the actual living human personal body who is the image of God and provide the grammatical paradigm for theological accounts of human being. (1009)

Let us pause briefly to consider the implications of Kelsey's construction that, epitomized in the quotation directly above, relates the anthropological formula with the image of God.

Recall how Kelsey's final coda draws together many of the key movements of *EE*, demonstrating how the three narratives speak to the three anthropological questions by appealing to Jesus as the paradigmatic human being who is the image of God. It is in the context of the first narrative strand (creation) that the anthropological formula is drawn into a description of Jesus of Nazareth as the image of God and consequently into a description of human beings generally who image the image of God.

The narrative of creation has implications for each of the anthropological questions.[27] His basic construction in each case is as follows: Jesus of Nazareth—simply by being created as a basic unsubstitutable identity of an actual living human personal body—is the image of God. This is to say, Jesus of Nazareth is the image of God, he is who the image of God is, and he is how the image of God ought to be. Since Jesus is paradigmatic of human beings generally, all other human beings, as basic unsubstitutable identities of actual living human personal bodies, are images of the image of God by virtue of their creation.[28] This is concisely and clearly stated in the first aspect

---

27. See Kelsey, *Eccentric Existence*, 1010–16, 1027–28, 1045–46.

28. It must be remembered that we are speaking about Kelsey's coda, which follows more than 1,000 pages of discussions. As such, Kelsey's construction in this regard is highly complex and idiosyncratic, requiring an understanding of the formulaic elements that, up to this point in our project, have yet to be analyzed and expounded. For the interested reader, Kelsey's arguments are as follows: In the first aspect of the anthropological 'What?' question (Kelsey, *Eccentric Existence*, 1010–16), Kelsey argues that Jesus is the image of God "in his creaturely humanity" (Kelsey, *Eccentric Existence*, 1010) by virtue of God creating him. He expands on what he means by 'creaturely humanity' later by referring to the anthropological formula: "Canonical narratives that offer a description of who Jesus is render the unsubstitutable personal identity of an actual living human personal body-in-community in his concrete particularity" (Kelsey, *Eccentric Existence*, 1012). He goes on to apply this to humanity in general, arguing that "in their human bodiliness, they image Jesus's imaging God in his human bodiless" (Kelsey, *Eccentric Existence*, 1015). In the first aspect of the answer to the anthropological 'How?' question, Kelsey contends that it is "in his creaturely humanity" (Kelsey, *Eccentric Existence*, 1027) that Jesus flourishes as the image of God in

of the answer to the 'How?' question. Here Kelsey claims that Jesus "images God, whether he does anything or not, simply by being what he is—namely, the actual living human personal body that he is" (1027). He goes on to say that all other human beings image the image of God in the same fashion as Jesus—that is, simply by being what they are (1027–28).[29]

As such, when Kelsey speaks about Jesus and human beings as images of God, he does so by describing both in terms of the anthropological formula. Therefore, in answer to the anthropological 'What?' question, within the framework of the doctrine of the *imago Dei*, human beings may be described using the anthropological formula. Consequently, Kelsey's anthropological formula is to be taken as a description of human beings, who are the image of the image of God. The human being, as a basic unsubstitutable identity of an actual living human personal body, is the image of the image of God. Question: What is Jesus? Answer: He is the basic unsubstitutable identity of an actual living personal body that is the image of God. Question: What are human beings? Answer: They are the basic unsubstitutable identities of actual living personal bodies that are the image of the image of God.

Before continuing to consider a strategy for 'unpacking' the anthropological formula, it is important that we are clear about the limitations of its application within the doctrine of the *imago Dei* for our project. First, recall our discussions in chapter 1 where it was noted that the underlying questions of the substantive-relational debate are driven by the doctrine of creation and the anthropological 'What?' question. In this and the previous chapter, we have further noted that Kelsey develops his anthropological formula in part 1 of *EE* as he discusses the doctrine of creation and, in particular, the anthropological 'What?' question. Our discussions directly above have further indicated that the formula is most aptly applied within *EE*'s framework of the image of God in the context of the doctrine of creation. Since this project deals with *EE*'s construction of the image of God in light of the substantive-relational debate, we have chosen to focus on the anthropological 'What?'

---

responding appropriately to the way God relates to him creatively. On the same page he applies this to other human beings, saying they—referred to as "all other living human bodies" (Kelsey, *Eccentric Existence*, 1027)—image the image of God as they enact appropriate responses to God's creative relating. In the first aspect of the answer to the 'Who?' question, Kelsey contends that "Jesus of Nazareth is the image of God simply in his creaturely bodily humanity" (Kelsey, *Eccentric Existence*, 1045) and that "all other human beings image the image of God in their actual living human personal bodies inasmuch as, like him," (Kelsey, *Eccentric Existence*, 1046) God relates directly and indirectly through their quotidian and basic identities. During the course of our project the intricacies of this construction become clearer.

29. It should be noted that in this particular instance the discussion is about the anthropological 'How?' question.

question and the doctrine of creation. In this context the formula is fundamental. Kelsey describes human beings as images of the image of God simply because they are what they are created to be, that is, basic unsubstitutable identities of actual living human personal bodies. It is, therefore, only fitting that our discussions focus on part 1 of *EE*.

However, it must be noted that Kelsey applies the notion of the image of God principally to the 'Who?' (Jesus Christ) and 'How?' questions and only subsequently to the 'What?' question (1002).[30] Therefore, as with all projects of this nature, there are limitations to our discussions. Those that take place in our project have implications for the broader debates around the image of God, particularly the substantive-relational debates, as these relate primarily to the 'What?' question and the doctrine of creation. Kelsey's doctrine of the image of God, however, speaks not only to these debates but also to who we are and how we ought to be as images of the image of God. Although we inevitably touch on the 'Who?' and 'How?' questions at different points in our project, the implications of the doctrine of the *imago Dei* on these questions, as well as parts 2 and 3 of *EE*, are left for other projects to explore.

More importantly, we must keep in mind that Kelsey does not define what the image of God is. Rather, he seeks to describe 'Who?,' 'How?,' and 'What?' human beings are as images of the image of God. During the course of our project we often note the implications of Kelsey's postliberal move away from definitions to descriptions—particularly narrative descriptions—for the doctrine of the image of God. We have much to say about this in our concluding chapter.

Strategy for Analyzing the Formula

From our discussions above, we can draw the following conclusion: Kelsey develops what is effectively, in his own words, an anthropological formula to describe human beings in general, Jesus in particular and (as a consequence of his construction) the image of God. This formula is composed of five elements: 1) *basic identity* (in distinction to quotidian identity), 2) *living body*, 3) *actuality*, 4) *personal* and, 5) *unsubstitutable individuality*. In many respects, the order of the formula is immaterial; *personal* for example, is intimately connected with both *basic identity* and *living body*. Yet Kelsey displays

---

30. It is interesting to note that Kelsey begins each of the three parts of his project with the 'What?' question and only subsequently moves on to discuss the 'Who?' and 'How?' questions. Furthermore, his final coda follows this same pattern beginning with the 'What?' question and only subsequently discussing the 'How?' and 'Who?' questions. One can, therefore, question the primary application of the *imago Dei* in *EE* in this regard.

a preference for an order as follows: the human being may be described as the basic unsubstitutable identity of an actual living human personal body. 'Unpacking' this formula is the main task of our project.

Providing a constructive, critical analysis of Kelsey's anthropological formula requires us to think carefully about our strategy in examining it. We are presented with a few options. One option is to approach the formula at will. As mentioned, the order of the formula is relatively immaterial. Each term or element speaks to a specific feature of human being, yet is inter-related to other terms and features of human existence. With this in mind, one may simply choose a random approach to discussing the formula, perhaps beginning in alphabetical order with *actuality* and ending with *unsubstitutability*. However, such an approach fails to recognize any development of thought within Kelsey's project, and it does not take into consideration the primary importance of some terms in relation to others, for example, Kelsey's central conviction that the basic structure of creation is to be understood in reference to God's relating. Such eccentricity speaks primarily to the feature of human beings' basic identity and only secondarily to features such as *actuality* or *unsubstitutability*.

Alternatively, one could approach the formula in terms of its grammatical structure, that is, consider the object and analyze the qualifications in ascending order. For example, one could begin with *living body* and proceed to discuss the qualifications of *actual, personal, unsubstitutable,* and *basic* and *quotidian* identity. Approaching the formula in this way, however, would give the misleading impression that the formula is a grammatically correct sentence that speaks about a particular object with increasing levels of qualification. As noted above, the formula is not a sentence and does not follow normal rules of grammar. It would be difficult to identify the object. Is the formula primarily speaking about living bodies, personal identities or personal bodies? Furthermore, although a hierarchy is evident in the qualifications *basic* and *quotidian* identity, it is not immediately evident what hierarchy exists among other qualifications such as *actual, personal* and *unsubstitutable*.

Another option is to approach the formula in the order in which Kelsey prefers to present it: discussing *basic* first and then proceeding to *living body*. While there is certainly merit in this approach, not least of which is its recognition of Kelsey's preferential order, such an approach focusses too heavily on the order of the formulaic elements while ignoring the intricacies of Kelsey's argument. As demonstrated in a previous subsection, while Kelsey makes frequent use of this preferred order, he also makes ample use of alternate arrangements as well as numerous derivatives and abstractions.

For example, in some cases Kelsey refers to *personal identity*[31] and in other cases *personal bodies*.[32] Thus, the formula may be ordered as the *unsubstitutable basic personal identity* of *actual living human personal bodies*. *Personal*, in such uses, may be introduced either at the beginning or the end of the formulaic clause.[33] Therefore, this approach is not appropriate.

There is another approach open to us. Considering that identity is one of the most important questions for our contemporary society and the global Christian church,[34] and that the doctrine of the *imago Dei* speaks to the heart of human identity in relation to God, it is arguable that the most appropriate approach for constructively and critically evaluating Kelsey's anthropological formula is to begin with Kelsey's notion of identity and then discuss the ontological status of this identity and its location. This is the approach we take in the next five chapters. Let us explain further.

Kelsey qualifies his "sense" (334) of identity with the terms *basic* and *quotidian*, *personal* and *unsubstitutable*. Following a brief introduction to Kelsey's sense of identity, we begin the next chapter with the terms *basic* and *quotidian*, which, speaking to the ultimate and proximate contexts of human being, form a binary pair. We note that this binary pair speaks to the gift and vocation of human existence, enabling Kelsey's construction to hold both static and dynamic elements.

We then discuss *personal identity* in chapter 6, where it is noted that this sense of identity establishes the foundation for human dignity and value in *EE*. It is noted that this foundation is entirely eccentric to the human being and that no list of characteristics or human relationality can establish human value.

In chapter 7 we turn our focus to the question of individual identity, that is, what distinguishes one human being from another, or—more precisely—what makes one human being unsubstitutable with another. These three chapters (5, 6 and 7), which discuss the qualifiers *basic* and *quotidian*, *personal* and *unsubstitutable*, together illuminate Kelsey's conception of human identity as images of the image of God.

Human *basic unsubstitutable personal identity*, according to *EE*, has the ontological status of being an actuality (384), and it is for this reason that we

31. See especially Kelsey, *Eccentric Existence*, 378–85.

32. Kelsey, 309–32, 354, 355, 404, 407, 410, 412, 413, 419, 443, 445, 480, 481, 498, 501–29, 606, 893, 1034, 1038, 1041, 1044.

33. Moreover, as we have noted, the concept of *living body* is considered in *EE* to be one term. Yet in the formula, the two words are often separated so as to read *living human personal bodies*. As such, it makes little sense to speak of *living* followed by *human*, *personal* and *body*, but rather to speak to *living body* as one concept.

34. Our next chapter establishes this point.

discuss *actual* in chapter 8. We see that in Kelsey's construction *actual* speaks to the gift and vocation[35] of humanity whereby the human being, in its 'complete reality,' works to remain what it already is. These notions have parallels in Kelsey's understanding of the gifted and vocational identity elaborated on in our discussions on *basic* and *quotidian identity*.

Along with the ontological status of actuality, *EE* argues that human identities in the image of God have their locus in living bodies. Chapter 9 considers this aspect of Kelsey's construction. Bearing in mind that (as chapter 1 of our project has noted) human embodiment has played a diminished role in conversations about the *imago Dei*, the fact that Kelsey incorporates this aspect into his description of the image of God is significant. We see that Kelsey speaks to human embodiment in a way that encompasses both pre- and post-mortem embodiment and in so doing draws human embodiment into the very heart of this doctrine.

To this end, let us begin in earnest.

---

35. This is a concept applied specifically to Jesus of Nazareth and to human beings in general (Kelsey, *Eccentric Existence*, 1045).

Basic and Quotidian Identity

FOR AS LONG as human beings have been conscious of themselves they have been questioning themselves and others in an attempt to understand the human condition. For the contemporary human being, the question is encapsulated in the modern notion of *identity*.[1] This is a highly complex notion, compounded by the conundrum that what is being searched for is doing the searching.[2] Many have attempted to provide a definition,[3] yet no single definition is widely accepted. Others have turned their attention to where identity may be located: Is it in number, unity or somewhere between the two? Is it, as Gottlob Frege contends, located in the relation between the names of objects rather than the objects themselves? Or perhaps in Bertrand Russell's notion of the difference between sense and meaning?[4]

Considering the complex debates around identity, it is no wonder that there are some, such as Derek Parfit,[5] Ludwig Wittgenstein[6] and Kai

---

1. Both Taylor and Bauman have provided in-depth research into the rise of the modern concern for identity. We should keep in mind that, as moderns, and even postmoderns, when we contemplate the biblical text through the optic of identity we bring to the text modern concerns that are not necessarily shared with the biblical writers. In both Taylor and Bauman's accounts, although given through different structural schemes, the modern concern for identity is characterized as one of inwardness. In Taylor's account this is a 'family of traits' characterized by disengaged, radically reflexive inwardness. Bauman contends that this identity is placed within a 'liquid modernity' in which individuals must choose their identity in the context of diverse options. See Taylor, *Sources of the Self*; Bauman, *Individualized Society*.

2. Ricoeur, *Oneself as Other*, 128–29.

3. For example, see Musschenga, "Personalized Identity," 23–24; White, *Identity*, 20–21.

4. For more on these debates consider Frege, "Über Sinn Und Bedeutung"; Black, "Translation of Frege"; Hume, *Treatise of Human Nature*; Wittgenstein, *Tractatus Logico-Philosophicus*, § 5.53–5.5303. For a comparative discussion of Frege and Wittgenstein, see White, "Wittgenstein on Identity." For discussions on Hume's understanding of identity, see Fang, "Hume on Identity"; Neujahr, "Hume on Identity"; Robison, "Hume on Personal Identity." Consider also White, *Identity*; Williams, *What Is Identity?*

5. Parfit, *Reasons and Persons*, 245–80.

6. Wittgenstein, *Tractatus Logico-Philosophicus*, § 5.53.

Wehmeier,[7] who have attempted to dispose of the notion altogether. Although there are technical reasons for not accepting their proposals,[8] it is the prevalence of the contemporary concern for identity that must be taken seriously. According to a World Council of Churches report, identity is the most frequently discussed theme in Christian communities, as they seek to understand themselves and their ministries in a pluralistic world.[9] Bearing in mind the "explosion"[10] that has triggered an "avalanche"[11] of interest in human identity, it is both necessary and unavoidable that a contemporary theological anthropology like *EE* would wrestle with this notion.

Within *EE*, the concept of identity is an enigma. The term is scattered throughout Kelsey's anthropology and forms a central part of *EE* and the anthropological formula. It is in chapters 9A and 9B that *identity* is discussed in some detail. Here Kelsey is acutely aware that the term *identity*, and in particular *personal identity* (which we come to in the next chapter), is difficult to define. Rather than attempting a definition himself, Kelsey speaks of his "sense of the term 'identity'" (334, 337, 378, 380).

His ambiguous reference to 'sense' rather than 'definition,' 'description,' 'meaning,' etc., attunes us to the intricacy of Kelsey's construction. Although he does not define what he means by 'sense,' we deduce that Kelsey is using the term to speak to an intuition, feeling or perception. He is suggesting a construction that does not allow a clean, neat and tidy explanation. In this construction, *identity* is "qualified" (357) by *personal*, *basic* and *quotidian* (which form a binary pair) and *unsubstitutable*. Our focus is on a constructive, critical analysis of his sense of the term within the context of these three qualifiers. We discuss Kelsey's sense of identity over three distinct chapters, beginning here with *basic* and *quotidian*. The emphasis in each chapter is on the qualifier in question, and it is across these three chapters that Kelsey's sense of identity will take shape. Before we begin, let us pause to consider a central concern raised by the notion of identity that is applicable to the substantive-relational debate.

---

7. Wehmeier, "How to Live Without Identity."

8. Trueman gives a compelling reason why this is not possible. See Trueman, "Eliminating Identity."

9. Crawford and Kinnamon, "In God's Image," 3.

10. Bauman, *Individualized Society*, 140.

11. Bauman, *Individualized Society*, 140.

Identity: Enduring and Dynamic

Ricoeur highlights a major problem with identities of living objects that is pertinent to our discussions: sameness in the face of change across time.[12] The notion of an enduring identity that is subject to radical change appears self-contradictory, especially in the case of human beings who experience significant changes throughout their earthly careers.[13] For example, in the contemporary world, we are familiar with those who have transitioned from one gender to another. Such instances pose a problem for enduring identity. An individual may have been born a male named Bruce, but during the course of their life, they may transition to be a female named Caitlyn. Such transitions raise deep questions about what remains of one's identity in the face of such radical change.

Hille Haker exclaims: "identity requires a certain amount of continuity, which must ultimately outweigh the discontinuity, even when a person moves between the two poles."[14] Where this is not the case, one risks the danger of associating identity with different states of living objects that just happen to bear the same name.[15] Although one can appreciate the necessity for such continuity of identity, establishing it is no easy task.[16]

Indeed, in recent years there has been a move to question the idea of an enduring identity based on the notion of individuality as received in the West.[17] Jacob Kruger provides us with a useful overview of the history of such Western concepts of individual identity since Augustine. Augustine contends for human identity on the basis of the *imago Dei*. As such, the structure of human identity was at the time understood analogously to that of the divine identity. Since God is a self-contained subject, it was only natural to consider the human being in like fashion—as an individuated entity.[18] This analogous theory is evident in Western thinking all the way through Luther (who places

---

12. Ricoeur, *Oneself as Other*, 115–25.

13. The problem of continuity and change that we deal with in this chapter speaks only to the earthly career of the human being. When we come to discuss *living body* in chapter 9, we consider the eschatological continuity question.

14. Haker, "Narrative and Moral Identity," 60–61.

15. Haker, "Narrative and Moral Identity," 60–61. In our example above, the 'object' in question does not even bear the same name.

16. We have briefly alluded to the complex debates around this issue, especially in discussions between Frege, Wittgenstein, and Hume in footnote 4 of this chapter.

17. Ward, *Giving Your Self Away*.

18. Kruger, "Christian Identity," 120–22. A different approach is available in Musschenga, "Personalized Identity," 23–30. One should keep in mind that many historical writers did not use the term 'identity,' and as such it is important to note that authors such as Kruger interpret these historical writers through a particularly modern optic.

his focus on the individual believer)[19] and Descartes (who displays a decisive turn to the subject with his thinking human ego, which becomes the point of reference for everything else) to Hegel (who argues that subjectivity is "pure self-recognition in absolute otherness"[20]).

Yet individuated identity poses many challenges. First, there is the risk of overly objective or subjective understandings.[21] Objectively, if we are to claim that identity is a fixed, crystallized characteristic that remains unchanged over time, we run the risk of establishing an identity that is judged to be representative of what others should be. Such an objective identity allows no space for individualization or freedom. Human beings who do not display this fixed identity are in danger of having their humanity called into question.[22] As shown in chapter 1 of our project, such has been the position and danger of the substantive understanding of the *imago Dei*.

On the other hand, a subjective identity allows every human being to establish their identity as they see fit.[23] Such subjectivity runs the risk of the subject turning from the outside world and withdrawing into itself, or what Buhler terms the "immunisation"[24] of identity. Although it is arguable that relational thinkers can help prevent the 'immunization' of identity in their outwardly focused construction, the fluidity of subjective identity questions the notion of a universality for human identity. The consequence of this charge, which is levied against the relational camp (see chapter 1 of this project), is just as destructive to those who have their human identity (and consequently their status as dignified and valued human beings) questioned.

Second, there is the risk of excluded otherness.[25] Identity in terms of individuality risks the dualistic construction of placing oneself over and against another. The dangers of establishing one's identity in contradistinction to others has been seen in divided communities rife with violence, prejudice and xenophobia.[26] The horrors of such xenophobia and violence,

---

19. It is arguable that Luther, contrary to Kruger, does not emphasize the individual identity but should be read with an actualist understanding of God's word addressing individual believers.

20. Hegel quoted in Kruger, "Christian Identity," 121.

21. Bühler, "Christian Identity," 22–23.

22. This is a concern for McFarland. See McFarland, *Difference & Identity*, chaps. 1, 2.

23. A concern raised by Bauman. See Bauman, *Individualized Society*.

24. Bühler, "Christian Identity," 22–23.

25. Kruger, "Christian Identity," 122–25.

26. Volf, *Exclusion and Embrace*; Kruger, "Christian Identity."

as epitomized in the Jewish Holocaust of the twentieth century, seriously question identity as excluded otherness.[27]

Problems such as these have led some to challenge the notion of an independently enduring identity altogether. Heather Ward, for example—using a very relational understanding—argues that (anthropologically speaking) when one speaks of human identity, one speaks primarily to the consistent inner identity uniting all humankind, an identity that is not so much based on the individual human being as on the human race as a whole.[28] Such an identity is not individually established or described, but understood dynamically in the relations and interactions of human beings with each other and their everyday context. As relationally conceived, this identity is understood as that which emerges from the crossroads of a complex, interrelated system of psychological, biological, social, political, ethical and religious exchanges that interact with an individual's identity to form, shape and adjust that identity. This complexity forbids a static notion to identity: "it is a dynamic process of constant integration of different aspects."[29] Ward contends that human identity is particularly dynamic. It is an identity that opens itself to what is offered to it. It is, in the words of Pierre Buhler, "only given to man in partial and precarious syntheses in which he feels in harmony with himself without ever being able to halt the movement of his life which risks taking him far away from himself again."[30]

Along these lines, Kruger argues for the disappearance of the self-identical individual, to be replaced by the subject that is formed, deformed and reformed by the innumerable interactions with itself, others and the quotidian context.[31] Such thinking is now widespread, from Erik Erikson's monumental work, *Identity: Youth and Crisis* (1968),[32] and Zygmunt Bauman's theory of 'liquid modernity,'[33] to Bühler, who draws on the positive and creative force of identity crises that reminds human beings of their unfixable identities that are constantly recast through the shocks and questions of their existence.[34] In

---

27. Kruger, "Christian Identity," 122–23; cf. McFarland, *Difference & Identity*, chap. 1.

28. Ward, *Giving Your Self Away*, 6–7. Others have argued for human historicity as a universal structure of humanness or human existence (*da-sein*). This is particularly evident in Heidegger. For more, see Heidegger, *Being and Time*; cf. Pannenberg, *Anthropology in Theological Perspective*, 485–532.

29. Bühler, "Christian Identity," 21.

30. Bühler, "Christian Identity," 21.

31. Kruger, "Christian Identity," 124.

32. Erikson, *Identity*.

33. Bauman, *Individualized Society*.

34. Bühler, "Christian Identity." See also Macquarrie, *Principles of Christian Theology*, 76–77, 229–32.

Kruger's words, this is the "deconstruction of identity"[35] that allows the self to be open to the other: "it is an inviting way of being in the world; always saying 'come' to the other—the new and the different."[36]

The consequence of such a deconstruction of identity is that the search for human identity becomes life-long.[37] One cannot describe an identity by pointing to a single moment in time or even to a number of key events.[38] All that one can describe is an identity at one time, at one moment in its development, with the understanding that this is only a small part of the picture of a developing and dynamic identity that is open to change across time. Such dynamic understandings go some way to help disentangle the notion of identity from substantive arguments, which, as shown in chapter 1, are problematic. However, if human identity is purely dynamic, something that is constantly developing and changing, without objective definition, is there really anything substantial to the human being? Is the image of God anything tangible, or is it simply ethereal, indefinable and ever changing? How can such an ethereal identity become anything at all? Are we not simply saying that what we are is nothing but change?

The question remains: While acknowledging the necessity to hold both enduring and dynamic notions of identity together, how is it possible? This is the challenge we keep in mind as we now turn to consider the sense of identity in *EE*.

Identity and Eccentric Existence

What Kelsey Is Not Asking

In chapter 9A, Kelsey turns his focus from the anthropological 'What?' to the 'Who?' question and contends that the notion of identity is best discussed in this context.[39] He begins his discussions of his sense of identity as it is used in *EE* by stating that his understanding is "ambiguous" (335) and requires some clarification. As such he negatively contrasts his sense with four other senses (234–37; cf. 380–81). First, the question 'Who is she?' may be confused with a request to identify one person out of a group of people,

---

35. Kruger, "Christian Identity," 122–26.
36. Kruger, "Christian Identity," 126.
37. Bühler, "Christian Identity," 22.
38. We have more to say about this in our discussions on Frei's identity description tools later in this chapter.
39. This approach is not unique. McFarland has argued for a similar approach. See McFarland, *Difference & Identity*, chap. 1.

so as to ask: 'Of all the people at this party, which one is she?' To Kelsey this poses a problem. One may ask a 'Who?' question not only of others but of oneself, yet it would make very little sense for one to ask about the identity of themselves in the given example. Such would be tantamount to asking of oneself: 'Of all the people at this party, which one am I?'

Second, one may use a 'Who?' question in order to obtain mathematical or strict logical identity. Kelsey argues that asking a 'Who?' question in this sense is not what he is attempting to do. He states that when he asks the question 'Who am I?' in *EE*, he is asking a different question than "Am I identical with the eldest child of Mildred and Hugh Kelsey?" (335).

Third, the question of 'Who?' someone is may be answered with reference to a psychological phenomenon sometimes referred to as a 'self-image.' This self-image may be conscious, unconscious or both. It may be realistic or distorted. Such a self-image, argue psychologists, helps determine a person's behaviors and attitudes. In the case of a distorted self-image, it may help explain why a person's behaviors or attitudes are perceived as being misleading about who that person really is. 'Who?' questions like these tend to be asked in the form of 'Who is he *really*?' or 'Who am I *really*?' Such phrasing of the question promotes an understanding of identity that allows for a disconnect between a person's perceived identity and their real identity. Kelsey contends that he is not seeking to identify the 'real' person that lies somehow behind a mask.

Fourth, 'Who?' questions may be answered in the context of philosophical discussions of the perduring identity of temporal and physical entities across time and through change. In systematic metaphysics, answers have included appealing to the perduring soul, basic human substance or even the enduring memory. Such metaphysical principles of identity may lead to the impression of an identity that somehow lies behind, beyond or beneath what is visible. In such answers one seeks to identify the 'real identity' (very much as psychologists do) that may lie beyond what is accessible to the observer or person posing the 'Who?' question—even if that person is themselves.

Kelsey contends that, although his sense of the term *identity* may overlap with these four senses, what he is referring to by the notion of *identity* is decidedly different from these other senses (337). However, as he himself notes, negatively contrasting his sense from other senses "goes only a little distance to clarifying what it does mean" (357). Thus, he picks up the notion of *identity* again in chapter 9B, entitled "Basic Unsubstitutable Personal Identity." In that chapter, he "seeks to explain more fully the phrase and some reasons for using it" (357). It should be noted, however, that chapter 9B does not present a clear, concise or sufficient explanation of the notion of *identity* in a single discussion. Rather, his sense of the term is expounded upon throughout the chapter as he builds on extensive previous discussions and on the qualifiers *personal, basic and quotidian* and *unsubstitutable*. It is here argued that the best way of drawing out his sense of the term is to consider the particular question he is asking and how he shapes both the question and the answer.

The 'Who?' Question

Kelsey contends that *identity* speaks primarily to the anthropological 'Who?' rather than 'What?' question (33). As such, instead of asking 'What is identity?' Kelsey poses the question as follows: "What is being asked for in 'Who?' questions?" (335). More accurately, Kelsey attempts to give a description of "the subject of a 'Who?' question" (335).[40] By rephrasing the question, Kelsey is able avoid the problematic question 'What is identity?' and instead seeks to answer the question "Who are we as God's creatures?" (339). He contends that what is being asked for, exactly, is not a definition of *identity* but a description. Speaking in the context of *personal identity* he states:

> An important clue to the sense of 'identity' intended here is the fact that answers to 'Who?' questions that are deemed maximally adequate to precisely personal (or communal) identity are normally given in selected types of stories about the personal bodies or communities of personal bodies in questions. (334)

In this way, Kelsey moves away from trying to define identity toward placing the concept within the context of narrative theology and, in particular, giving a description of the subject of a 'Who?' question. Kelsey argues that the reason why narrative is able to provide an adequate answer to the question of identity is that it is able to describe the subject of a 'Who?' question as "she or it persists through change across time" (335). In postliberal fashion, he argues that narrative is able to hold together the notions of an enduring yet changing identity.

In order to achieve his goal of providing a narrative description of identity, Kelsey relies heavily on his Yale colleague's theory of identity description.[41] Frei's work *The Identity of Jesus Christ* (1997)[42]—which is dedicated

---

40. See also Kelsey, *Eccentric Existence*, 334–37.

41. Kelsey, *Eccentric Existence*, 334–35, 385–87. See also Kelsey, "Biblical Narrative," 123–31. Here, Kelsey looks at Frei's attempt at narrative theology to describe the human being's personal identity.

42. It is interesting to note that this work was dedicated to Kelsey. Consider also the article written by Frei, which is very closely associated to this work (Frei, "Theological Reflections" [1993]; "Theological Reflections" [1966]).

to Kelsey—sets out to provide a description of the identity of Jesus Christ. He, like many, considers the notion of *identity* to be "difficult"[43] and refers to it as the "puzzle that the sages of Western culture since the time of Plato and Aristotle have not been able to solve."[44] Like Kelsey, Frei contends that "it is important for us to understand that there is such an argument [what is identity], but also that we need not and must not enter into it."[45] Frei concerns himself not with the question 'What is identity?' but with "purely descriptive talk."[46] The basis of this descriptive talk is Frei's contention that the identity of the human being "is not attributable to a super-added factor, an invisible agent residing inside and from there directing the body, or what Gilbert Ryle has called 'a ghost in the machine.'"[47] It is not the case that human identity somehow lives behind, beyond or above the perceivable acts humans undertake and suffer. Frei contends that the narrative of human action is enough to provide an adequate description of their identity. This description is supplied by making use of two identity description tools.[48]

The first tool is what Frei terms intention-action description: "for a person is not merely illustrated, his is *constituted* by his particular intentional act at any given point in his life."[49] Here Frei distinguishes between occurrences and actions. For him, there is a unity between one's intention and one's actions: "an intention, unless impeded or frustrated, is no intention and has no mental statues at all except as a plan to be executed."[50] Without an action, there is no true intention. Conversely, "an event that happens accidentally or without intention is an occurrence rather than an action."[51]

Kelsey picks up on this aspect of identity in *EE*. In postliberal fashion, he argues that pre-modern descriptions of human beings as agents construe the relation between intentions and actions as dialectical rather than an event-cause-and-effect relation. Kelsey contends: "In explanation of events, causes and effects must themselves be events defined independently of each other, or the explanation will be viciously circular" (386). However, he argues that if we are to understand intentional actions as being describable only in dialectical

---

43. Frei, *Identity of Jesus Christ*, 95.
44. Frei, *Identity of Jesus Christ*, 98.
45. Frei, *Identity of Jesus Christ*, 98.
46. Frei, *Identity of Jesus Christ*, 98.
47. Frei, *Identity of Jesus Christ*, 99.
48. Frei, *Identity of Jesus Christ*, 14–26, 100, 132–44; Kelsey, *Eccentric Existence*, 334–35.
49. Frei, *Identity of Jesus Christ*, 100.
50. Frei, *Identity of Jesus Christ*, 136.
51. Frei, *Identity of Jesus Christ*, 136.

terms of intentions-to-act and enacted intentions, one is able to retain the integral unity of the agent who enacts intentional actions (386).

The result of such an understanding of human action is Frei's contention that "a person is what he *does* centrally and most significantly."[52] Therefore, if we are to provide a description of a person's identity, we need only look at their intentional actions. These are accessible to us through their narrative. Within this narrative, one may point to instances or events in which a person has acted in such a way that is "characteristically himself."[53] In Kelsey's words, these instances exemplify ways of acting and interacting that are "just like her" or "her when she is most fully herself" (386).

Such anecdotal stories are able to "describe the subject of a 'Who?' question entirely by reference to the subjects own intentional actions within its given circumstances" (334). In this way, the "patterns of intentional action . . . constitute the personal identity of the subject of a 'Who?' question at the time in which the narrated intentional interactions occurred" (334). Simply by looking at these anecdotal stories one can describe identity.

The second identity description tool is, in Frei's words, "self-manifestation" description.[54] This tool seeks to describe the subject of a 'Who?' question "as she or it persists through change across time" (335, 386–87). Such a description involves describing the continuity of a person across time while acknowledging and describing genuine changes. According to Frei, to describe unity in disunity is the talent of a good story teller who is able to demonstrate the changing actions, states and properties ascribed to the central character and yet demonstrate that no set of changing states, properties or actions exhausts the self so that it cannot also provide the bond of continuity that is held together by the same identity across time.[55] To Kelsey it is only in a narrative of the agent's actions that the agent, its circumstances, the actions and the identity can be held together in dialectical tension (387): "simply by the way in which such stories are told, they render the self-manifestation-in-difference of personal bodies" (335).

This is the first clue to Kelsey's sense of the term *identity*, that—regardless of what is being asked for in identity questions—identity is describable by appealing to narrative. Yet Kelsey's discussion of his sense of identity does not stop there. He goes on to discuss three qualifiers. It is in these qualifiers that Kelsey seeks to locate identity, as such, they provide further

---

52. Frei, *Identity of Jesus Christ*, 136.
53. Frei, *Identity of Jesus Christ*, 136.
54. Frei, *Identity of Jesus Christ*, 100, 138–44.
55. Frei, *Identity of Jesus Christ*, 99, 133.

'clues' for his sense of the term. Let us turn our focus now to the qualifiers *basic* and *quotidian*.

Identity: Basic and Quotidian

Kelsey notes that the term *identity* is used in a wide variety of contexts and that in contemporary culture it carries certain senses associated with terms such as 'racial identity,' 'ethnic identity,' 'sexual identity,' 'gender identity,' etc. Kelsey groups these senses under the broader banner of "identity politics" (381). He does not define what he means by 'identity politics,' one is left to deduce this oneself. While Kelsey's sense of identity partially overlaps these other senses, he enters into a discussion to distinguish between his sense of identity and the sense of identity entailed in 'identity politics.' He does this through a distinction between *quotidian identities* and *basic identities* (381).[56] Let us begin with *quotidian identity*.

In chapter 5A Kelsey expands on the proximate contexts into which humans are born. Using Wisdom literature to expound on his understanding of creation, Kelsey argues that the created order denotes the lived world as the quotidian: the everyday finite realities of all creatures in the routine networks constituted by ordinary interaction. He states that "taken together, they (we!) are a society of everyday being" (190). To Kelsey, these ordinary and everyday networks and interactions together are termed the quotidian.

The quotidian is situated in the myriad complex interactions of multiple energy systems.[57] These include inorganic energy systems such as subatomic particles, atoms and molecules and varying organic energy systems that appear emergent from these basal systems. Emergent systems include biological life (complex and simple) as well as the consequences of complex biological sentient beings. These consequences include culture, language and social and political structures. As such, it is immensely complex, having

---

56. In Kelsey's distinction between the basic and quotidian identity, one may read a reference to the double interpretation of Genesis 1:26 (common in patristic thinking) of *tselem* (image) and *Demuth* (likeness). The debates around the distinction, or lack thereof, between these two terms are extensive. See, for example, Barth, *CD* 3/1:197–206; Berkhof, *Systematic Theology*, 203; Cairns, *Image of God in Man*, 20, 73–86; Hoekema, *Created in God's Image*, 13; Middleton, *Liberating Image*, 45. Indeed, it is no wonder Miller argues that the biblical writers were intentionally vague. See Miller, "In the 'Image' and 'Likeness,'" 297; cf. Berkouwer, *Man*, 69; Grenz, "Jesus as the Imago Dei," 263. Kelsey is well aware of this patristic distinction (Kelsey, *Eccentric Existence*, 895); however, he does not follow in this line of thought, arguing instead for his proposals to be seen "Against the Tradition" (Kelsey, *Eccentric Existence*, 895–97).

57. Kelsey refers to the notion of 'energy systems' regularly without definition. See Kelsey, *Eccentric Existence*, 251, 265, 554–56, 643–44.

a history that is diverse, sometimes fractured and marred by conflict. These interactions are not themselves the container in which the created order sits but are integral to the quotidian; "they are part and parcel of the everyday that God creates" (192).

One should be careful not to misinterpret Kelsey on this. Just because the created order is ordinary or everyday does not mean that it is without value. Kelsey argues that Wisdom theology understands the quotidian as something more than simply an appearance or social construct that is culturally shaped and, as such, has value invested into it by human beings. Nor is it to be understood as a reality that is waiting for a better future state. In Kelsey's view, Wisdom literature does not display a teleology to quotidian creation. Kelsey urges us to understand the ordinary everyday state of the created order as having value and meaning simply in its "everydayness" (191).[58]

The quotidian is formative for the human being and decisively shapes human creatures' identity. God relates to the human being creatively by forming them as part of and setting them in this quotidian context. Therefore, "we may call whatever identity a human creature develops in its interactions with its quotidian proximate contexts its 'quotidian identity'" (383).

The quotidian identity involves a degree of negotiation between external constructs and internal or self-constructs. External constructs refer to both physical and non-physical influences on the quotidian identity. This includes the physical environment as well as the socially constructed environment of culture, language and politics. The shape of one's quotidian identity is partly influenced by the degree of acceptance or rejection of external influences. Alongside these external influences is the internal particularity of the quotidian identity, which displays some form of originality, if only slight or subtle (382).

Using Peter and Bridgett Berger and Hansfried Keller's study of modernization and consciousness in *The Homeless Mind* (1973),[59] Kelsey describes four aspects of the quotidian identity in modern culture. 1) Human being's identity is 'peculiarly open' in the sense that it is "peculiarly 'unfinished'" (383) even into adulthood. 2) Since modern individuals live in a plurality

---

58. One should be careful not to confuse Kelsey's affirmation of the ordinary life with modern affirmations of ordinary life, which affirm the quotidian value to the degree to which it lives, or exists, according to its design. Kelsey does not affirm that the quotidian is valuable because it has a certain design or it obeys natural laws. He affirms its value simply in its being created by God. For the modern affirmation of the ordinary life see Taylor, *Sources of the Self*, pt. 3.

59. Kelsey, *Eccentric Existence*, 383. The notions that follow are referenced elsewhere. For example, Bauman speaks of the fluidity of modern identity in Bauman, *Individualized Society*. Taylor, on the other hand, traces the rise of modern notions of identity in terms of its radical reflexive inwardness. See Taylor, *Sources of the Self*.

of social worlds, their identity is 'peculiarly differentiated.' Their individual identities seek to find their "foothold" (383) in reality internally rather than externally: "one consequence of this is that the individual's subjective reality (what is commonly regarded as his 'psychology') becomes increasingly differentiated, complex and constantly changing" (383). 3) Modern identity is 'peculiarly reflective' partly as a result of the kaleidoscope of social experiences that cause both internal and external subjective reflectivity. 4) Modern identities are 'peculiarly individuated' in that individual freedom, autonomy and rights are taken for granted as moral imperatives.

Such an understanding of modern identities highlights both the complexity of the quotidian identity and its dynamic and ever-changing nature. Modern identities are peculiarly unfinished, differentiated, reflective and individuated. They are open to, and subject to, radical change as they interact with the quotidian.

Yet, as we have noted, this ever-changing nature is problematic for an understanding of identity. If the human being is to be understood as only changing and dynamic, the consequence would be the loss of the coherence and wholeness (the unity) of identity over time. To counter this tendency, Kelsey references the concept of a *basic identity*.

> From a theological point of view, however, quotidian identities, including modern ones, are themselves included in a larger context for which the term of art here will be human creatures' 'basic identity.' (383)

While the creaturely realm forms the proximate context of human existence, Kelsey emphasizes that we exist within a far broader context: "the ultimate context into which we are born is God's relating to [human beings] as their creator" (160). It is this context that "ultimately defines what and who we are and how we are to be" (162). This broader context is defined by the triadic way God relates to all that is not God in creative blessing, eschatological consummation and reconciliation. Kelsey derives a different aspect of human beings' basic identity from each of the three ways God relates to us.

First, that God relates creatively to the human being defines their basic identity in a double way. As God relates directly to them to create and sustain them in their creaturely finitude, the answer to the 'Who?' question is that human beings are those who are radically contingent on God's call to be. It is God himself who defines their identity directly as he relates in creative blessing. On the other hand, as God relates in creative blessing indirectly through the quotidian proximate context, human beings may be described as those who are "called to be wise in their actions for the well-being of our quotidian contexts" (384).⁶⁰ In this second sense, their quotidian identity is reliant on their basic identity in that it is God who ultimately relates, albeit indirectly, through the quotidian context.

Second, as God relates in eschatological consummation, the human being's basic identity may also be described in a double way. On the one hand, we are elected by God. This election does not bestow upon us a special status or role that may be considered of higher importance than those who are not elected. Rather, this election speaks to a distinctive relationship with God. It speaks to the human being's ultimate destiny to live in relation to God, alongside and in community with other human creatures. However, while this may be our ultimate destiny, in the present state, human beings are "those to whom the catastrophe of final judgement is now happening" (384).⁶¹

Third, as those who are being reconciled to God in Christ, the human being's basic identity may be described as an identity *in* Christ's identity.⁶² In Kelsey's understanding, the narrative plot of God's relating to reconcile us through the incarnation becomes the descriptive plot of our own dynamic singular identities (384).⁶³ As such, our basic identity is defined and described in the singular person of Jesus of Nazareth.

These three aspects of the human being's basic identity are not to be taken as three separate strands or even three alternative identities. Rather, they are three aspects of a single basic identity that is given to the human being by God. This identity has the characteristic of a gracious gift with the status of an actuality. Our basic identity does not speak to either the

60. See also Kelsey, *Eccentric Existence*, chap. 4A, 9A.

61. See also Kelsey, *Eccentric Existence*, chap. 12A, 15A.

62. The formula 'in Christ' appears frequently in *EE*. For Kelsey's interpretation of the Pauline texts dealing with this formula, see Kelsey, *Eccentric Existence*, 695–702.

63. See also Kelsey, *Eccentric Existence*, chap. 18. Although we shortly come to critique the role of narrative in identity description, here one may question the relation of humanity narratively 'in Christ.' To be sure, Kelsey is not unique in this approach. Grenz notes that narrativity enables us to interpret 'in Christ' insofar as we are incorporated into the transcending narrative of Jesus' story and in that we allow this narrative plot to shape our own lives. Yet there are questions that threaten to take us on a tangent to the topic at hand. First, how is it possible to narratively describe an individual identity if their narrative is defined and shaped by another narrative? Second, dogmatically, how is this achieved? In Calvin and Grenz, it is pneumatologically achieved as the Spirit gives us to Christ. In *EE*, it appears that the Son is the driving force behind the narrative of reconciliation (Kelsey, *Eccentric Existence*, 120–22). Third, what exactly happens when our narrative is transformed by the narrative of Jesus of Nazareth? If our identity is narratively located, and we are incorporated into another's narrative, what does that do for our identity? Since these tangents do not impact either the qualifiers *basic* and *quotidian* or Kelsey's 'sense' of identity, we do not attempt to explore them further here. The interested reader is encouraged to see Kelsey, *Eccentric Existence*, chap. 18, 19A, 19B, 20B; cf. Grenz, *Social God*, 328–31; Calvin, *Institutes of the Christian Religion*, 20:3.1.

possibility of or the potential to be such an identity. Rather, since this identity is eccentrically rooted in the triadic way God relates to us, it is already a reality, it cannot be destroyed or lost.[64]

The same cannot be said of our quotidian identity, which has the characteristic of a vocation (193–99).[65] Although our basic identity has the status of an actuality—that is, the human being cannot actualize this identity through their practices (384–85)—in our quotidian identity, we are called to live in congruence with this basic identity. We are called to acknowledge our basic identity by enacting practices that are in line with the ultimate context of God relating to us. By doing so, the quotidian identity does not replace the basic identity, nor is it replaced by the basic identity. Rather it is taken up into the basic identity and shaped by it (385).

One may interpret Kelsey's understanding of our 'call' in line with Barth's motif of actualism.[66] When Barth speaks of notions such as 'call,' he does so in terms of events and relationships rather than monadic or self-contained substances. It is not something that one can possess once and for all, but rather God's call is continually established anew. As Kelsey speaks to God's call, and alongside this his "address" (337–40), he does so in such a way as to indicate that God's address is an ongoing process in the quotidian context as the human being lives and responds to the call of God.

The vocation implicit in our quotidian identity has ethical implications, as we are continually called to engage in appropriate practices. Since this vocation is lived within our proximate contexts, we are called to be wise in the way we respond to non-human, human and social contexts on an ongoing basis. This, however, is not always the case, as human creatures may or may not respond to this vocation appropriately. We may, and often do, enact practices that are unwise or even foolish:

> In one of the few cases where concession of the obvious is at the same time an important theological claim, it is stressed in each of the three parts of this project that living human personal bodies are fully capable of living as though the three aspects of their basic identity do not obtain, are not in fact their basic identity, indeed have nothing to do with their personal identities. Human beings can live quotidian identities that totally ignore

64. We have much to say about human actuality in chapter 8 of this project.

65. It should be noted that Kelsey also considers the quotidian to be a gracious gift. See Kelsey, *Eccentric Existence*, 212–14.

66. For a good overview of this motif in Barth, see Hunsinger, *How to Read Karl Barth*, 30–32, 66–70. Although not expressly stated, one can interpret Kelsey's notion of *basic identity* in a similar vein. One's basic identity is a continual 'call' upon one's life, as God continues to relate to human beings moment by moment.

the gift of their basic identity. They can live quotidian identities that do not wholly ignore their basic identity, but rather fail to cohere with it so that they amount to distortions of it. They can live, as it were, at cross-grain to themselves, in that sense, they can live with divided identities. (385)

To Kelsey, such a reality is not only possible but common and results in a paradox. The human being becomes what it is not. When a human being lives at cross-grain to their basic identity, their quotidian identity is distorted and marred. The result is what Kelsey calls "bondage in living death" (385).[67] It is a bondage because the human being suffers from a divided identity. This divided identity cannot be self-overcome because it is self-contradictory. In answer to the question 'Can humans save themselves?' Kelsey responds with a resounding 'No!' For "who would it be that would take steps to overcome the self-division except a self-divided, self-contradictory identity or some community of them?" (385). If the human being is to rectify its identity so that it may live its quotidian identity in congruence with its basic identity, it requires a savior: one who is not self-contradictory, one whose quotidian identity is not incongruent to its basic identity and one who is not in bondage to living death. That savior is Jesus of Nazareth.

Narrative Identity?

Much of Kelsey's position is unobjectionable. That humanity has a dual identity is referred to in one form or another throughout theological literature, albeit in slightly differently nuanced forms. Alistair McFadyen, for example, talks about vertical and horizontal identity;[68] Richard Rohr talks about the true and false self;[69] and Douglas Hall speaks of "essential humanity" and "existential humanity."[70]

As such, reference to our ultimate and proximate context is widespread. George Carey,[71] Stephen Neill[72] and Emil Brunner[73] all refer to God as the

---

67. See also Kelsey, *Eccentric Existence*, 194. The concept is explored throughout Kelsey's anthropology. See Kelsey, *Eccentric Existence*, chaps. 11, 17, 25; cf. Kelsey, *Imagining Redemption*, 75–79. Here, Kelsey considers living death as the endless cycle of excluding others so as to affirm oneself and, in so doing, diminish oneself.

68. McFadyen, *Call to Personhood*, 18–39.

69. Rohr, *Immortal Diamond*.

70. Hall, *Imaging God*, 128.

71. Carey, *I Believe in Man*, 26–41.

72. Neill, *Man in God's Purpose*, 13–17.

73. Brunner, "Christian Understanding of Man," 159.

ultimate context in their claims that "man is what he is, as *reaction* to the *action* of God."[74] Indeed, while Christopher Schwöbel may argue that this is the distinctive thesis of a Christian theological anthropology,[75] Vernon White argues that numerous non-Christian ideologies have identified ultimate reality with God. This is true of the socio-biological evolutionary theory of random mutations, Heraclitain views, Marxist theory, Plato's Republic and modern scientific rationalism. Even the mathematical physicist who claims that he may soon know the mind of God when he identifies a unified theory of everything is claiming that the ultimate meaning of everything is God.[76]

Equally, the impact of our quotidian context on our identity is so well established it hardly needs referencing, as the endless debates around the role of nature and nurture in identity formation still ring heavily in our ears.[77] In such debates, at least within Christian theology, lies the challenge of the disconnect between the quotidian and basic identity.[78]

However, questions are raised when we turn to consider the narrative nature of Kelsey's construction. Considering Kelsey's postliberal heritage and his insistence on narrativity as the basis for identity description, it is necessary that our critique of Kelsey's sense of identity takes this aspect of his construction seriously. Although Kelsey's reliance on Frei is not unique,[79] there are those who question Frei's tools on a number of grounds. First, there are questions surrounding the relationship between intention and action. Is it really possible, as Frei does, to say that intentions and actions are essentially a unity without distinction? Robert King questions this contention, arguing that a fully intentional action is an exception rather than the rule. It is far more common for a person to fail to achieve their intentions or

---

74. Brunner, "Christian Understanding of Man," 159.

75. Schwöbel, "Human Being as Relational Being," 142–45.

76. White, *Identity*, 17–18. God here is used symbolically rather than personally as asserted by the Christian faith. It may, therefore, be more accurate to refer to 'god' rather than 'God' and to claim that such ultimate reality has taken the place of God, rather than being identified with God.

77. There is little need to reference this point, any basic/introductory psychology book will make reference to this. In Christian theology innumerable references have been made; as examples, see Carey, *I Believe in Man*, 1–25; Haker, "Narrative and Moral Identity," 61; McFadyen, *Call to Personhood*, 13–18; Neill, *Man in God's Purpose*, 6–16; White, *Identity*, 46–47.

78. Many of the authors referenced directly above, while not using the exact terms, engage in some form or another in the debate between our ultimate and proximate identities. See as examples Rohr, *Immortal Diamond*; McFadyen, *Call to Personhood*, 18–39.

79. Ratzinger, *Introduction to Christianity*, 114–37; White, *Identity*, 21–37. White references others who also rely on Frei, such as Ryle and King.

objectives.[80] How often have we heard someone say, 'I did not intend that' or 'I am sorry, that was not my intention?' Of course, as we have noted, Frei would contend that any action a human being enacts that is not intended is merely an occurrence, not an action. Nevertheless, King's argument makes intentional actions rare.

Second, even if we are to contend that actions are always intentional and therefore provide access to the identity of the subject of a narrative, there remains an enormous amount of interpretation when providing identity descriptions. King argues that we infer rather than observe what a person's intentions are when witnessing their actions. This results in the observer dividing a person's history, and with it their identity, into an inner history—which only that person has access to—and an exterior history—which others can observe. Although King acknowledges Frei's distinction between an occurrence and an action, he is nevertheless perturbed. It is not always easy to distinguish between an action and an occurrence in human behavior. While the agent may recognize the difference between intentional action and unintentional occurrence, an observer often finds them difficult to distinguish.[81]

Third, more problematic than the paradox of intentional action is the conflating of narrative and identity that occurs both in Kelsey and Frei. To be fair to both authors, however, this conflation is widespread. Rolf Jacobson argues that the modern consensus among divergent academic disciplines is that identity is narrative.[82] Although acknowledging a simplification, Jacobson demonstrates that narrative is nothing more than one event after another. Since all human experience happens in time, it, too, is the experience of one event after another, and, therefore, "we are our stories."[83]

The conflation of narrative with identity has arisen in part due to the paradox of sameness and distinction that is evident in the lives of living objects. Paul Ricoeur[84] expounds on this point in his theory of *idem* (Latin for 'sameness') and *ipse* (Latin for 'selfhood'). Ricoeur notes that the human being experiences radical change over the course of its lifetime. From an embryo to childhood, adulthood and eventually old age, very little *idem* is observable. The problem arises of how to speak of a permanence in identity that *ipse* implies without relying on an unchanging substance. In other

---

80. See King, *Meaning of God*, chap. 3, esp. 59–63.
81. King, *Meaning of God*, 40.
82. Jacobson, "We Are Our Stories," 124.
83. Jacobson, "We Are Our Stories," 124. See also Bühler, "Christian Identity," 21; White, *Identity*, 47–49.
84. Ricoeur, *Oneself as Other*, 115–25.

words, "is there a form of permanence in time which can be connected to the question 'who?' inasmuch as it is irreducible to the question of 'what?'"[85] To answer this question, Ricoeur calls on the notion of character.[86] Character is a set of distinctive marks that allows one to re-identify a human individual as the same as that human being in preceding moments. This set of distinctive marks is acquired over time as the identity changes and forms habits as a result of both external and internal factors.[87] Since character is acquired over time, it is best described through narrative identity:[88]

> Without the recourse to narration, the problem of personal identity would in fact be condemned to an antinomy with no solution. Either we must posit a subject identical with itself through the diversity of its different states, or, following Hume and Nietzsche, we must hold that this identical subject is nothing more than a substantialist illusion.[89]

Through his theory of emplotment, Ricoeur argues that identity is held together within the story. He goes so far as to claim, "it is the identity of the story that makes the identity of the character."[90] Yet we should understand him clearly on this point. Rather than claiming we can know the intention of an identity through their actions (Frei and Kelsey), Ricoeur argues that a dialectic is formed whereby a character's identity is not only known through their actions, but also formed by the acts they enact and undergo. It is here that the lines between identity description and identity formation become blurred.[91]

Fourth, Jacobson questions the ability of a narrative to accurately reflect the identity of its character. In terms of self-stories, Jacobson has

85. Ricoeur, *Oneself as Other*, 118.

86. It is possible to note that character is often related to the notion of virtue, which would bring ethical issues into our discussion. However, these questions are secondary to the discussion at hand, and we therefore leave them unanswered for now.

87. See McFadyen's theory of sedimentation: McFadyen, *Call to Personhood*, chaps. 3, 4.

88. Ricoeur, *Oneself as Other*, 112–28. See also Ricoeur, *Time and Narrative*, 1:140–68.

89. Ricoeur, *Time and Narrative*, 3:246.

90. Ricoeur, *Time and Narrative*, 3:148.

91. In Ricoeur and Haker, this is particularly evident as stories are told and retold in which the narrative continually shapes the identity of the character. For more on this concept consider Ricoeur's theory of mimesis (Ricoeur, *Time and Narrative*, 1:52–77; Haker, "Narrative and Moral Identity," 62–64). This point also raises questions about the role of names within narratives. In modern story telling, someone is re-named following a significant event in their lives (e.g., King Slayer), while in biblical stories, a name often precedes the narrative (e.g., Emanuel).

reservations. If we are both the narrator and the character, then what of the fact that we are finite, fallible sinners not capable of either knowing or telling the whole truth? Jacobson argues that there are parts of our story that we simply will not tell anyone, not even ourselves. This is this reason that one cannot rely solely on one's own narrative to provide either a description of an identity or to prescribe that identity itself: "We are our stories, but our stories—from both a theological and an ethical perspective—are inevitably inadequate."[92]

Jacobson raises a good point. Frei's identity description tools rely heavily on the veracity of the encountered narrative. However, questions remain as to the extent of knowledge we have of that narrative. Although Kelsey may acknowledge that this knowledge is limited (385–86), he (along with Frei) would contend that there are moments in the narrative that sufficiently epitomize a character.[93] Yet, when we consider Jacobson's point, how is it that we can trust even these moments? As Paul Tournier notes, "It is no use trying to arrive at an exact picture by adding all the many false images together."[94]

Even Ricoeur, who argues that there is no understanding of personal identity apart from narrative, is forced to place a caveat on his position. Not only are we unable to know all aspects of the narrative, but we often compose several plots for the same character. Think of how many biographies exist of characters such as Martin Luther, St Paul or, indeed, Jesus Christ. Ricoeur demonstrates that it is possible that some of these narrative plots may even oppose and contradict each other. Narrative identity, understood this way, continues to make and unmake itself at the same time. It is no wonder, therefore, that Ricoeur refers to narrative identity as "the name of a problem at least as much as it is that of a solution."[95]

When we consider these critiques, are we not forced to conclude that narrative offers shaky ground upon which to develop a description of human identity? There are questions at every turn: about the relationship between intention and action, the sufficiency of information regarding intentional actions and the descriptive versus formative aspects of stories. In short, one is left unconvinced that we can describe the identity of the human being using such narrative description tools.

---

92. Jacobson, "We Are Our Stories," 126.

93. This is particularly evident in the first descriptive tool in which key moments in a narrative are picked out in which the person is "most fully themselves" (Kelsey, *Eccentric Existence*, 385–86; cf. Frei, *Identity of Jesus Christ*, 14–26).

94. Tournier, *Meaning of Persons*, 21.

95. Ricoeur, *Time and Narrative*, 3:249.

In light of this, the question now posed is: What value, if any, does Kelsey's postliberal understanding of human basic and quotidian identity offer theological anthropology?

The Gift and Vocation of Human Identity

Although there are serious questions around the suitability of narrative to be "deemed maximally adequate" (334) to provide identity descriptions, this does not necessarily spill over to Kelsey's entire construction. On the contrary, while Kelsey insists that his sense of identity is placed in the context of narrative and that Frei's narrative tools can be used to describe identity, the utilization of these tools in Kelsey's discussions of human *basic* and *quotidian* identity is minimal at best.[96] Beyond a rudimentary mention that our basic and quotidian identity is described in the narratives of God relating in creative blessing, eschatological consummation and reconciliation, his locating of basic and quotidian identity in the ultimate and proximate contexts of human existence is not conceptually reliant on Frei's identity description tools. Therefore, let us explore the value of this aspect of his construction for the topic at hand.

Recall how it is we began this chapter: noting that an important conundrum posed by identity is that of the enduring yet dynamic nature of human existence. In chapter 1 we noted that this conundrum is at the heart of the substantive-relational debate. Substantive thinkers, working with the language of 'noun' and 'gift,' seek to emphasize the enduring, universal nature of human existence. On the other hand, relational thinkers, working with the language of 'verb' and 'vocation,' emphasize the dynamic, developmental aspects of human beings.

Kelsey picks up the challenge of speaking about human identity in a way that demonstrates continuity over time while maintaining real difference and development. This challenge is at the heart of Kelsey's understanding of the basic and quotidian identity as he constructs a notion of "identity-in-difference" (336; cf. 334–37). Kelsey's first step in meeting this challenge is to reshape the question. He is acutely aware of the impact different questions have on anthropological discussions (1–2). In phrasing the question 'What is a human being?' one is compelled to seek out characteristics that define human beings in contradistinction from the rest of the created order. This, as we have noted, is evident in both substantive and relational thinkers. In Western thinking, the answer is often given within the

---

96. Consider that he makes no use of these tools in his description of our basic and quotidian identity. See, for example, Kelsey, *Eccentric Existence*, 337–40, 382–85.

context of individuated excluded otherness: calling on a single or limited set of features in human beings to distinguish them from the rest of creation. This feature(s) is sometimes considered the root of human identity. In substantive thinking, an intrinsic feature such as rationality is that root, while in relational thought it is the relationality of humanity.

Rather than speaking to a single aspect as that feature that may define human identity, Kelsey reshapes the question to ask, 'How does one describe the subject of a "Who?" question?' Not only is his description of that subject (at least in his construction) narrative in shape, it is also qualified by three qualifiers: *personal*, *unsubstitutable* and *basic* and *quotidian*.

Qualifying his description of human identity by locating it in the binary pair of the basic and quotidian identity enables Kelsey to draw out his sense of identity in the context of two distinct, yet intertwined, notions of identity. Unlike substantive and relational thinkers who both appeal to a single basis for human identity, Kelsey speaks of two notions of identity that together (along with *personal* and *unsubstitutable*) illuminate his sense of identity as a description of the subject of a 'Who?' question. Using this binary pair, Kelsey incorporates elements of both substantive and relational concerns: a human identity that universally endures and is simultaneously dynamic, open to change and development.

In this construction, Kelsey is able to speak substantially about the human being without investing substantive qualities into the human being itself or appealing to a non-physical dualistic argument about human identity. In his claim that our basic identity is a gift given by God as He creates us, Kelsey—using the language of 'noun'—is able to claim that the human being has an enduring identity that is universally present. All human beings are created by God. They are God's creatures. This is the eccentric root of their basic identity. Kelsey speaks of *their basic identity* as a 'gifted identity' that cannot change across time and space. It is, for all intents and purposes, a substantive identity. It is part of the very structure and nature of the human being: universally present in all human beings.

As with relational thinking, Kelsey is able to avoid the problems associated with assigning substantive identities to living objects that radically change over time by rooting the human being's identity eccentrically. However, unlike relational thinking, this identity is gifted, not developed. The human being's *basic identity* is not dependent on whether an individual human being displays a unity of identity across time and change, or that every human being displays the same characteristics. Rather, our basic identity is rooted in God's faithful creative blessing, which does not change. Whether a human being is young or old, male or female or intellectually capable or challenged, the fact that the human being is God's creature means that they all have the same basic identity.

At the same time, Kelsey's construction appeals to a *quotidian identity* that is dynamic and changeable. Using the language of 'verb,' Kelsey speaks of the quotidian identity as a vocation the human being is called to live out. References to the quotidian identity enable Kelsey to appeal to an identity that is open to radical change, development and progress. It takes seriously the dynamic nature of humanity.

Furthermore, both of these identities are eccentrically rooted in the relational character of God. The substantive *gifted basic identity* of human beings is, albeit consistently present, relationally conceived. It is as God relates directly to us in creative blessing that we obtain a *basic identity*. In like fashion, as God relates indirectly through our quotidian context we receive our quotidian identity.

The basic and quotidian identities are not distinct or separate but are intertwined in the notions of gift and vocation.[97] In the words of Alistair McFadyen, identity—as it relates to the *imago Dei*—"is both an 'is' and an 'ought.'"[98] The human being *is* God's creature, related to in creative blessing, eschatological consummation and reconciliation. In addition, it *ought* to live its life in congruence with this identity. This is very much the struggle Paul talks about in Romans 7. Here, Paul discusses a quotidian identity that lives at cross-grain to his basic identity. In the words of Edmund Hill: "We discover what we are by becoming what we are. And we always run the risk of failing to discover what we are by becoming what we are not."[99]

---

97. Kelsey understands human being as both a gift and a vocation, rooted in two ways Job tells of his creation: as having been given a living body and being a living body. These two ways help to balance the notions of gift and vocation, or substantive and dynamic anthropology. See Kelsey, *Eccentric Existence*, chap. 6; cf. 284–85.

98. McFadyen, *Call to Personhood*, 17; cf. Visala, "Imago Dei," 117–18.

99. Hill, *Being Human*, 13.

6

Personal Identity

THE SECOND SENSE OF identity in *EE* is qualified by *personal*. Kelsey contends that "much of the theological work usually done in anthropology by the notion of 'image of God' is done here by the theological notion of the 'personal'" (281).[1] Kelsey does not explain this statement, and the reader is left to deduce his meaning. As we note later in this chapter, a reading of chapter 7 of *EE* (esp. 286–291) indicates that Kelsey understands the term *person* to be used, among other things, with "evaluative force" (288–91). That is to say, entities with a personal identity are evaluated to have unqualified dignity and value. As such, within *EE*, this sense of identity is the foundation upon which subsequent claims about human dignity—and the ethical/moral implications that follow—are founded. The focus of this chapter is on this foundation. We leave for others to explore the ethical/moral implications of those claims.

A contemporary theological anthropology cannot avoid taking cognizance of the fact that terms such as 'person' and 'personal' are readily available in ordinary secular contemporary discourse.[2] Kelsey notes: "Arguably the most important family of concepts borrowed by contemporary theologians from modern secular culture's anthropological wisdom includes concepts of 'person,' 'personality,' 'personhood,' and the like. There is no way to avoid borrowing them."[3]

The concept of *personal*—and as Kelsey states, "by extension 'person'" (286)—raises many questions,[4] not least of which is about a definition of the

---

1. Kelsey is not alone in associating personal with the imago Dei. Grenz's work *Social God* has the sub-heading, "A Trinitarian Theology of the Imago Dei." See also McFadyen, *Call to Personhood*, 17–44; McFarland, *Difference & Identity*, 22–25; Zizioulas, "Human Capacity and Human Incapacity," 411, 424.

2. Kelsey, *Eccentric Existence*, 357–58, 363, 377; cf. Kelsey, "Personal Bodies," 153.

3. Kelsey, "Personal Bodies," 149. It should be noted, however, that there is still debate as to whether human beings should be associated/conflated with the notion of 'person.' See Rudman, *Concepts of Persons*, 4–5.

4. Indeed, there is much debate as to whether personhood should be considered distinct from human being entirely. After all, there are non-human persons, e.g., angels,

term. In secular discourse, the notion is associated with (and often substituted for) other conceptions such as 'person,' 'personhood,' 'personality,' 'self,' 'subject' and 'consciousness.'[5] It is often used in radically distinct contexts, for example, the legal persona[6] of a company or the freedom in self-making and self-constitution.[7] A theological anthropology that is to be taken seriously needs to be conscious of these other uses. Yet, as David Grant argues, personhood "is incapable of precise definition,"[8] and is—in Penelhum's words—"a very untidy concept."[9] Tidying up this concept and providing neat definitions is a task beyond the scope of this chapter. Indeed, Kelsey himself argues: "It is no part of this project to defend a claim about what the English word 'person' really means in theological contexts or otherwise" (357). Although we briefly consider some of the challenges associated with this theme, we limit our discussions, as far as possible, to issues relevant to Kelsey's understanding of the term.

The Challenge of Persons

Kelsey, like Stanley Rudman, is all too aware that "the concept of 'person' has a long and complicated history in both theology and philosophy."[10] Theologically, many have argued that divine personhood functions as the foundation and precondition for the model of human personhood.[11] How to construe Trinitarian personhood and its relation to human personhood

---

corporations and even animals. Rudman believes such debates hinge on the attempt to distinguish the essential criteria of personhood without reference to accidental properties of human being. Engelhardt, for example, claims that "persons, not humans, are special" and thus valuable. Such a reduction of human being and the exaltation of personhood, Rudman argues, is the result of "an attempt to *exclude* certain human beings who have previously been included as persons (namely, the senile and foetuses)." Rudman ultimately concludes that there are distinctions but argues for a very close connection between the two. See Rudman, *Concepts of Persons*, 4–5, 42–59, 75–100.

5. See as examples Engelhardt, "Beginnings of Personhood," 20–21; Grenz, *Social God*, 58–97, esp. 59, 60, 99; Pannenberg, *Anthropology in Theological Perspective*, 185–224; Shutte, "What Makes Us Person," 69; Kelsey, "Personal Bodies," 149; Kelsey, *Eccentric Existence*, 286.

6. Hellegers, "Beginnings of Personhood," 16; cf. Kelsey, *Eccentric Existence*, 360.

7. Kelsey, "Two Theologies of Death," 350.

8. Grant, "Personal and Impersonal Concepts," 79.

9. Penelhum quoted in Grant, "Personal and Impersonal Concepts," 79.

10. Rudman, *Concepts of Persons*, 123; cf. Kelsey, *Eccentric Existence*, 31–33, 287–91, 363–78; "Personal Bodies," 149–52; "Human Being," 141–56.

11. See as examples: Hudson, "Dementia and Personhood," 127–28; McFadyen, *Call to Personhood*; McFarland, *Difference & Identity*, vii; Scott, "God as Person," 161–62; Rudman, *Concepts of Persons*, 144–45.

is widely debated.[12] It is commonplace to use personal language to talk of the Trinitarian God,[13] and some have even gone so far as to claim: "If God does not exist, the person does not exist."[14] John Zizioulas, for example, argues that the very notion of personhood is a theological one: "purely the product of patristic thought."[15] As such there is general agreement that an analogy between God's personhood and human personhood exists, be that an *analogia entis, relationis or transcendentalis*.[16]

Yet, the question of whether God may be considered a person,[17] especially if understood within modern concepts of individuality, self, consciousness or agency, is still open to debate.[18] Indeed, some commentators consider

---

12. See as examples: Grenz, *Social God*; McFadyen, *Call to Personhood*; McFarland, *Difference & Identity*; Scott, "God as Person"; Torrance, *Persons in Communion*, 213–306; Zizioulas, *Being as Communion*. Kelsey considers three such proposals (Kelsey, *Eccentric Existence*, 358–59).

13. Rudman goes so far as to argue that this is a biblical imperative based on the narrative of God as a personal being. Rudman, *Concepts of Persons*, 160.

14. In Rudman, *Concepts of Persons*, 129. Rudman does not go so far.

15. Zizioulas, *Being as Communion*, 27. See also Scott, "God as Person," 162; Rudman, *Concepts of Persons*, 160.

16. The debates around which analogy is appropriate are numerous and beyond the scope of this project. For the interested reader, consider Torrance's in-depth analysis between the different constructions: Torrance, *Persons in Communion*, 129–90. For Kelsey's understanding of the *analogia transcendentalis* see Kelsey, *Eccentric Existence*, 376.

17. It should be noted here that, on the whole, Christians speak of God as three persons rather than one. See Emmet, "Could God Be a Person?," 3; Rudman, *Concepts of Persons*, 161. However, there are exceptions; see, for example, Swinburne, *Coherence of Theism*, 99–100.

18. Kelsey himself is very aware of this debate (Kelsey, *Eccentric Existence*, 68–72). Although Aquinas feels that it is only fitting to attribute this concept to God, he is very much aware that God, as a notion, is not a person or being in the sense of any human classification of being. See Aquinas, *ST* 29.3; cf. Emmet, "Could God Be a Person?," 7. It is interesting to note that Aquinas takes pains to note that only the present (his contemporary) meaning of *hypostasis* should be applied to God, and not the original meaning. Emmet argues that modern notions of individual conscious persons are incompatible with theological notions of God's omnipotence, omniscience and omnipresence. See Emmet, "Could God Be a Person?," 5–7. Furthermore, modern conceptions of personhood often entail embodiment, which appears to be incompatible with God. See Penelhum, *Survival and Disembodied Existence*, 103–8. Of course there are debates about the embodied nature of God expressed in the doctrines of the *Logos asarkos* and *ensarkos*. Also, there are questions about human beings necessitating embodiment. Swinburne, for example, is able to give an intellectually coherent concept of personhood that does not necessitate a body, yet Rudman believes this is disputable. More than this, there are intellectually coherent ways of speaking about God as being in time in the history he reveals. See Rudman, *Concepts of Persons*, 144–70. Considering these complications, it is perhaps no wonder that Augustine argues that one refers to God as 'three persons' simply so that one does not remain wholly silent on the topic, it is simply a matter of

divine personhood a red herring.[19] Notions of independent, embodied, spatial individuality are alien to Trinitarian constructions of personhood and, as Dorothy Emmet warns, if assigned to God would push the analogy of God as a person beyond any real meaningful notion of personhood.[20] The disparity between those theologians who insist God is a person and those who refuse to designate him as such is understandable.[21]

Even if we do insist that God is a person, what that means for persons elsewhere is not entirely clear. Kelsey considers three ways of using the word 'person' in different theological *loci* (358–59). The first is in fourth-century Cappadocian doctrines of the Trinity where 'persons' names the unique way in which Trinitarian members are related. To Kelsey, it is not clear that this usage can cover human beings elsewhere. Only God is capable of having the generative relations that describe 'persons' in this *locus*. To use *person* this way to encompass human beings would be such an extension "that its illuminating power would be very dim" (358). Second, Kelsey notes Richard of St Victor's use of 'divine being' as understood in terms of divine love as a personal category with analogues in human experience. However, using St Victor's understanding of divine love as a personal category to cover human beings can only be done by "abstracting the defining characteristics of a human person from God's nontemporality and nonphysicality" (359), ultimately resulting in a human being having their existence in themselves and nothing else. Third, in the context of Boethius's clarification of 'person' as "an individual substance of a rational nature" (359), 'person' is not constituted through relationships but "by its individual subsistence as a concrete instance of a particular kind of being—a 'rational' kind" (359). While such usage may work to speak of an analogy between 'person' in Christology and humanity generally, to speak about Trinitarian persons in this way would "yield doctrinal incoherence and polytheism" (359). Considering these uses, Kelsey's conclusion is to question the viability of a single, universally valid theological definition of personhood.

As with theological usages, the historical development of personhood is fraught with challenges. Such developments have been plotted and

---

necessity or a manner of speaking rather than being inherently accurate. See Brown, "Trinitarian Personhood and Individuality," 48, 64–73.

19. Rudman, *Concepts of Persons*, 7.

20. Emmet, "Could God Be a Person?," 5.

21. Rudman considers a vast range of theologians, such as Swinburne, Pannenberg, Ott, Tillich, Rahner and Moltmann with differing views on this point. Rudman, *Concepts of Persons*, 161–66. Kelsey himself is very cautious about such designations and prefers to use the term *hypostasis* than person (Kelsey, *Eccentric Existence*, 68–67).

debated by many,[22] each with their own unique take. We do not digress into those debates here. For reference one may note Stanley Grenz, whom Kelsey uses in his discussions on personhood, who has provided a useful discussion on this development.[23]

In brief, Grenz interprets Augustine as inaugurating the modern self[24] characterized by inward cogitation.[25] This becomes the basis of Boethius's "normative"[26] definition of person as the "individual substance of a rational nature"[27] (*naturae rationalis individua substantia*). To Grenz this definition instils what is to become an almost unshakable pillar of personal identity: rationality. Aquinas uses rationality as the foundation upon which to categorize something as a person: "among all other substances individual beings with rational nature have a special name, and this is 'person.'"[28] Kelsey understands Aquinas's definition to be the "standard classification" (289) that still has influence on contemporary thinkers. It is arguable that substantive thinkers have drawn extensively on this type of understanding of personhood in their doctrine of the *imago Dei*.[29]

To both Grenz and Kelsey, the Enlightenment's "turn to the subject"[30] inaugurated a shift toward a stance of radical disengagement: the disengagement of the self from the objectified world and ultimately the disengagement from oneself with oneself (as object) so as to remake oneself. Charles Taylor has argued that this disengagement is a particular characteristic of the modern conception of the self, a conception that assumes a radical subjectivist understanding within which individuals are called to separate themselves (both from themselves and others) through self-objectification.[31]

In late modernity and latter postmodernism, the concept of a radical inwardly centered individual subject comes under pressure.[32] The indi-

---

22. See as examples Grenz, *Social God*, 60–97; Gunton, *One*, pt. 1; McFarland, *Difference & Identity*, 6–10; Rudman, *Concepts of Persons*, 5–7, 75–143.

23. Grenz, *Social God*, 60–97. Kelsey actively engages this with this. For more see Kelsey, "Human Creature," 129–30.

24. Grenz, *Social God*, 60.

25. Grenz, *Social God*, 60–64.

26. Grant, "Personal and Impersonal Concepts," 79. See also McFarland, *Difference & Identity*, 7–8; Pannenberg, *Anthropology in Theological Perspective*, 235–36; Rudman, *Concepts of Persons*, 134–37.

27. Boethius quoted in Grenz, *Social God*, 65.

28. Aquinas, *ST* 29.1.

29. See chapter 1 of this project.

30. Kelsey, "Spiritual Machines," 7.

31. Grenz, *Social God*, 71–74. See also Taylor, *Sources of the Self*, 143–76.

32. Grenz, *Social God*, 128–37.

vidual, in such thinking, becomes a structure of intersecting relations rather than an inner, self-centered and self-sufficient center. The person finds their identity only in their place within a larger system. Personal identity no longer exists simply in the self as a liberated, autonomous, rational subject distinct from the world of objects, but as a result of the inter-relational structures that govern human social and cultural interactions. Such thinking echoes relational understandings of the *imago Dei*. Here, the self and personhood are considered constructs of social and cultural structures.[33]

In Grenz's view, not only do postmodernists acknowledge the loss of the self, they embrace its demise.[34] Yet the postmodernist is unable to entirely dismiss the concept of an inner personal identity. The self remains within postmodernism as a self-referential system that is continually self-producing through a selective reorganization of the surrounding world within itself. Zygmunt Baumann contends that this is the problem of "liquid modernity,"[35] in which the self is continually dismantling and rearranging itself.[36] The effect of the postmodernist self is the "psychic fragmentation"[37] that gives birth to a "chaotic self."[38] The dangers of this conception are serious. Benno van den Toren, for example, argues that the person is left adrift, with no moral direction as they search for a "home."[39]

Against such a backdrop, it is unsurprising that Kelsey is critical of terms like 'person,' 'personhood' and 'self' in the context of ordinary secular Western discourse.[40] He contends that "the major problem with framing a Christian anthropology as a theological concept of person lies in the inherent power and current cultural dominance of the modern concept of

---

33. For more on the relationship between structuralist, poststructuralist, and pre-Kantian philosophy, see Grenz, *Social God*, 128–37.

34. Grenz, *Social God*, 133–37.

35. Bauman, *Individualized Society*, 146.

36. Bauman, *Individualized Society*, chap. 11.

37. Fredric Jameson quoted in Grenz, *Social God*, 136.

38. Johann Roten quoted in Grenz, *Social God*, 136.

39. Here, van den Toren references Lyer. See van den Toren, *Christian Apologetics*, 56–58.

40. We have already noted his concern with respective culturally relevant referencing of certain sets of human powers, particularly rational powers (Kelsey, *Eccentric Existence*, 289; cf. Kelsey, "Spiritual Machines," 7). His objections to his understanding of contemporary philosophical notions of personhood are numerous. See for example his notion of the manner in which 'person' is used in contemporary culture as either classificatory, descriptively metaphysical or evaluative and the "worrisome tensions" these uses raise for theology (Kelsey, "Personal Bodies," 149–52). Compare with his concerns over pre-modern substance/distinction operations, which he argues are still evident in modern constructions (Kelsey, *Eccentric Existence*, 31–33).

person" (363). Kelsey argues that the conceptual power of the modern concept of persons to coherently integrate Enlightenment interests with human individual uniqueness, equality, autonomy and perfectibility is attractive to Christian theological anthropology, which shares similar interests (366–67). Yet Kelsey also believes that the modern conception is "insufficient to articulate its own Enlightenment interests" (363; cf. 364–78). He justifies this claim through a lengthy discussion in chapter 9B of *EE* (363–78). His discussions in this regard are highly technical and draw on the work of Welker, Frei and Schwöbel, who use the term 'person' in a way that distinguishes their usage from contemporary secular discourses.[41] His conclusion is that these authors "give strong reasons not to adopt the modern concept of person in Christian theological anthropology" (376).

> So dominant is the modern concept in modern culture, and such is its power that, it seems to me, it is virtually impossible to use the English word 'person,' however much it is qualified, without leading the listener or reader to absorb what is said or written into this already-well-known concept of person. The very use of the word 'person' to name the subject of the discussion would invite confusion of the received modern concept of person with what is proposed as a theological alternative, regardless of how explicit, clearly different, and intellectually powerful the theological formulation of the alternative concept might me. (377)

Therefore, Kelsey suggests "going beyond anything either Welker or Schwoebel [*sic*] suggests—simply setting aside completely the word 'person' as the name for the subject of theological anthropology" (377). In place of 'person,' Kelsey prefers to use the term 'personal.' Let us follow the contours of his argument.

---

41. In sum, Kelsey's analysis of their positions revolves around the conflict in current modern concepts between public and private personhood. Kelsey interprets Welker as arguing for the insufficiency of the Enlightenment's "*subjectification* of the person" (Kelsey, *Eccentric Existence*, 366) on the basis of thinly structured public environments which challenges persons' ability to mediate public and private subjectifications. As the person mediates between their private and public identity in such diverse contexts, conflict, confusion and ultimately contradiction ensue. As a result, the contemporary notion of person "has proved incapable of illuminating the relation between the 'outer' and the 'inner' dimensions of the person and has left itself conceptually unable to integrate the entire 'public dimension' of the person" (Kelsey, *Eccentric Existence*, 373). For further theological objections implied in Kelsey's understanding of secular contemporary discourse which are not elucidated here, see Kelsey, "Human Being," 154–66. Kelsey ultimately contends that narrative is the preferred scheme for describing a personal identity in a way that takes cognisance of both the private and public personal identity (Kelsey, "Biblical Narrative and Theological Anthropology," 122–31).

Personal Identities, Not Identities of Persons

Kelsey develops his view of human personhood over the whole course of part 1 of *EE* and in particular chapters 7 and 9B. As we have shown, Kelsey argues that in both historical and theological discourse, the term 'person' has a variety of meanings, which are often technical and valid for their own contexts (357–58, 363). It is impossible, with such complex and diverse *loci*, to establish a single correct meaning of the term (357–58, 360, 363). He contends that while one cannot help but borrow one's host culture's concept of personhood (377),[42] one should be careful about adopting such terminology uncritically (357). Therefore, he argues for a "bending"[43] of this concept for his specific purposes.

In *EE*, chapter 7's discussion of *personal* begins by considering two ways in which conventional ordinary discourse makes use of 'person.' The first is identified in P. F. Strawson's theory of M-predicates (material predicates) and P-predicates (personal predicates).[44] Strawson argues that in ordinary discourse, 'person' is informally used in a metaphysical way to speak of a logically 'primitive' concept that cannot be explained in terms of any other, logically more basic concepts (287–88). In Strawson's theory, "the content of the concept of person simply is that of which both M-predicates and P-predicates may and must be predicated" (287).[45] Although acknowledging the necessity for such a primitive concept, Kelsey is unconvinced that 'person' is used consistently in either theological or ordinary discourse in this way. Therefore, he questions the term's ability to replace an Aristotelian notion of substance as the logically primitive human concept.[46]

---

42. See also Kelsey, "Personal Bodies," 153.

43. Kelsey, "Personal Bodies," 153.

44. What exactly the 'M' and 'P' stand for in Strawson's theory is open to debate. Here we have followed Kelsey's presumption of "material" and "personal" (Kelsey, *Eccentric Existence*, 287) simply because we are discussing Strawson in the context of *EE*. However, 'personal' is misleading as it is placed within a discussion of personhood, which, according to Strawson, is logically more basic than either M- or P-predicates. A better translation may be 'consciousness' as it is better suited to the immediate discussion of Strawson on P-predicates, although here we recognize that it does not begin with 'P.' See Strawson, *Individuals*, 104–6.

45. Strawson, *Individuals*, chap. 3. Strawson's theory of M- and P-predicates is widely used in discussions of personhood. See as examples Cooper, *Body, Soul, and Life*, 18–20; Ricoeur, *Oneself as Other*, 30–39; Rudman, *Concepts of Persons*, 145–51. Swinburne is not convinced that both M- and P-predicates are necessarily ontologically primitive, see Swinburne, *Coherence of Theism*, 99–100. Zizioulas is dubious about the entire construction, Zizioulas, "Human Capacity and Human Incapacity," 415.

46. See also Kelsey, "Personal Bodies," 149–51.

The second way 'person' is used in conventional discourse is with both classificatory and evaluative force (288–91). Thus, by assigning beings who adhere to certain types of conventional standards—for example, psychological, moral, intellectual, etc.—to a specific class, one may make the evaluative judgement that beings of this class have intrinsic value. While acknowledging the usefulness of the two forces, Kelsey questions the relationship between the classificatory and evaluative forms. He argues that—bracketing God out of the discourse—there is no viable reason why certain classes of beings should be so positively evaluated. In short, In Kelsey's view, ordinary discourse about 'person' fails to provide either an ontological primitive principle or grounds for evaluating human dignity (287–91).[47] Kelsey, therefore, seeks to establish a theological concept of 'person' that overlaps these discourses while avoiding the limitations (291). Here, his primary concern is to establish a viable foundation upon which to lay the grounds for human value and dignity.

Kelsey establishes this foundation throughout part 1 of *EE*, which deals primarily with the 'What?' question in the context of God relating in creative blessing. Kelsey argues, relying heavily on Westermann's analysis of the Genesis account, that Wisdom literature and Job 10 in particular is the most appropriate narrative of God's relating to create human beings (Chps. 4B, 6, 7).[48] Retaining this approach, Kelsey argues that the use of 'person' in *EE* is guided both by a reading of Job 10 and by a reading of Genesis 2:4b—3:24 in light of Job 10 (291). According to *EE*, both narratives assume that a human creature is the unity of a "personal body" (291).[49] *Personal*, in the phrase *personal body*, refers to "the distinctive way in which God relates to them, not because of the ways in which they relate to God" (291–92). In both accounts, God's relating in creative blessing is narrated in such a way as to express God's giving and human receiving of the gift of creation within a public space. As such, "the distinctive way in which God relates to creaturely human bodies to personalize them is 'address'" (292).

---

47. See also Kelsey, "Personal Bodies," 149–53.

48. Kelsey notes that his reliance on Westermann is entirely "one-sided" (Kelsey, *Eccentric Existence*, Chp. 4B), and he engages solely with Westermann to justify his preference for Wisdom literature at the expense of the Genesis creation narratives. It is interesting to note that he agrees to reject the Genesis narratives of creation in favour of the narratives in Job 10 based on Westermann's argument that they are "bent" by the narratives of reconciliation, and yet he is very happy to 'bend' his notions of personhood, thereby questioning the detrimental impact of bending narratives and theological concepts to suit one's ends (Kelsey, *Eccentric Existence*, 153).

49. Kelsey acknowledges that the term is Ricoeur's. See Kelsey, "Personal Bodies," 7, 155; Ricoeur, *Freedom and Nature*, 8–13.

In these accounts, God's relating to human creatures in creative blessing correlates to God's relating to personalize them. In creative blessing, God relates directly to the human being. On the other hand, in relating to personalize them, God relates indirectly by addressing them through the medium of the quotidian context (291). His address is mediated in the quotidian context by culture and, usually, ordinary language (291). This address is analogous to a social space between God and human beings and, indirectly mediated by the quotidian context, personalizes the human creature.

Kelsey demonstrates that this address is narrated in slightly different ways in Job and Genesis. In both texts, ordinary human language is privileged as the medium of personhood. In Job, both God and Job respond to each other using human speech, while in Genesis, God's command to the human being creates the possibility of the human response. Kelsey terms this the 'happening' of a relationship that personalizes the human creature (293–95).

In Both Genesis and Job, God's address to personalize human beings is given within the context of a public space which is constituted, in part, by the use of ordinary language. It is by virtue of the fact that God speaks to the human being, granting them a status in a social space, that they are personal beings. Theologically speaking, the *personal* is necessarily a public and social reality: "Indeed, it is a social construct—that is, the construction of a society by God through the social practices of language use" (296). In sum:

> They are 'persons' inasmuch as the living bodies that God creates are personal bodies (as opposed to impersonal bodies) by virtue of the distinctive way in which God creatively relates to them indirectly: through their creaturely proximate contexts, and in particular through use of ordinary language. God, as it were, talks living human bodies into being personal. (293)

Using this construction, Kelsey is able to claim that *personal* is logically prior to 'person':[50] "it is only because human creaturely living bodies are 'personal' that they may, for that reason, also be called 'persons'" (292). Yet this primitive concept is not used as a surrogate for an Aristotelian substance that designates which various properties are predicated. M- and P-predicates, as well as 'person'/'personal,' are all predicated: They have their status in God (292). Furthermore, Kelsey is able to avoid reliance on human creaturely capacities as the basis for personhood. The consequence is that

---

50. Here Kelsey differs slightly from Zizioulas, who argues that 'person' (the Father) is the ontologically primitive concept. Kelsey contends that *personal* precedes person. It should, however, be noted that Kelsey is speaking anthropologically, while Zizioulas is speaking in the context of the Trinity.

the correlation between the classificatory and evaluative forces of the use of 'person' is grounded not in conventional standards—such as emotional, moral or intellectual—but in the distinctive manner in which God relates to human beings. Thus, one may classify a human being as a person and at the same time judge them to have intrinsic value only in reference to the manner in which God relates to them. This avoids the dire consequences of classifying human beings as persons based on creaturely capacities or relationality that may then be used to grant or remove intrinsic value.

Since human creatures are personalized by God's address, Kelsey refers to 'personal identities' rather than 'identities of persons.' *Personal* qualifies identity in a particular way: without specifying which entities' identities are thus qualified (357–58, 363). If one uses the qualifier 'personal' adverbially, then the human creature is used to name a member of a distinctive class of entities without reference to the evaluative force of the term, while 'personal' is used to evaluate those entities in a certain way. That is to say, it evaluates them as having unqualified dignity and value.[51]

Kelsey's model, in his own opinion, avoids the negative implications of using the term 'person' while establishing a logically primitive principle for human being in God's personal address (rather than personhood itself). Simultaneously, it solves the problems with the classificatory and evaluative uses of 'person' (377–78). It is here argued, however, that Kelsey has attempted to achieve this end by borrowing from and 'bending' certain Trinitarian anthropologists. Let us spend a little time justifying this claim.

A Trinitarian Anthropological Influence

Kelsey's article "The Human Creature" (2007), in which he speaks to the concept of *personal identity*, deliberates on this theological notion by considering the constructions of Stanley Grenz, Alistair McFadyen and Ian McFarland in detail.[52] These authors, along with Kelsey, reference John Zizioulas. Let us briefly note each in turn.

The central thesis of Zizioulas's work *Being as Communion* (1985) is that person, not substance, is primitive, and personal being—as understood through Trinitarianism—is being in communion. Zizioulas contends that it was the Cappadocian Fathers who were able to provide a philosophical

---

51. Chapter 9B elaborates further on this contention. Kelsey addresses the reason for not simply defining 'person' in theological terms so as to avoid the problems associated with the classificatory and evaluative ways the term is used in ordinary discourse. His central argument is that the modern concept of person is too powerful to simply amend, yet it is inadequate (Kelsey, *Eccentric Existence*, 357, 363–78).

52. Kelsey, "Human Creature," 128–37.

and theologically coherent account of God's life as being caused by the personhood of the Father.[53] It is the Father who, in relationship, brings about God.[54] This latter turn in Zizioulas's work establishes personal communion as the primary ontological basis for all being.[55] In Zizioulas's words, personhood implies an "openness of being"[56] an "*ekstasis*,"[57] that is, a move toward communion. To Zizioulas "ekstasis and hypostasis represent two basic aspects of personhood."[58]

---

53. Zizioulas, *Being as Communion*, 40–41. Torrance queries this radical claim, arguing that Zizioulas may be read as identifying the being of God with the person of the Father almost exclusively: Torrance, *Persons in Communion*, 288–89.

54. One should note the difference between Eastern and Western theologians on this point. There are echoes here of the *filioque* controversy. The manner in which Kelsey uses Zizioulas does not take this into account.

55. During our project, when we refer to 'primary ontological basis' and other such derivatives, we are speaking with Strawson's understanding of this concept in mind. That is, "Suppose, for instance, it should turn out that there is a type of particulars, β, such that particulars of type β cannot be identified without reference to particulars of another type, α, whereas particulars of type α can be identified without reference to particulars of type β. Then it would be a general characteristic of our scheme, that the ability to talk about β-particulars at all was dependent on the ability to talk about α-particulars, but not vice versa. This fact could reasonably be expressed by saying that in our scheme α-particulars were ontologically prior to β-particulars, or were more fundamental or more basic than they." Strawson, *Individuals*, 17.

56. Zizioulas, *Being as Communion*, 44–45n40.

57. Zizioulas, *Being as Communion*, 44–45n40.

58. Zizioulas, *Being as Communion*, 27–49. See also Zizioulas, "On Being a Person," 33–46; Zizioulas, "Human Capacity and Human Incapacity," 408. Zizioulas's work is rooted in highly complex questions surrounding Greek philosophical categories of substance and relationship and in particular a shifting emphasis between these notions within Augustine. How exactly this new link between substance and relationship is established by Augustine is a very complicated question. Zizioulas's argument revolves around his interpretation of the early fourth-century debates between Greek monism and Christianity's conception of an entirely independent God. This led to a terminological quarrel between East (Latin) and West (Greek) as to how to describe the dual nature of the single hypostasis of Jesus Christ. Zizioulas argues that a solution came with the Cappadocian qualification of *ousia* (substance) with hypostasis, which referred to what was distinct between the three members of the Trinity. According to Zizioulas, *hypostasis* morphed from its original connotation of substance to acquire a connotation of independence and to become identified with person. See Zizioulas, *Being as Communion*, 36–41; Zizioulas, "Human Capacity and Human Incapacity," 408–9. Zizioulas's approach is widely referenced. See as examples McFarland, *Difference & Identity*, 9–11; Rudman, *Concepts of Persons*, 125–28; cf. Gunton, *One*, 191; Kelsey, *Eccentric Existence*, 68–72; Torrance, *Persons in Communion*, 120–25, 287–89. Although held in high esteem, it should be noted that some have argued that these terminological quarrels have not entirely been resolved. Barth, for example, had grave reservations with the term 'person' and as a result prefers *Seinsweise* to refer to the three members of the Trinity. However, there is a connotation of modes of being within Barth

McFadyen's work *The Call to Personhood* (1990) makes use of a relational Trinitarianism that understands the Trinity as a unique community of persons in which "person and relations are interdependent moments in a process of mutuality."[59] He, like Zizioulas, describes Trinitarian personal identities as "ex-centric."[60] That is to say, the persons of the Trinity are themselves personal centers but only through the pattern of communication and response in which they are engaged.[61] A personal identity is dependent upon a person's "incommunicable personalities,"[62] which designate the character of the relations one has with others and yet are not reducible to these relations. Upon this basis he argues that persons are unique centers only in their interactions with other unique centers, who are themselves centered in their interactions with other centers of communication. This is the "basic conception"[63] of his book: "it is other people who enable us to become persons."[64]

Grenz's work *The Social God and the Relational Self* (2001) considers the impact of the "return of the Social Trinity"[65] on the doctrine of the

---

that the fourth-century Fathers may have been trying to avoid. See Torrance, *Persons in Communion*, 213–62. Kelsey notes that these two terms were vague and often used in overlapping/interchangeable ways (Kelsey, *Eccentric Existence*, 69) and that while the Cappadocians are credited with this innovation, the formula "one *ousia* in three *hypostases*" is not used often by the Cappadocians (Kelsey, *Eccentric Existence*, 68). More than this, there is reason to question Zizioulas's argument that this was a Cappadocian move. Dörrie has argued that it predates the Cappadocian Fathers. See Mikhailovsky, "Anthropology of Hypostasis," 157–59.

59. McFadyen, *Call to Personhood*, 27.
60. McFadyen, *Call to Personhood*, 40.
61. McFadyen terms this the "sediment" of personal identity that is laid down through communication history. He states that the Father is "a sedimentation of his significant history of relations" (McFadyen, *Call to Personhood*, 40). This poses major questions, not least of which concerns the conception of the Father as a changeable and developing sedimentation of layer upon layer of history that personalizes Him. Such questions are beyond the scope of this project. For more on his theory of personal identity as sedimentation, see McFadyen, *Call to Personhood*, 7–8, 40–42, 86–90, 93–95, 102–3.
62. McFadyen, *Call to Personhood*, 28.
63. McFadyen, *Call to Personhood*, xi, 9.
64. McFadyen, *Call to Personhood*, xi.
65. Grenz, *Social God*, 3–9. There are questions that arise about the viability/suitability of social Trinitarianism. It was first introduced, arguably by Moltmann, at the height of the Cold War, in which Western individualistic capitalism was in a life-and-death struggle with Eastern collectivistic communism. It is arguable that social Trinitarianism arises out of this context. See Moltmann, *Trinity and the Kingdom*. Questions emerge about how it is possible, within a social Trinitarian model, to avoid projecting our own sense of relationality onto the Trinity, thus further baptizing Trinitarianism

imago Dei. Grenz contends that Trinitarian members are to be considered persons subsisting in three subjective centers. His understanding of the social Trinity is that "God is [not] three persons who have relations, but three subsistent relations that are in fact persons."[66] As a consequence, human personal identities can only achieve "wholeness"[67] in personal relationship, most aptly characterized/illustrated in human sexuality (drawing on Barth's contextual understanding of the *imago Dei* as human beings made male and female[68]). Ultimately this is only achieved at the *eschaton*.[69]

McFarland's work *Difference & Identity* (2001), considers the role played by personhood in Trinitarian debates. Arguing that a major modern strategy to counter discrimination is to find common denominators on which to establish universal human value, he contends that the common approach is to coalesce claims to human value with human status as persons. According to McFarland, this homogenizing approach questions the value of those who fail to exhibit the necessary common denominators.[70] He, however, argues that (from a theological perspective) the concept of person is diversifying rather than unifying. In his understanding of Trinitarianism, the personhood of the Trinitarian members speaks to their irreducible distinction rather than what they have in common.[71] Using Jesus as the primary means by which we come to know of Trinitarian personhood, McFarland contends that personhood establishes distinction relationally.[72]

These theologians construct a picture of a relationally conceived Trinitarian understanding of personhood. In sum, drawing on Zizioulas, they reject substance in favor of relation as the ontological primary reality. Zizioulas argues that persons are eccentrically constituted by relations. McFadyen picks up on the eccentric nature of personhood in the dialogical and dialectical dimensions of persons. Persons are dynamic; that is, persons are formed through the address and response of social interactions (ex-centered) and yet never come to rest in a single ultimate unity. Persons' centers are centered in other persons, who themselves are likewise centered. McFarland draws our

---

in our contemporary culture. Furthermore, if this was a very contemporary question when first introduced, there are questions as to its honesty with regard to patristic Trinitarian thought.

66. Grenz, *Social God*, 50–51.
67. For Grenz's understanding of Wholeness see Grenz, *Social God*, 277–79, 294–98.
68. Barth, *CD* 3/1:185–88.
69. Grenz, *Social God*, pt. 2.
70. McFarland, *Difference & Identity*, 2–10.
71. McFarland, *Difference & Identity*, 30–48.
72. McFarland, *Difference & Identity*, 49–61.

attention to the heterogeneousness of personhood.[73] While many attempt to use the concept of personhood to establish a homogeneousness to humanity (thereby establishing universal human value), McFarland highlights that personhood (in Trinitarian terms) is at its core a differentiating rather than unifying principle. To claim that there is one characteristic of personhood is impossible. Grenz pulls much of this together to speak of an analogy of human personhood that is built on a social Trinitarianism. We are persons, as the Godhead consists of persons, through relational communion that is ultimately only perfected at the *eschaton*.

What is most significant in these theologians is their notion of the eccentric nature of personhood. Personhood is not a feature that is internally and individually rooted homogenously in a person, as modernism might contend. Rather, these authors refer to personhood in ways that are opposed to modernism's attempt to discover the self through interiority.[74] Personhood is socially assigned. Persons are personalized as they are personally related to.

The point is most aptly made when considering an infant. By all accounts, apart from DNA and a vague physical resemblance, infants display very little of the characterized nature of fully developed human beings. Yet we naturally consider them persons. H. Engelhardt argues that this is because of the role the infant plays in the mother-child relationship. The child is treated as a person by the mother, as though it were a person in its own right. It is the mother who personalizes the infant, and as a consequence, it *is* a person.[75] Similarly, personhood in theological terms is not a definition of a category of a being that possesses certain qualities. Rather, it is a description of a being as it is personally related to by God.[76] Although there are different

---

73. The same notion is picked up by Gunton who argues for the unity-in-diversity of the Triunity. It may be argued that this unity-in-diversity is very similar to Kelsey's notion of human eccentric existence as a wholeness-in-complexity. Gunton, *One*, pt. 2; cf. Kelsey, *Eccentric Existence*, 893.

74. Grenz makes this point quite emphatically. Grenz, *Social God*, 58–97.

75. Engelhardt, "Beginnings of Personhood," 22–23. See also Macmurray, *Persons in Relation*, 2:44–63. For a more technical version, see Shutte, "What Makes Us Person," 71–77. Brümmer places the emphasis slightly differently in his argument that personal identity involves others recognizing and endorsing the personal identity that one conceives themselves to be. See Brümmer, "Religious Belief and Personal Identity," 157–58. See also Brown, who, using the example of the infant-mother relationship, may be interpreted as conflating soul with person in his argument that our soul is originally endowed through the process of being related to (Brown, "Cognitive Contributions to Soul," 123–25).

76. For a discussion on the difference between definition and description in this context see McFarland, *Difference & Identity*, 10–13.

models of how this personalizing relationship is conceived,[77] there is some consensus that: "We are persons because Jesus claims us as such, not because we possess a certain set of intrinsic ontological properties."[78] McFarland expounds on this point quite eloquently when he states:

> If, however, we reconceive our analysis of persons in terms of who makes us persons rather than by trying to define what a person is, then the situation changes. Once this switch is made, our status as persons, instead of being understood as a function of some *thing* supposed to inhere in our physical or psychological makeup, can be reconceived as the result of some *one* acting toward us in a particular way. The activity of this someone may be a factor that all persons share in common, but it remains external to the individual.[79]

Kelsey is not uncritical of these authors.[80] He recognizes the problems associated with pure relationality that we have raised in chapter 1 of this project:

> This thesis [the relational thesis] is subject to serious critique: If relationality is the ontological structure of persons, then "we are landed with a logical problem of positing relations between relational entities, and so perhaps a never-ending regress of relations.... Persons are ontologically prior to relations."[81]

---

77. Zizioulas, for example, argues that salvation is a personalizing action (Zizioulas, *Being as Communion*, 49–65). Scott elucidates and questions Barth's construction of a mimetic personalizing relationship between human beings and God (Scott, "God as Person," 168–81). McFarland talks about a person as a character to whom God proclaims the good news (McFarland, *Difference & Identity*, 19–23).

78. McFarland, *Difference & Identity*, 23. Jesus here may be substituted for God without loss to the core point being made. It should also be noted that McFadyen may add that our response is important.

79. McFarland, *Difference & Identity*, 9 (cf. 10–11).

80. This is not to say that Kelsey is uncritical of them. For example, he criticizes their uncritical use of the term 'personal identity' as if they take for granted what they are talking about. See Kelsey, "Human Creature," 137. He further raises questions regarding McFadyen's call-response analogy (Kelsey, *Eccentric Existence*, 762), questions Grenz's eschatological ecclesial self which threatens the personhood (and with it the universal value) of non-Christians who may never reach eschatological consummation (Kelsey, *Eccentric Existence*, 901–4; cf. Kelsey, "Human Creature," 130) and is unconvinced by Zizioulas's metaphysical dialectic between human beings and God as a basis of the *imago Dei* (Kelsey, *Eccentric Existence*, 1009–10; cf. Kelsey, "Human Creature," 133).

81. Harris quoted in Kelsey, *Eccentric Existence*, 37. White, critiquing McFadyen's position on personhood, argues that a definition of personhood that has no "substantial personal core" is a weak definition that could amount to nothing more than an abstractivist claim. That is to say, without substance, personhood is simply abstracted from

Nevertheless, Kelsey's construction has clearly borrowed and bent their respective constructions. This is evidenced in a number of ways. First, we see it in his use of *personal* as a logically primary principle. He argues that theological anthropology requires a notion of person that is logically primitive (288)[82] and supplies this notion, very much as Zizioulas does, by referencing a personal reality (God) as the ontological basis for human personhood (291–92). Second, as with Zizioulas, Grenz, McFadyen and McFarland, Kelsey argues that the ontology of human personhood is both relational and eccentric. His construction, with minor amendments, sits easily with these Trinitarian anthropologists. The "person-constituting relation between human creatures and God" (294) is analogous to a social space (Grenz) that personalizes the human being through God's address (McFadyen). Human persons, who are personal centers, are ex-centered (McFadyen); they are centered in the call and response of another center (God), who himself is centered in other personal centers (Father, Son and Holy Spirit). This ex-centered existence is an *ekstasis* (Zizioulas): It is an openness of being that becomes hypostatic (bears its nature in its totality, according to Zizioulas). As a hypostasis it is differentiated (McFarland) from God; it is not the same personal being as the personal being (God) who relates to it.

Creating Personal Identities in *EE*

Kelsey's construction raises a number of questions. Minor questions, for example, are introduced about the consistency of his use of the terms 'personal' and 'person.' While he urges theological anthropology not to use the term 'person' in favor of the adjectival 'personal' (357), in *EE* the terms are very closely related (286) and he even makes use of 'person' himself (e.g., 286, 292).[83] He contends that personal bodies may be called 'persons' as long as this description is highly qualified, contrary to his argument against theological anthropology stipulating a technical theological concept of 'person' (292; cf. 363).

Perhaps a more problematic issue is raised in his very postliberal approach to the question. Rather than seeking an answer to the question

---

the concrete individuals with which one is faced (White, *Identity*, 45–46). It should be noted that White is not convinced that McFadyen actually makes such an abstractivist claim. This may be the reason McFarland prefers to speak of a description, rather than definition, of human personhood. See McFarland, *Difference & Identity*, 10–13.

82. See also Kelsey, "Personal Bodies," 153.

83. It should also be noted that his preference for 'hypostasis' as opposed to 'person' is short lived, with 'hypostasis' appearing very rarely in his anthropology (Kelsey, *Eccentric Existence*, 68–69).

'What is a personal identity?' Kelsey employs what can be described as an inverse methodology. He states: "The sense of the phrase 'personal identity' intended in this theological anthropology project is best brought out by clarifying the kind of question to which a narrative description of someone's personal identity would be the appropriate answer" (378).

As one can see, he begins with the answer—a narrative description of someone's personal identity—and proceeds to find a question that leads to this answer. Naturally, such a methodology is open to serious problems, as presuppositions and assumptions dictate the questions to be asked.[84]

Of note is his heavy reliance on ordinary language and speech.[85] This is very much in line with his postliberal heritage. However, here Kelsey is not using the 'traditional' reference to the *logos* as God's way of creating. Although acknowledging that human beings may respond to God's personalizing address in ways that are not necessarily verbal (296), the inclusion of ordinary language as the means of personalization remains troubling. Setting aside the highly philosophical discussions around the adequacy of ordinary human language that arose in the debates surrounding the *vestigium trinitatis*,[86] why does God address us in such a problematic and easily misunderstood medium if His personalizing relation is not dependent on human response (296–97)? This is especially the case considering the many problems with ordinary human language (many lack the ability, there is widespread miscommunication, etc.). Surely God does not need our ordinary language to relate to us? Since we do not need to respond to God to be personalized, why build such a problematic model?

One may also ask questions about whether Kelsey is being honest with where he himself borrows from his secular and theological host culture. There are echoes of secular postmodernism in his approach: He understands personhood as arising out of the structure of intersecting relations (in this case with God) rather than an inner, self-centered and self-sufficient center. At the same time, there is ambiguity in his relationship with his theological host culture. Kelsey raises questions about Zizioulas's construction. He believes that the family of concepts associated with 'person' (often borrowed from secular discourse) cannot be used usefully to

---

84. It is not necessary at this point to once again critique the narrative approach, the discussion in chapter 5 of this project will suffice.

85. Kelsey is not alone in referencing human language as a medium of God's address and call. See as an example Pannenberg, *Anthropology in Theological Perspective*, 339–96.

86. For more, see Jüngel, *God's Being Is in Becoming*, 17–27; cf. Kelsey, *Eccentric Existence*, 376.

embrace ontologically different realities such as the Triune God. Speaking on Zizioulas Kelsey states:

> Even if there were a genetic historical link with the fourth-century Father's borrowing-and-bending of technical Greek metaphysical categories in service of elucidating the doctrine of the Trinity, the disanalogies between the uncreated triune Persons and created human persons are so great as to render equivocal the use of the term "person."[87]

As we have noted earlier in this chapter, Kelsey argues that the terms 'person' and 'personal' have technical and properly theological meanings in Trinitarian contexts, but he does not contend that such senses of the terms also constitute their theological senses in theological anthropology (286–87). He therefore claims that he is not using Trinitarian-based understandings of 'person' and 'personal' for his anthropological proposals in *EE*. He goes so far as to "brackets use of the same terms in reference to God (as in, 'God is personal,' or 'God is a person') and in reference to nonhuman creatures (as in, 'Angels are persons,' or 'Sufficiently complex robots are persons')" (286–87).[88] In doing so, Kelsey means to focus on 'person' and 'personal' as they apply only to human creatures.

His reference to a non-Trinitarian theological basis for 'person' used in *EE* is puzzling. To explain the remark, he points the reader to the very same chapter in which the remark is made: chapter 7 of *EE* (286–87). A reading of this chapter does not yield any further clarification on the point. Furthermore, he insinuates that Trinitarian doctrines have, at times, argued for a univocal use of the term 'person' in theology proper and theological anthropology. Here he contends that it is impossible to use the term univocally for such ontologically distinct realities (70–71, 358–59).[89] However, it is not immediately clear that such Trinitarian doctrines are using 'person' univocally.[90] Indeed, it is almost universally accepted that whatever the re-

---

87. Kelsey, "Personal Bodies," 153; cf. Kelsey, *Eccentric Existence*, 358. The point is widely acknowledged. For a concise example see Emmet, "Could God Be a Person?"

88. Cf. Kelsey, "Personal Bodies," 153–54.

89. Kelsey, "Personal Bodies," 153.

90. Kelsey argues that this is the position of Zizioulas, which both he and Grenz reject (Kelsey, *Eccentric Existence*, 904, 1010). One is not convinced this is either Zizioulas's position or Grenz's understanding of Zizioulas's position. Zizioulas's argument is not that human persons are exactly the same as divine persons, but that personhood is ontologically primitive in relational communion and that human persons can truly become persons as they engage in communion with God. Furthermore, Grenz argues—based on Zizioulas—for a communal/ecclesial human personal ontology. See Zizioulas, *Being as Communion*, 27–65; cf. Grenz, *Social God*, 51–53, 304–66.

lationship between divine and human personhood may be, it is not univocal but analogical.[91] Kelsey states that it is possible to speak of divine and human persons if it is done analogically (358), that he is aware this is the route taken by many Trinitarian anthropologists,[92] and that he himself heavily borrows from Trinitarian anthropologists such as Zizioulas, McFadyen, McFarland and Grenz. Therefore, one is at a loss as to explain exactly why he so fervently rejects a Trinitarian basis of personhood.

All this is not to say that his model does not offer value. Indeed, it is here argued that his nuances, while minor, are important for a doctrine of the *imago Dei*. Let us turn to these now.

The Personal *Imago Dei*

As noted, Kelsey indicates that much of the work that is traditionally done by the *imago Dei* is done by his notion of *personal*.[93] After considering his arguments laid out in chapters 7 and 9B of *EE*, one can deduce that Kelsey is speaking of the classificatory and evaluative forces of the terms *personal* and *imago Dei*. In debates surrounding the image of God, the term *imago Dei* has been used to classify a certain type of being that subsequently is evaluated to have dignity and respect. In substantive thinking, human beings possess certain characteristics. The possession of these characteristics is the basis on which to classify them as members of a distinctive class of beings: those who are the image of God. For example, beings that have a certain rationality or morality are made in God's image. In relational thinking, human beings are relational creatures. The attainment and development of a particular relationality is the basis on which to classify human beings as members of the class of beings that image God. Members of the class of beings whose categorical marker is the *imago Dei* are subsequently evaluated to have unqualified dignity and respect. The term 'person' is used in like fashion. *Homo sapiens* are included in the class of beings whose membership is classified by

---

91. Numerous others expressly state this point. Indeed, Schwöbel's analysis of Christian theological anthropology's core claims includes it as the third of three corollaries to the unacceptability of the modern concept of person (Kelsey, *Eccentric Existence*, 375). Torrance, speaking of the relationship between human and divine persons, spends an enormous amount of time on this very point (Torrance, *Persons in Communion*, 129–79). See as some examples Barth, *CD* 2/1, §28.1; McFarland, *Difference & Identity*, 50–51; Rudman, *Concepts of Persons*, 7–8, 159–70; Scott, "God as Person," 164; White, *Identity*, 21.

92. He has read many of these theologians and even includes this point in his summary of Schwöbel (Kelsey, *Eccentric Existence*, 375).

93. It is not entirely clear what he means by this, as there are questions about the "traditional work" done by the image of God (Kelsey, *Eccentric Existence*, 281).

the ascription of personhood. Since persons have unqualified dignity and respect, *Homo sapiens* have unqualified dignity and respect.[94]

A *prima facie* assessment shows that Kelsey fits neatly in the relational camp. His conclusion to his in-depth analysis of Grenz, McFarland and McFadyen is that "they share the intuition that, however it is understood, 'personal identity' can only be adequately understood 'relationally.'"[95] Similarly, his construction in *EE* his highly relational (286–97). Recall what we have said about Zizioulas, who posits a person (the Father) as the ontologically primary principle and in this way substitutes an Aristotelian substance for a relational *hypostasis*. Kelsey adopts Zizioulas's concern for a non-monistic, relational primary principle as far as human personhood is concerned. God's distinctive relating to human beings is the ontologically primary principle for human persons. Persons are only deemed such because of the manner in which God personalizes them through personal relations.

However, on closer inspection, the nuances of his approach become apparent. We have already noted his concern with the problems associated with the relational intuition shared by Trinitarian anthropologists, an intuition that may lead to a never-ending regress of positing relations between relational entities.[96] There are two ways Kelsey nuances his proposals to avoid this never-ending regress. First, he avoids talk of God's personal nature entirely. He is quite clear that his remarks on personhood are to be viewed entirely within anthropological discussions (286). There is no never-ending regress in his construction, simply a linear progression: God relates to human beings to personalize them, and as a result they may be called persons. As to how God himself is a person, Kelsey leaves this question unanswered.

Second, his construction is entirely one-sided. This one-sided approach is distinct from relational *imago Dei* thinking. Within that thinking, it is as human beings develop and attain certain relationships, they are classified as

---

94. McFarland is a prime example of relational understandings conflating personhood with the image of God resulting in the devaluation of those who do not obtain the required relationality. Basing his arguments on Aquinas, *ST* 8.3; 93.4, McFarland argues that "because only those who are incorporated into the body of Christ are saved, ultimately it must be the case that only the elect are persons. Those not acknowledged as persons by the Father or the Son are by definition excluded from life in relationship with God (Matt 10:33; Luke 12:9; cf. John 12:48; 1 John 2:19). Because the possibility of such exclusion is reserved for the *eschaton*, however, it cannot be used as grounds for treating anyone as a nonperson in the present" (McFarland, *Difference & Identity*, 56–57; cf. Kelsey, *Eccentric Existence*, 904–5).

95. Kelsey, "Human Creature," 137.

96. Kelsey, "Human Creature," 137. It is perhaps puzzling that this quotation ends with "Persons are ontologically prior to relations," referencing Harris. Yet Kelsey's argument in *EE* is that *personal* (itself relationally understood) is ontologically prior to persons.

a member of the class of beings that images God and consequently evaluated to have dignity and respect. However, according to Kelsey, it is immaterial what relationality humans attain as far as their personal status is concerned. God personalizes them, irrespective of their relational response to Him. Within Kelsey's construction, obtaining personhood through human relationality is impossible. Consequently, one cannot classify members of the species *Homo sapiens* as being either a *person* or as imaging God on the basis of their relationality. Nor can one evaluate them as having dignity and respect on this basis.

On the other hand, this one-sided approach addresses substantive concerns for universality. Although Kelsey is non-substantive in his rejection of inherent human characteristics that classify them as either *images of God* or as persons, he is very much substantive in his universality. In Kelsey's construction, God has freely chosen to relate to all human beings in order to personalize them. Thus, there is a universality to *Homo sapiens*. All *Homo sapiens* are personally related to by God and as such may be classified as images of God and consequently evaluated to have unqualified dignity and respect.

This latter point has far-reaching consequences for our understanding of human dignity and value. It helps to clarify why certain human beings have intrinsic value while displaying almost none of the features often associated with being human. For example, infants, the senile and the mentally and physically challenged often have severely diminished physical, emotional, moral, intellectual or relational capacities. Yet as a mother personally relates to her infant to personalize her—thereby granting the infant the status of person with all the associated rights and duties—God relates to all human beings to personalize them. Their capacities (physical, emotional, moral or intellectual) and/or their relational responses are not the basis for their personal identities and consequently not the basis for their value and dignity (291–92). This is of great advantage to both the substantive-relational debate and the debate surrounding human rights.

It must be noted, however, that while Kelsey's proposal avoids many of the pitfalls associated with substantive-relational notions of human beings as personal images of God, it also opens the door for some troubling consequences. If persons are created through personal relation, what is to stop other persons from personalizing the rest of creation? Indeed, human beings have personalized non-human entities. For example, companies have personas with certain rights and duties, and an animal was recently granted the status of non-human person.[97] The latter occurrence was un-

---

97. In 2014, an orangutan from Buenos Aires Zoo was granted 'non-human person' status along with the associated basic rights. See Bawden, "Orangutan Inside Argentina Zoo."

dertaken for the express purpose of using 'person' in the evaluative sense. Sandra the orangutan was granted rights associated with personhood based on her non-human personal status. If Sandra can attain this position, why not other apes? And if apes can, why not other animals,[98] and if animals can, why not other created realities?

If we are to adopt Kelsey's proposal, it must be done with qualification. Kelsey is quite clear that, while his theological proposals may apply to other beings, within *EE* they apply first and foremost to human beings.[99] As such, Kelsey does not address this challenge. Considering that personal status, as far as Kelsey's anthropological formula is concerned, does not describe human distinctiveness, the potential for other beings to be personal beings is not detrimental to his construction. We have much more to say about this in our concluding chapter, but for now let us leave this discussion and turn our attention to the third qualification of identity in *EE*: *unsubstitutable identity*.

---

98. There is already evidence of such a move, as the town council of Trigueros del Valle voted in 2015 to grant cats and dogs the status of 'non-human residents.' See Dawber, "Human Rights for Cats and Dogs."

99. For more, see Kelsey, *Eccentric Existence*, 252–59.

7

Unsubstitutable Identity

IN OUR PREVIOUS CHAPTER we noted that the image of God has been used with classificatory and evaluative force. That is to say, because human beings possess certain characteristics (substantive position) or develop a certain relationality (relational position), they belong to a class of beings whose distinctive mark is the image of God (classificatory force). This class is evaluated as having unqualified dignity and value (evaluative force). When used with classificatory force, the image of God acts to ascribe commonality to human beings, but this is problematic. Recall chapter 1 of this project, where we questioned the ability of substantive and relational thinkers to establish a viable commonality for all human beings. Consider also Ian McFarland's concern that the drive to establish human dignity and value based on commonly shared attributes has resulted—paradoxically— in acts of human cruelty.[1]

It seems prudent, therefore, to address the question of human differentiation. Indeed, theological anthropology is interested in more than simple taxonomy. While a zoologist is primarily interested in the question of classification (e.g., what makes each ant the same, but unique as a group?), anthropologists—and in particular theological anthropologists—are keen to address the question of individuality: What makes one human being different from another? Very rarely, however, has the doctrine of the *imago Dei* been used to address the question of human individual distinction, even though this question is fundamental to human identity:

> Identity can only exist when a person is capable of being distinguished from other persons or objects. With reference to a person's identity, this means that the someone is 'particular' in the sense that he is different from other persons and that this difference is significant.[2]

---

1. See our discussions on Ian McFarland in chapter 6 of our project.
2. Haker, "Narrative and Moral Identity," 62.

What Kelsey means by 'particular' and why it is significant are the central questions of this chapter. There are a number of ways these questions can be asked. For example, a common approach would be, 'What makes one individual different from another?' Such a question would invariably lead to a process of individuation through differentiation, or asking what the differences or uniquenesses are among instances of *Homo sapiens*.[3]

Kelsey is not convinced that such an approach is adequate to the task at hand (381, 691). It may help identify a person in the sense of making it possible for us to pick someone out of a crowd, yet Kelsey argues that "it would fail to convey her unsubstitutable identity" (691).[4] This quotation indicates that Kelsey is seeking something very specific in the notion of individuality, something more than simply a list of distinguishing characteristics:

> The question of how best to describe the unsubstitutability of a human being's personal identity is in part the question of how best to describe her personal identity in a way that brings out what it is about her human being's personal identity that keeps her from ultimately being interchangeable with any other human being. (392)

As one can see from the quotation above, Kelsey's concern is primarily with the interchangeability among individual human beings. Although issues of distinction and uniqueness invariably come into play (and we need to consider them), they are principally the means to address the question's end. As this chapter seeks to address issues of individuality by critically evaluating Kelsey's construction, it is important that we keep in mind the nuances of his question. With this in mind, let us clarify what this chapter is not about.

This chapter does not deal with issues of individualism versus collectivism. Such anthropological debates are wide and far reaching as they move to-and-fro in addressing the 'chicken and egg' question of the relationship between individuals and the collective. Kelsey notes that "contemporary theological anthropologies include a great deal of polemic against strands of individualism alleged to be implied in much theological anthropology and to be explicitly affirmed in characteristically modern or Enlightenment

---

3. For more on these versions and similar alternatives to the problem of individuality, see Paasch, "Scotus and Ockham," 46. See also Kelsey, *Eccentric Existence*, 335–36, 380–81, 691.

4. It should be noted that Kelsey does not contend with the question of God's unsubstitutability. For Kelsey this is not a problem. He does not appear to be aware that biblically this may be an issue, as God is often considered in the midst of other gods, for example in Elijah's fight against the Baal prophets (1 Kgs 18,) or in Paul's apologetics among the Greek gods (Acts 17).

theological anthropology" (391; cf. 400).⁵ So rife are these anthropological issues that Alistair McFadyen states, "the individualistic way of regarding personal being is so ingrained in us that we need to be shocked somehow into a new cognition and consciously unlearn it."⁶ Although Kelsey hardly attempts to shock his audience out of individualism, using Steven Lukes's analysis of individualism and collectivism to evaluate the individualistic tendencies of *EE* (392–401), Kelsey is quite clear that his theological anthropology is not to be construed through the lens of individualism.⁷ While it is impossible to entirely avoid drawing on sources involved in the individualism-collectivism debates, we follow the contours of Kelsey's argument and avoid unnecessary tangents.

The Challenge of Particularity

Let us begin our search for unsubstitutability by considering what is here argued to be an important source for this topic: Colin Gunton's *The One, the Three and the Many* (1992). In this work, Gunton casts issues of divine (and with it human) individuality against the wider debates surrounding generality and particularity. He contends that the question of individuality is a recurring question that has occupied Western culture since the debates between Heraclitus and Parmenides.⁸ Heraclitus argued for the notion of a universe in constant flux, which leads to plurality and motion (the foundation of particularity in opposition to generality). On the other hand, Parmenides contended that true reality is unchanging, timeless and uniform: "the many do not really exist, except it be as a function of the one."⁹ According to Gunton, these two Greek philosophers exemplify two contending ontological positions that continue to play out even today. The opposing views manifest

---

5. Cf. Gunton, *One*, 28–34; Brown, "Trinitarian Personhood and Individuality"; Pannenberg, *Anthropology in Theological Perspective*, 157–79. It should be noted that Kelsey questions the distinction between these two concepts, arguing that it is impossible to speak of one without the other (Kelsey, *Eccentric Existence*, 399–400). Cf. Gunton, who argues that "collectivism is but a corollary of individualism" (Gunton, *One*, 31–32).

6. McFadyen, *Call to Personhood*, 9.

7. Kelsey is not alone in relying on Lukes. See also Brown, "Trinitarian Personhood and Individuality," 49. This is not to say that Kelsey does not address the question of the relationship between the individual and the collective. His project often considers the relational character of human beings to their quotidian context which includes a great deal of social and collective institutions. Here we are simply saying that his discussions of unsubstitutable individuality are not crouched in those conversations.

8. Gunton, *One*, 17–18; cf. Zizioulas, "On Being a Person," 33–37.

9. Gunton, *One*, 18.

at different points in Western culture: between Plato and Aristotle,[10] Scotus and Ockham[11] and, more recently, modernism and postmodernism (neither of which adequately solves the dispute).[12]

The question Gunton poses is, "what makes things and people particularly and distinctively what they are?"[13] In the words of John Zizioulas, this is a question of "personal ontology."[14] What is ontologically primary: particularity or universality? This question is fundamental to the notion of unsubstitutable individuality. Is human individual particularity of ontological significance or is it simply accidental? Is the particular simply the "*pars* of a *totum*,"[15] or is it, to use R. H. Reeling Brouwer's illustration, like manna, a loose piece of bread that "stands by itself and knows its own relationship to the *Adonai 'ehad*."[16] If the general gives rise to the particular, then the particular is contingent on the general and of secondary importance to the non-predicable generality. If this is the structure of being, then human particularity and individuality are of diminished significance, arising accidentally from humanity in general. The ontological claim of absolute being, stated in its simplest form as "I am who I am,"[17] becomes nonsensical. In such a case, 'I am' is an abstraction from the common, predicated on the universal and, stripped of these abstractions, ultimately non-identifiable as an individual. One's individuality becomes insignificant and, as Harker warns, ultimately non-existent.[18] In this situation, while accidentally unsubstitutable for another human being, ontologically one human may be substituted for another.

The ontological primacy of unsubstitutable individuality is an important point in our quest to answer the questions surrounding this notion. Any answer must satisfy this criterion; it must be ontologically primitive.

---

10. Gunton, *One*, 16–21.
11. Gunton, *One*, 28, 198–99.
12. Gunton, *One*, pt. 1. In his inaugural lecture at the Protestant Theological University (based on the work of Zizek), Reeling Brouwer argues that the notion of God's singularity and unity, expressed biblically in the "Hear, O Israel, Adonai our God, is Adonai '*ehad*,"(Deut 6:4) may be a solution to this conundrum. He proposes a triadic focus on particularity, generality, and singularity (Reeling Brouwer, "[This One Is] One").
13. Gunton, *One*, 74.
14. Zizioulas, "On Being a Person," 35.
15. Reeling Brouwer, "(This One Is) One."
16. Reeling Brouwer, "(This One Is) One."
17. Zizioulas, "On Being a Person," 33.
18. Haker, "Narrative and Moral Identity," 62.

Yet where do we look to find a characteristic or feature of human beings that satisfies this criterion?

It is arguable that the debate surrounding individuality reached its pinnacle in medieval philosophy, where, according to Paul Spade, it attained "a level of insight and rigor it has never enjoyed since."[19] In this context, no two medieval philosophers epitomize this debate better than John Duns Scotus and William of Ockham,[20] and it is in Scotus that a notion of unsubstitutability begins to emerge. Indeed, it is almost inevitable that when one talks about individuality one thinks of Scotus's notion of haecceity.[21]

Although Scotus's work is considered to be encyclopedic in scope,[22] his *Ordinatio* (which he continued to revise until his death) is generally taken to be his premier work.[23] The *Ordinatio* contains a revision of his Oxford lecture on the topic of individuals.[24] The lecture is broken up into six questions. In typical medieval philosophical fashion,[25] his first five questions outline the problems associated with individuality and the various responses proposed by respected thinkers.[26] After considering and rejecting these competing theories, Scotus turns in question six to his own understanding of individuality:

> Again, every difference among the differing is reduced ultimately to some items that are diverse primarily. Otherwise there would be no end to what differ. But individuals [in the same

19. Spade, *Five Texts*, vii.

20. For more on these two opposing views, see Paasch, *Debates in Medieval Philosophy*, 371–94; Spade, *Five Texts*; Tweedale, *Scotus vs. Ockham*.

21. Were this a paper in philosophy, we would pause here for an extended discussion on these important contributions. However, many have noted that the texts of Scotus and Ockham are "especially difficult" and "dense and forbidding" (Spade, *Five Texts*, xi–xv) even for those trained in philosophy (Tweedale, *Scotus vs. Ockham*, 11–12). These texts contain "a large battery of technical terms which have now either fallen out of use or are used with quite different meanings" (Tweedale, *Scotus vs. Ockham*, 12). Furthermore, it is arguable that their views remain obscure, which is why the secondary literature is vast, confusing, difficult to understand and riddled with technical ambiguities (Paasch, "Scotus and Ockham," 1, 39). Since this is primarily a project in theological anthropology and it is assumed that the reader is uninitiated in complex philosophy, we refrain from extensively engaging in such philosophically rich debates.

22. Hause, "John Duns Scotus."

23. The critical edition of which was only completed in 2013. See Williams, "John Duns Scotus."

24. For an English translation, see Scotus, *Early Oxford Lecture*.

25. For a very brief overview of medieval philosophical methodology see Spade, *Five Texts*, xi–xii.

26. For a good overview of his argument see Spade, *Five Texts*, xii–xiii; Scotus, *Early Oxford Lecture*, xci–xvii.

species] differ, properly speaking, because they are diverse beings that are yet something the same.[27]

Here Scotus is speaking about a primary distinction between two individuals of the same species. He notes that such distinction cannot rest in the distinct nature of the individuals because this nature allows the same instance to be "really distinct from something and yet really agree with it."[28] Think, for example, of two identical spoons; both have a 'spoonish' nature by which they are grouped together in the category of 'spoon,' yet they are distinct—there are two spoons.

In addition to this 'spoonish' nature, Scotus argues that each spoon must have a positive and fundamental *per se* attribute that primarily distinguishes one from the other. Scotus claims that a quality is added to the nature of an individual that distinguishes two similar objects: *this* one from *that* one.[29] The quality that makes one object *this* has come to be known as haecceity (Latin *haecceitas*, from *haec*, meaning 'this'[30]).

Scotus argues that individuality cannot be established through extrinsic factors. One must make an appeal to something internal or intrinsic to the individual in question, as such individuals are comprised of a common nature and a unique haecceity.[31] In a realist reading of this view, one may claim that the natures of individuals are in some sense a universal particularized by the haecceity. This particularity creates a singleton that is unrepeatable. While two identical spoons both have a 'spoonish' nature, *this* spoon is unrepeatable in its *thisness*, or its haecceity.[32] In the words of J. T. Paasch, "the crucial feature of a haecceity is that it cannot be repeated or copied. Each haecceity is itself a singleton."[33]

Defining what haecceity actually comprises has proven to be complicated.[34] Allan Wolter[35] notes that 'this' and 'that' are indexical terms that philosophers of language contend are used for what one cannot ultimately

27. Scotus quoted in Spade, *Five Texts*, 101–2.
28. Scotus quoted in Spade, *Five Texts*, 102.
29. Scotus quoted in Spade, *Five Texts*, 104–5.
30. Cross, "Medieval Theories of Haecceity."
31. Paasch, "Scotus and Ockham," 39; Paasch, "Scotus on Universals and Individuation."
32. Paasch, "Scotus on Universals and Individuation."
33. Paasch, "Scotus on Universals and Individuation."
34. Wolter quoted in Scotus, *Early Oxford Lecture*, xiv–xvi. Wolter, for example argues that "Like the quanta and quarks of theoretical physics, Scotus's 'Haecceity' is a rational fabrication" (Scotus, *Early Oxford Lecture*, xii–xiii). He goes on to demonstrate how Bergmann has misunderstood it.
35. Wolter quoted in Scotus, *Early Oxford Lecture*, xi–xii.

describe. The coining and usage of haecceitism achieves two functions. First, it makes each individual incapable of duplication, even by God, and second, it radically differentiates one individual from another even if they are from the same species or group. This radically primitive quality means that one cannot conceptualize what haecceity ultimately is. It is, as *this* is, an indexical term: "it does not really tell us what a particular individual's individuality really is."[36] It is here that the usefulness of Scotus's notion of haecceity comes to an end. Although his notion provides the conceptual tools to speak of individuality as intrinsic to an object that is unrepeatable, its vagueness leaves something to be desired.[37]

In context of the debate between Scotus and Ockham, Martin Tweedale draws our attention to the implications these discussions have for Christianity and in particular the doctrine of the Trinity, which "seems to require at least the conceivability of something completely singular in itself being common to many singulars, namely the divine essence being common to the divine persons."[38] In the Trinity, the general and the particular coalesce so that one struggles to distinguish between them.[39]

It is not possible here to engage in extensive discussions on Trinitarianism. The crucial point Tweedale makes is that particularity is at the very heart of the being of God, and if persons are like the persons of the Trinity by virtue of their creation in the *imago Dei*, then their particularity is central to their being: "it is not an unfortunate accident but our glory that we are other: each unique and different."[40] As Trinitarian particularity originates relationally,[41] so too does the particularity of all that is not God:

> All particulars are formed by their relationship to God the creator and redeemer and to each other. Their particular being is a being in relation, each distinct and unique and yet each inseparably bound up with other, and ultimately all, particulars.[42]

---

36. Wolter quoted in Scotus, *Early Oxford Lecture*, xii.

37. See, as examples, Gunton, *One*, 198–99; Paasch, "Scotus on Universals and Individuation," 25–26.

38. Tweedale, *Scotus vs. Ockham*, 10.

39. Gunton, *One*, 150. For some solutions to the conundrum, consider Davis, "Haecceities," 205–8.

40. Gunton, *One*, 196.

41. Theologically, Trinitarian generality and particularity is often solved by referring to relationality. There are many different ways this is conceived. Consider as examples Swinburne, *Christian God*; Grenz, *Social God*; Zizioulas, "On Being a Person," 33–46; Gunton, *One*, 180–209.

42. Gunton, *One*, 207.

As one can see from the quotation above, Gunton establishes a notion of particularity that is highly relational. Gunton suggests a framework of coordinates for dealing with the general-particular debate: "the term 'coordinates' is the crucial one here, for it implies a system in which particulars are truly related to one another, and yet in such a way that 'space' remains between them."[43] One may read Gunton here as urging us to consider the many and the one—the general and particular—as entwined in much the same way coordinates are: each a particular position on the grid, yet each only occupying this particular position in relation to other coordinates.

From this overview of the broader challenges of the general-particular debate we can draw out two essential aspects for a viable conception of human unsubstitutable individuality. First, we must affirm particularity as ontologically primitive and primary. Unrepeatable individuality must be an ontological part of humanity if it is to be of any significance. Second, taking relational Trinitarianism seriously compels us to affirm relational particularity. Gunton concludes that "everything must be what it is and not another thing, but it is also what it uniquely is by virtue of its relation to everything else."[44]

Unsubstitutable Individuality

Kelsey argues that "the identities of living human personal bodies are repeatedly characterized in this project as 'unsubstitutable'" (387). He himself acknowledges that the "term calls for some clarification" (387). A reading of his table of contents may give the impression that his process of clarification is straightforward. After all, chapter 9B, entitled "Basic Unsubstitutable Personal Identity," includes a sub-section on the term *unsubstitutable* (387–91). Yet reading only this section fails to provide the full nuances of his construction. For this reason, our critical analysis incorporates diverse sections of Kelsey's work in a single discussion. Our primary aim is to establish how Kelsey understands the term *unsubstitutable individuality* by considering his understanding of what can and cannot work to define and describe human individuality. Let us begin by considering what Kelsey believes cannot work.

---

43. Havel referenced in Gunton, *One*, 71.

44. Gunton, *One*, 173. There are others who affirm a similar notion. Consider, for example, McFadyen, *Call to Personhood*.

Descriptive Dead Ends

Kelsey contends that there are a number of attempts that fail to define and describe the unsubstitutability of individual human beings. On the one hand, one may attempt to make use of a body of theory about what individual persons are (69-70). However, each of these theories construes persons in a manner congruent with their own presuppositions. As such, each body of theory—be they human sciences, philosophy, theology, etc.—develops a conceptual grid against which to map out human personhood. Where this is done, Kelsey argues:

> Any given person can never serve as more than an instance of a type of person defined by the conceptual grid of one of the human sciences, an instance interchangeable with and thus substitutable for other instances of the same type. (690)

Although such a systematic conceptual scheme may be able to describe how individual human beings are unique in certain respects, Kelsey believes: "'Unique' is too abstract to index the difficulty with trying to use some body of theory about persons to describe someone in his unsubstitutable personal identity" (690). As such, in *EE*, although it is right to contend for the uniqueness of each individual human being, this does not equate to their unsubstitutability.

Similarly, a person's individual unsubstitutability cannot be adequately conveyed by simply attributing a list of properties to a subject with a proper name and then comparing this list with others attributed to other subjects (690, 1022-23).[45] Kelsey gives an example to illustrate the point. One cannot describe the unsubstitutable individuality of Maria by the successive predication of *her* attributes as 'female,' 'five feet three inches tall,' '120 pounds,' etc. Although this may help to identify someone in terms of picking them out of a crowd, it fails to convey unsubstitutability (691).

The reason for this failure is threefold. First, such a list is potentially exceptionally long, resulting in near impossibility of producing an adequate list to which the sum total could sufficiently define and describe a person's individuality and unsubstitutability. Second, and more seriously, such an approach assumes that the subject in question (the unsubstitutable identity)

---

45. McFadyen's theory of sedimentation is very much in line with such an approach, as he argues that human personhood is the sum total of an extensive and complex process of sedimentation, each layer (attribute) placed upon the next as the human being proceeds through their life. This process of sedimentation is unique in each instance of human being and as such is responsible for individual uniqueness. It may be argued that each sedimentary layer is an item on an exceedingly long list of attributes. See McFadyen, *Call to Personhood*, 7-8, 40-42, 72-73, 93-95 (cf. 103-9).

is "an otherwise featureless subsistent individual entity that somehow exists behind or below the properties ascribed to it" (691). This "ghost in the machine," as Ryle terms it,[46] has received much criticism.[47] It is at times presented as a featureless and obscure reality without true form or content, lying somehow beneath or behind the perceptible facade. Indeed, the Christian appeal to the featureless soul as the root of human individuality is arguably tantamount to just such a 'ghost in the machine'.[48] Kelsey is opposed to this notion. Using Steven Lukes, he refers to it as "abstract individualism."[49] Lukes explains as follows:

> According to this conception, individuals are pictured abstractly as given, with given interests, wants, purposes, needs, etc. . . . This givenness of fixed and invariant human psychological features leads to an *abstract* conception of the individual who is seen as merely the bearer of those features, which determine his behaviour, and specify his interests, needs and rights.[50]

According to the theory of abstract individualism, human individuality is a given, independent of society or political institutions. Individuality appears ready-made in the human being, and society responds to this individuality.[51] The individual is conceived of in abstraction from the concrete particularities of its social, historical and cultural context. Kelsey contends that such an abstract individualism is theologically inappropriate as it fails to take seriously the eccentric rooting of human beings in their quotidian context or their fundamental relationality (400–401). As such, "Insofar as the target is abstract individualism, the anthropological proposals promoted [in *EE*] have explicitly joined the theological polemic against individualism" (401).

Third, a list of attributes describes human individuality in terms of contingent predication and abstracted from commonly shared characteristics. This approach, although demonstrating uniqueness in terms of the unique collection of attributes one has, ultimately diminishes unsubstitutability.

---

46. Ryle quoted in Frei, *Identity of Jesus Christ*, 99.

47. Frei, *Identity of Jesus Christ*, 98–100, 139, 142; Aldwinckle, *Death in the Secular City*, 71.

48. Hill, *Being Human*, 31–36. See also Gunton, *One*, 46, 48. It is also telling that people speak of inanimate objects as having a soul, for example 'the soul of the building' or the 'soul of the country.' In these cases, 'soul' indicates individuality and unsubstitutability without reference to what exactly that is.

49. Kelsey, "Spiritual Machines," 7.

50. Lukes, *Individualism*, 73.

51. Lukes, *Individualism*, 73–77.

Attributes such as height, weight, age, gender, nationality, skin color, socioeconomic status, etc. exist independently of the actual living human body in question. To establish individuality on this basis is to compare and contrast one instance of *Homo sapiens* with another and to abstract attributes and features from what is common to humanity in general. This process of comparison and contrast predicates human individuality on an ontologically more primary list of attributes shared by other instances of *Homo sapiens*, and as such particularity loses its ontologically primary place.

Such an approach is widely criticized. Frei, for example, explains that identity—which to Frei incorporates human uniqueness[52]—cannot be established by comparison:

> Identity is the specific uniqueness of a person, what really counts about him, quite apart from both comparison and contrast to others. Even a contrast between two things means that there must be a common basis for judgement between them. The uniqueness of a person, however, goes beyond the possibility of contrast or comparison with others.[53]

Kelsey takes such cautioning seriously. Speaking on the limitations of terms such as 'individual,' 'individuality' and 'uniqueness' (378), Kelsey argues that a human being's basic personal identity as an actual living human body is more than simply the sum of attributes that may be shared by other human beings. One cannot argue, for example, that one's uniqueness is simply the product of his red hair or her blue eyes. To do this is to make individuality an abstraction from the basic personal identity of an actual living human personal body. As such, what is left—the basic personal identity of an actual living human personal body—may be interchangeable with other basic personal identities of actual living human personal bodies. Established this way, individuality fails to establish ontological primacy or grasp unsubstitutability.

---

52. Frei, *Identity of Jesus Christ*, 94–100.

53. Frei, *Identity of Jesus Christ*, 95. I am not convinced that Frei is consistent in his contention. He goes on to state that "A person's identity is the total of all his physical and personal characteristics referred neither to other persons for comparison or contrast nor to a common ideal type called human, but *to himself*" (Frei, *Identity of Jesus Christ*, 95). He seems to indicate that human uniqueness does indeed refer to a list of uniquely possessed attributes, but that they are self-referent rather than socially referent: "The point of reference is purely *internal* to the individual person who constitutes a self-relatedness that is continuous over a period of time" (Frei, *Identity of Jesus Christ*, 98). This leads to a circularity whereby individual uniqueness is defined not by comparison or contrast to others, but by self-reference. Yet surely the very notions of uniqueness, individuality, unsubstitutability, etc. are extrinsically referent? For more, see Frei, *Identity of Jesus Christ*, 94–100; cf. McFadyen, *Call to Personhood*, 99.

Limited Substitutability

To be sure, Kelsey does not claim that human beings are absolutely unsubstitutable (273). He contends: "Within limits, human beings can be substitutes for one another in filling roles" (387).[54] Examples of such substitution are readily available. We think, for example, of substitute teachers or understudies in theatrical plays. Furthermore, there are many social roles that can be filled by a number of individual human beings, such as national president, church pastor, customer, etc. (273). Here roles are defined "independently of the description of any individual human being's personal identity" (387), and it is therefore "proper to say that roles can be filled by any of several individual human beings who can be substituted for one another in filling the role" (387). However, such claims are made at a high level of abstraction; that is, an individual is abstracted from a concrete living human personal body in the role they fulfil.

Kelsey notes that there are some exceptions. In some instances, one may claim that an individual is unsubstitutable in terms of the roles they fulfil. As an example, Kelsey speaks of the conceivability for a surgical procedure to be so complex that only a single living surgeon has the required skills, expertise and experience to perform it. In this case, one may claim that only they can perform that procedure. Such unsubstitutability, however, is the result of "a historical accident that at a particular moment in time she is the only one capable of filling the role" (387). In such a case, "she would be contingently unsubstitutable" (387). Her unsubstitutability would be contingent on her training, experiences, intellect, age, social standing, etc. It would not be an unsubstitutability based on her basic personal identity as an actual living human personal body.

Contingent unsubstitutability poses a number of challenges. First, it is dependent on features of the quotidian identity which could have been different (388). For example, the surgeon could have had a debilitating accident in childhood, thereby preventing her from studying further. In such cases, their unsubstitutability would come to an end. Furthermore, as their age progresses, their ability to fulfil such roles diminishes and eventually ends altogether. As such, their unsubstitutability is temporary. It is for these reasons that contingent unsubstitutability—such as role fulfilment—cannot be, properly speaking, a viable answer to the question "What makes one human being unsubstitutable for another?"[55]

---

54. Kelsey's discussion on substitutable role performance closely follows Frei's discussion on the same topic. See Frei, *Identity of Jesus Christ*, 105–14.

55. Kelsey notes, presumably based on Frei's discussion that follows a very similar route, that such role substitutability may not be applicable to God in terms of certain

Kelsey proceeds to note that "concretely speaking, a human being, simply *as* 'human being,' does not fill any role" (388). Therefore:

> The sense in which 'unsubstitutable' is used in this project in the phrase 'unsubstitutable personal identity,' [is not] the contingent unsubstitutability that might be ascribed to the human being who is the sole human being capable of filling a given role. . . . Instead, 'unsubstitutable' is used here in sense [*sic*] of 'absolute unsubstitutability.' (388)

Considering that earlier in his project Kelsey claims that human beings are not absolutely unsubstitutable (273), it is important that we clarify what Kelsey means exactly. To do this, it is helpful to differentiate between Kelsey's understanding of concrete singularity and unsubstitutable individuality.

Concrete Singularity

Kelsey equates 'concrete individuality' with singularity (378–80; cf. 387–401). In a fashion similar to Frei, Kelsey argues that the sense of the term 'identity' used in his project is rooted in a "very particular intuition about the integral dynamic singularity of each human creature's life across time in community and its proximate contexts" (387).[56] A person's unconditional value and dignity does not lie in their abstract individuality nor "does it lie in one of those respects that is unique to that individual, or a set of such respects, abstracted from the full complexity of the concrete human creature" (379). Kelsey uses the term 'singularity' to describe humans in terms of their concrete particularity, dignity and value:

> The way I use 'singular' is largely stipulative. 'Singularity' is used to pick out the inseparable conjunction of value, dignity, and messy complexity of detail that, following the intuition underlying this notion of 'personal identity,' constitute a concrete living human personal body's identity across time in its proximate contexts. . . . Given the singularity of the personal identity of a concrete living human personal body, an adequate description of that identity needs to render at once what she is like in her singularity and that she is of unconditional value and dignity in, and not somehow

---

roles/titles such as Lord, creator, king, saviour, judge, priest, etc. In these instances, unlike baseball player, teacher, pastor, etc., it is God himself that defines these roles (Kelsey, *Eccentric Existence*, 388–89; cf. Frei, *Identity of Jesus Christ*, 2–4, 105–14).

56. Cf. Kelsey, "Biblical Narrative and Theological Anthropology," 139–40; Frei, *Identity of Jesus Christ*, 94–100.

behind or underlying or despite, the complex and not necessarily very orderly details of her life across time. (379)[57]

Here, 'singularity' refers to three features of a human being: a) concrete uniqueness, b) dignity and c) value. It refers to them in a way that does not abstract that uniqueness from a single, or limited set of attributes commonly shared. It is the combination of these three features that is a person's singularity, rather than the addition of them to an already pre-existing 'behind-the-scenes' human being. Although 'singularity' speaks to human particularity without abstraction, it does not necessarily speak to human unsubstitutability. It simply states that one human is different from another in such a way that their value, dignity and complex concrete life across time (in their proximate contexts) differs.

It is interesting to note that the term 'singularity' does not take root in Kelsey's project. It appears only twice after his discussion on human singularity (386, 387), and Kelsey later substitutes it by qualifying individuality with the term 'concrete' in order to speak about "concrete individuality."[58]

From what has been said, one can interpret Kelsey as saying that individual uniqueness is contingent on the quotidian identity. Individual uniqueness does not refer to an individuality that is simply given, existing somewhere behind, beneath or above a quotidian identity (abstract individuality). A person's peculiar singularity is not abstract but concrete. It arises from and displays itself in the quotidian context. It is an inherent part of being an actual living human personal body. Every human being has this concrete individuality: "The intuition behind the concept of 'identity' under discussion here is that every human creature has a singular identity. . . . Regardless of its degree of vividness, however, singularity is inherent in being a living human personal body" (380).

Although every human being has a singular, peculiar, concrete individuality, it is evident that an individual's peculiar singularity is contingent on the actions, interactions and interpretive relating that the human being undertakes and undergoes (379, 390). These actions, interactions and interpretive relations are themselves contingent on the quotidian identity of the person in question. Since the notion of singularity and concrete individuality is contingent on the quotidian context, it is arguable that it corresponds to a list of attributes that a human being has accidentally rather than primarily. Of course, this list is highly complex. Nevertheless, the items on the list are

---

57. Cf. Frei, *Identity of Jesus Christ*, 171–73.

58. Kelsey does not expressly state this substitution. Rather, it is deducible as one reads later sections. Ultimately, even this term is later succeeded by the term "absolute individuality" (Kelsey, *Eccentric Existence*, 387–401).

commonly shared by every human being. For example, every human being has height, weight and age. These attributes are defined independently of the individual in question. Being part of the quotidian context implies that such singularity is accidental to the basic, and more fundamental, identity of the human being.[59] Therefore, while singularity establishes particularity, it does not necessarily equate to unsubstitutability.

Unsubstitutable Individuality

The notion of unsubstitutability first appears in chapter 6 of *EE* as Kelsey describes Job's second retelling of his story of creation:

> In light of the second description of Job's birth as [God's] creature, we may say that in certain definite but quite limited respects, human creatures are, precisely by virtue of God's relating to them as their creator, unsubstitutable one for another. (272)

Kelsey introduces the "limited" and "restricted" (272) sense in which human creatures are unsubstitutable for one another in the context of their response to God's triple-helix relationality. From this response, Kelsey derives his notion of absolute unsubstitutability:

> None can respond to God in place of another. No one is accountable for another's response to God. It is in being responsible and accountable, to the extent that we are capable, that we are each unsubstitutable by any other human living body. Absent this context, it would be difficult to find strong reasons for stressing our unsubstitutability by one another. (274)[60]

Furthermore, Kelsey argues that we are unsubstitutable in the way we respond to God for and on behalf of ourselves within the quotidian context, which includes other unsubstitutable identities:

> I am not accountable to God for the way I respond to God's creative relating all by myself. Rather always, and from the origins of my being, I am accountable for the way I respond as a

---

59. Although Kelsey may insist that the quotidian context is important for defining and describing the human being—and in this we do not disagree—his distinction between basic and quotidian identity indicates that the human being has a prior identity in their basic identity. Recall our discussion in chapter 5.

60. It should be noted that Kelsey does indeed find another context in which to contend for human unsubstitutability: the context of the human being as the beloved of God, which does not necessarily imply human response. We address this issue very shortly within this chapter.

> member of a society of fellow human creatures, all of whom are also accountable for their responses to God's relating to them creatively, and by whose network of relationships with me my capacities to respond and to give an account of my response are empowered and shaped. But I, only, give my account, I give it in onliness, though not alone. (274–75)

Each human being responds—as far as they are capable—in the quotidian proximate contexts, yet it is ultimately the individual that is responsible for their response before God. As such, Kelsey refers to individual instances of human creatures as "terminal individuals."[61]

> Thus, Job 10 leads us to stress that what God creates in creating each human living body is a terminally individual personal body. It is a personal body that is terminal to two lines of questioning. It is terminal in responding to fellow creatures and to God. Who responds to them? None can substitute for me, only I can respond to them for myself. Second, it is terminal in the giving of an explanatory account of intentional actions. How come just this intentional action by me? Finally the answer is, 'I did it.' (307)

Although chapter 6 contends that human beings are not absolutely unsubstitutable in that they may substitute for each other in the roles they fulfil, Kelsey again takes up the theme in chapter 9B. There he contends that his understanding of human unsubstitutable individuality does not refer to "abstract individuality" or "contingent unsubstitutability," but rather to "concrete individuality" and "absolute unsubstitutability" (391–401). Kelsey contends that human beings are not absolutely unsubstitutable in every respect, only in three respects. These constitute the limited and restricted sense of his use of the term 'absolutely unsubstitutable.' Let us explore this further.

1) In their quotidian identity. Human beings are unsubstitutable simply as the quotidian identities they are and have:

> No other quotidian personal identity can be substituted for the quotidian personal identity that simply is who a given living human personal body is. . . . The singularity of human creature's integrally dynamic identities means that in principle their quotidian personal identities are inalienable. (389)

The quotation above requires analysis. It is possible to interpret Kelsey as saying that singularity is inalienable to the quotidian identity, and

---

61. The term is taken from Hart (Kelsey, *Eccentric Existence*, 307–8)

therefore it is in the quotidian, concrete singularity of an individual's life that—simply as being what they are as quotidian identities—their absolute unsubstitutability exists. Yet this statement is troubling for two reasons. First, as we have demonstrated in chapter 5, Kelsey has previously argued that our quotidian identity is not simply given. It arises out of the quotidian context and is the dynamic vocation to bring itself into congruence with the basic identity (which is simply given).[62]

Second, as we have noted in this chapter, Kelsey has previously objected to contingent unsubstitutability. Yet the entire quotidian identity is contingent on the quotidian context. As we noted in the previous sub-section of this chapter, the contingency of the quotidian identity may be used to establish concrete singularity, but it is unable to establish unsubstitutability. As Kelsey is keen to avoid contingent unsubstitutability, questions arise as to why his notion of unsubstitutability is based on the quotidian identity, which itself is contingent.

For these two reasons, we must question this first aspect of human unsubstitutability and ask why Kelsey refers to the quotidian identity here rather than the basic identity. Kelsey leaves this question unanswered.

2) In human responsibility. Kelsey states that human beings are unsubstitutable in regard to their responsibility: "They are absolutely unsubstitutable in regard to their responsibility for the acts, interactions, interpretations of what befall [sic] them, and responses to what befalls them" (390).

In this second respect, Kelsey acknowledges that the "acts and so forth" (390) of what befalls a human being are "contingent on accidental features of their proximate contexts" (390). However, he contends that it is the individual human being who—in their quotidian personal identity—engages in these acts, interactions and interpretations. This personal identity remains unsubstitutable in its responsibility for these actions and interactions—even through the radical changes in both quotidian context and quotidian identity (390–91). Here he contends:

> No other personal identity can substitute in regard to that responsibility. That is a metaphysical claim that the relation between quotidian personal identities and the acts and so forth that constitute the lives of living human personal bodies makes the unsubstitutability of their personal identities absolute and not contingent on any accidental features of their proximate context. It is in their inalienable quotidian personal identities that human living personal bodies are terminal and absolutely unsubstitutable for any other in the order of responsibilities. (391)

---

62. See chapters 5 and 8 of our project.

This assertion raises serious questions. Although it is not controversial to say that, as a rule, human beings can be held accountable for their own actions (responses), there are a large number of exceptions to this rule. Apart from the complications of holding individuals responsible for "what befalls them" (390) rather than what they do, there are questions about the extent of human response and responsibility. Kelsey himself notes the limitations and states that "there is a great variety in the range of human creatures' capacities for intentional responses" (274). He recognizes that there are those whose capacity is significantly limited, yet he does not expand on the implications of these limitations for his understanding of unsubstitutable response. He simply acknowledges that all are accountable "for whatever response each is capable of making" (274). However, the question remains as to the unsubstitutability of an individual who is entirely unable to make a response. We think, for example, of serious mental deficiency or even those in vegetative states from birth. Such individuals may be entirely unable to respond to God's relating, and one questions if one can hold them responsible at all. Indeed, although an infant may respond to stimuli (such as God's relating), it is questionable that the infant can be held responsible for these responses. It is arguable that an infant's responses are simply instinct rather than active choice. If such human beings have no control over their responses and no responsibility for their actions, do they remain unsubstitutable in the presence of others who likewise have no response and responsibility?[63]

Of particular concern are the implications for this position on Christological soteriology. It is regular practice within Christological soteriology to conceive of Jesus as substituting for other human beings in order to take responsibility for their actions. Such doctrines of soteriology are problematic for Kelsey's claim of human unsubstitutability in responsibility. To be sure, Kelsey proposes a particular Christological soteriology. Although, as noted in chapters 3 and 4 of our project, Kelsey links Christology and anthropology very closely, his soteriology does not rely on Christological substitution.[64] Kelsey casts human estrangement not in the context of sin

---

63. We are in danger of being swept away on tangents about the possibility of such a state or who exactly finds themselves in this state, etc. The point being made is that it is conceivable for two or more human beings to be unable to respond or to have no responsibility and, as such, be substitutable for each other on these particular grounds. It should be remembered that we are not talking about dignity and value, but about unsubstitutability. For an alternate critique of establishing unsubstitutability on the notion of responsible response see McFadyen, *Call to Personhood*, 73–74.

64. A critical and in-depth discussion of his soteriology is beyond the scope of this project. What follows is a very brief overview. For more, see Kelsey, *Eccentric Existence*, part 3, esp. Chps. 18, 19, 1034–44.

or evil[65] and therefore the context of human responsibility, but in the context of distorted and self-destructive proximate identities in which human beings persistently resist being related to God (607). In this context, the Incarnation[66] is God's relating in reconciliation. Here,

> Estranged humankind is reconciled, not by the Son alone, but by the triune God perichoretically come among them to share their common lot. The Son is one among us who, in the power of the Spirit, has a unique relationship with the One he calls Father, a relationship that he turns to share with us. (622)

Salvation, in this scheme, is not achieved by substitution. It is achieved solely in Jesus' "turning" to and "sharing" with human beings.[67]

Recognizing the problem of referring to both human beings and to Jesus as unsubstitutable, Kelsey raises the question 'In what sense can others participate in Jesus' personal identity?' His answer typifies postliberal theology:

> The inalienable quotidian personal identities of living human personal bodies may be said to participate in Jesus' inalienable personal identity 'formally' to the extent that the pattern of the movement of the sequence of acts, interactions, and so on, that constitute the lives in which they have those identities begin to be shaped by the narrative logic of the life in which Jesus has his personal identity. (390)

Here Kelsey understands our participation in Jesus narratively. Kelsey argues that the dynamic movement of the sequence of human life has a pattern that may be shaped by the pattern of the narrative plot of Jesus of Nazareth. To the extent that our narrative plot is shaped by the narrative plot of Jesus

---

65. Kelsey puts the "Theological Carload before Its Theological Horse" (Kelsey, *Eccentric Existence*, 1034-44) by discussing reconciliation before sin, sins and evil. His argument is that doing otherwise risks theological concepts, such as grace, being conceived of functionally by becoming solutions to problems in the context of other options.

66. Kelsey understands incarnation to be "a theological shorthand for the entirety of a complex story whose protagonist is the triune God, and not simply the story of one Person of the Trinity—namely, the Second Person" (Kelsey, *Eccentric Existence*, 608). He argues that incarnation does not take place at a specific point in time, such as conception or birth, but "refers to the entirety of a life constituted by all that Jesus did and underwent in the context of a longer story of God's interactions with the children of Abraham" (Kelsey, *Eccentric Existence*, 703). In this he is very similar to Kathryn Tanner. See Tanner, *Christ the Key*, 257-61; *Jesus*, 26-33.

67. For more on Kelsey's understanding of Jesus as 'sharing' and 'turning' see Kelsey, *Eccentric Existence*, 619-23.

Christ we participate 'in Christ': "To be 'in Christ' is to have [our] stories included in Jesus' story" (698).[68] This understanding of participation 'in Christ' does not necessitate substitution in the sense of responsibility, and, as a result, Kelsey is able to claim that all human beings are unsubstitutable in their response to God.[69]

Such participation, it must be said, is participation "at some distance" (390) and requires extensive rethinking of soteriology, Christological substitution and hamartiology.[70] It is perceivable that a great deal of Christian thinkers would take issue with Kelsey on this point. Such a discussion, while valuable to the topic of soteriology, is beyond our discussions here on unsubstitutability. We are forced, reluctantly, to simply raise the question and move on. If one accepts Kelsey's view of participation in Christ, then indeed there are grounds for human unsubstitutability in the notion of human responsibility. If one holds to a closer participation 'in Christ' and to a form of Christological substitution, then one is forced to question the viability of establishing human unsubstitutability on human responsibility in the way Kelsey does.[71]

3) *In becoming the beloved.* Individual human beings are unsubstitutable with regard to certain ways that they are valued and loved. Kelsey argues that human beings are not loved and valued in their concrete quotidian personal identity without being cognizant of their existence as individual instances of *Homo sapiens* (391). Kelsey qualifies this as follows:

> [Love is] contingent on a host of accidental features of shared proximate contexts, of who meets whom, of peculiar sensibilities [etc.]. . . . Correspondingly, the unsubstitutability of the personal identity of the one who becomes the beloved is contingent; once the beloved has become the beloved, however, her or his personal identity is unsubstitutable by any other human creature in respect of being the beloved. (391)

Kelsey contends that it is as beloved that we are unsubstitutable. Although becoming the beloved is contingent on accidental features of the quotidian context and personal identity, once someone has become the

---

68. For Kelsey's interpretation of the 'in Christ' formula, see Kelsey, *Eccentric Existence*, 695–702.

69. Although not necessitating substitution, Kelsey does describe it in terms of "exchange"; that is, the overall movement of Jesus' life enacts a pattern of exchange between God and human beings, which constitutes the way God relates to all other human beings (Kelsey, *Eccentric Existence*, 1048).

70. Kelsey provides some of this reworking in part 3 of his project.

71. Of course, we make allowances here for other forms of establishing unsubstitutability on human responsibility.

beloved of someone else, they are unsubstitutable for another. Kelsey goes on to argue that this unsubstitutability applies not only in inter-human relations but between God and human beings. In God's triadic relating to concrete individuals, they become the beloved of God and as such are unsubstitutable. In this respect, their unsubstitutability is not founded on their quotidian identity but on their basic identity (391).

Within this third respect of human unsubstitutability, an aspect of contingency remains. In inter-human relations, such contingency is fundamental. The process is contingent on who we meet, when we meet them, how we meet them, etc. It is very conceivable that anyone's beloved may have been someone else's beloved. However, in divine-human relations, this contingency is diminished. If one is human, then one is inevitably the beloved of God.[72] As such, human beings and God's beloved are inextricable. Being an individual instance of *Homo sapiens* ensures that one is the beloved of God and, as such, unsubstitutable.

Since God has freely chosen to love all human beings, such unsubstitutability is not contingent on any other fact except that one is an instance of humanity. As such, it establishes unsubstitutability as an ontological primary concept. It is part of being human, not an addition or an accidental feature. It is not contingent on the accidental quotidian context, or even the accidental inalienable quotidian personal identity, but on the basic personal identity. Thus, all basic personal identities are unsubstitutable individuals.

Furthermore, such unsubstitutability—while expressed in the concrete singularity of an individual instance of *Homo sapiens*—is both eccentric and relational. One's haecceity is in being the beloved of God. God loves *this* human being, as such, *this* human being is the beloved of God. It is a structural feature of human being that is constituted eccentrically through God's relating to the human being in creative blessing, reconciliation and eschatological consummation. In this regard, it is ontologically primary, non-contingent,[73] and at the same time relational.

In sum, it is not clear that Kelsey's first two respects of human unsubstitutability are not based on contingent individuality or raise serious questions about Christological substitution. However, Kelsey's third respect

---

72. Of course, the contingency is not entirely removed. It is a contingent fact that one is born a human being, and it is conceivable that one may be born something else. Such conceivability is beyond the scope of this thesis and the current chapter, which deals with the individuality and unsubstitutability of human beings.

73. While it is contingent on God's relating, this contingency is ontologically primary. After all, what the human being is is the creature related to by God in a distinct manner.

offers a way of speaking about human unsubstitutability that is ontologically primitive and relational at the same time.[74]

Imago Dei as God's Beloved

Let us turn now to the implications of our discussions above for the doctrine of the *imago Dei*. In so doing, we must keep in mind the challenges of human particularity discussed above: 1) human particularity needs to be significant, that is ontologically primary, or fundamental and not accidental; 2) this necessitates a notion of particularity that is non-predicable and non-contingent; 3) although ontologically primitive, unsubstitutable identity is not an isolated term, the notion is relational. A coordinated understanding of particularity is required.

Our analysis of Kelsey indicates an understanding that combines both substantive and relational concerns. For example, in Kelsey's insistence on a concrete individualism rather than an abstract individualism, he suggests a possible union between substantive and relational anthropology in terms of human particularism. Considering Lukes's analysis of individualism, Kelsey contends that it is commonly held that a relationally conceived anthropology can counter the limitations of an abstract individualistic anthropology. The latter is very similar to Gunton's notions of wrongly conceived substantiality[75] in its focus on the underlying generalities that are simply given rather than the concrete particularity with which one is faced (398–99). However, Kelsey contends that Lukes's analysis of the contrast between individualistic and relational anthropologies "does not hold up historically or conceptual-

---

74. It must be noted, as we have done at the beginning of this chapter, that Kelsey is asking a descriptive question when referring to *unsubstitutable identity*. As such, he contends that "realistic narrative" is the most apt at "rending" (Kelsey, *Eccentric Existence*, 691) unsubstitutable identity. We have already taken issue with postliberalist reliance on narrative and Kelsey's reliance on Frei's narrative tools in chapters 3 and 5 of this project. For this reason, we have not discussed the narrative implications of human unsubstitutability here. It is interesting to note that Kelsey here argues that "only narrative provides the type of discourse adequate to give a uniquely individuating description of God as an unsubstitutable personal identity, that is, of God as singular" (Kelsey, "Biblical Narrative and Theological Anthropology," 140). While it is possible to apply narrative descriptions to Jesus of Nazareth and one can acknowledge that a description of Jesus is a description of God, there are questions as to how narrative (by definition a retelling of chronological events) can be applied to God *in se*, who is spirit and beyond chronological events. Moreover, considering God's singularity, simplicity and unicity, why Kelsey is concerned with giving a "uniquely individuating description of God" remains problematic. Consider Kelsey, "Biblical Narrative and Theological Anthropology," 140; cf. Reeling Brouwer, "(This One Is) One."

75. Gunton, *One*, 188–95.

ly" (399). In Kelsey's opinion, individualistic and relational anthropologies cannot be "played off against each other in theological anthropology" (see 399–400).

> I suggest that an individualistic concept of human being is not as such problematic in theological anthropology, if for no other reason than because it is conceptually impossible to talk about human beings without acknowledging that they are not only social beings standing in and shaped by many kinds of relations, but also are concrete individuals who are not wholly reducible to mental constructs abstracted from concrete social entities. (400)

Kelsey's insistence on concrete individuality is an insistence that human beings "are *at once* individual and relational" (400). The exact relationship between substantive and relational thinking is not drawn out by Kelsey on this point. He simply notes that individuality does not require the negation of relationalism. It is possible to speak of unsubstitutable individuals as concrete individuals who simply are what they are (substantive particularity) without having to jettison relational anthropology. Indeed, Kelsey's notion of humanity as God's beloved is just such a way of speaking. Here, the human being itself, in its existence as a concrete human being (ontological substantive particularity) is the beloved of God (relationality) and as such is unsubstitutable for any other human being. It is an ontologically unsubstitutable individual that is relationally constituted.

Yet Kelsey's answer to the question of human distinction goes beyond merely addressing concerns of substantive and relational thinkers. Recall how we began this chapter, noting that the doctrine of the *imago Dei* has been used to speak to what is common to humanity. Kelsey's inclusion of *unsubstitutable identity* in the anthropological formula takes the debate around the image of God in new directions. Not only does he enable us to speak about concrete individuals who are what they are (in their substantive particularity) through their relationality, but he makes their individual particular unsubstitutability an important part of the doctrine of the *imago Dei*. In Kelsey's construction, the *imago Dei* does not only speak to what is common to all human beings, but also to what is particular.

Basic Unsubstitutable Personal Identities

Before progressing, let us pause to consider what we have deduced from Kelsey's 'sense' of identity. Kelsey's unique approach to the important question of human identity is to speak about identity qualified by *basic and quotidian, personal* and *unsubstitutable*. These three qualifiers enable him to describe human identity without committing to a fixed definition. As such, his sense of identity is flexible and holds different notions—even competing ideas—together in the anthropological formula. For example, identity qualified by *basic* and *quotidian* holds together the notions of gift and vocation. One exists in the tension of having both a basic (gifted) identity and a quotidian (vocational) identity. To image the image of God is to exist in this tension; we must become what we already are.

At the same time, these three qualifiers speak to important aspects of human identity. To begin with, Kelsey's sense of identity demonstrates just how complex human identity is. It cannot be distilled to a single or limited set of features residing within the human being that distinguishes it from the rest of creation. Our concrete individuality, in its quotidian identity, incorporates myriad features into one unsubstitutable basic personal identity: physical, non-physical and transcendental. These features are fundamental to our identity, whose individuality cannot be described through abstraction or comparison of these characteristics either among human beings or other creatures. As such, human identity is not an abstract identity existing behind or beneath these features like a formless 'ghost in the machine.' Human identity is concrete, comprising myriad features both external and internal to the individual in question.

Apart from individuality, human identity has often been used to establish human value and dignity. In these schemes, all human beings possess certain qualities, characteristics or endowments (e.g., rationality or relationality), and the possession of these has acted as the foundation for subsequent claims about human value and dignity. However, history has demonstrated that such an approach is flawed. In the past, humans who failed to possess or display these characteristics have had their dignity and value questioned. Kelsey's approach to identity, qualified by his understanding of *personal*, makes the possession of certain characteristics, or displays of a particular form of relationality, immaterial to a concrete individual's value and dignity. Human value is established eccentrically in God's particular relating. God personalizes human beings through personal relations and as such creates persons who are evaluated to have dignity and value.

This personalizing relation, although applicable to humanity generally, establishes individual unsubstitutability. As God relates to human beings, they become the beloved of God, and in this they are unsubstitutable for any other being. Here Kelsey moves our understanding of human individual identity away from features and characteristics that distinguish one concrete individual from another and toward one-sided relational engagement with God. Concrete individuals are absolutely unsubstitutable, not because they have a unique array of characteristics that are abstracted from the common list of human characteristics, but because they are each uniquely the beloved of God. As unsubstitutable basic personal identities whom God has freely chosen to relate to, they are all individually (and therefore universally) the images of God who have yet to image God.

To this sense of identity Kelsey adds two further descriptive terms. In the first instance he describes human ontological status as an actuality in contradistinction to being mere possibilities or potentialities. Second, he claims these actual identities are located in living bodies. Let us turn now to explore these two aspects further, starting with human actuality.

Human Actuality

IN CHAPTER 5 OF this thesis we noted that, according to Kelsey, our basic identity has the logical status of an actuality. This chapter explores this concept further. At the heart of the substantive-relational debate is the ontological status of every human being *qua* human being: Are we potential or actual human beings?[1] To substantive thinkers, all human beings are already (actually) made in the image of God and therefore of intrinsic worth. On the other hand, implied in relational thinking is that human beings have the potential to image God as they develop the appropriate relationality. In such a construction, human actuality is "the eschatological goal toward which we are moving."[2] In chapter 1 we noted the degrading consequences for human beings who are considered only potentially the image of God. In some cases, such beings are referred to as "subhuman," "inhuman,"[3] "dehuman"[4] and, in the case of Calvin, "double beasts."[5] Kelsey is keenly aware of this challenge (902–5), and in this chapter we discuss how *EE* may be interpreted so as to affirm human actuality yet take cognizance of relational concerns.

Possible, Potential and Actual Human Beings

Kelsey first introduces the notion of actuality in chapter 6 of *EE* as he focusses his attention on the creation of the human being as interpreted through the lens of Job 10:8–19. Kelsey construes these verses as Job's creation narrative. This narrative drives Kelsey's doctrine of creation, which he understands "as a theology of birth, construing 'to be created' as 'having been born'" (159). In

---

1. As dynamic living objects, human beings possess much potential: the potential to grow from child to adult, for rational thought, for moral action, etc. However, in our discussions and in *EE*, the focus is on the potential-actual dynamic as it relates to humanity itself.
2. Hoekema, *Created in God's Image*, 28. Consider also Grenz, *Social God*, pt. 2.
3. Horst, "Face to Face," 267.
4. Hughes, *True Image*, 4.
5. Torrance, *Calvin's Doctrine of Man*, 73–81.

EE, the result is that the term 'created,' as far as human beings are concerned, is conflated with concepts of birth. Creation and birth are the same process. 'Having been born' is synonymous with being created and it bestows human actuality: "Having been born," claims Kelsey, "is the event in the past in which a living human body emerged into actuality" (251).

When Kelsey contends that human creation is a matter of 'having been born,' he does so with a specific understanding of this phrase in mind. In this regard, we should note three important implications; first, the phrase indicates that human creation is not *ex nihilo* (92).[6] To be sure, Kelsey does affirm such a doctrine with regard to creation in general (201). However, as far as human beings are concerned, all human beings arise from prior material through the process of human reproduction. Second, Kelsey contends that when he speaks of 'having been born,' he is not speaking in a physiological literal-minded sense; in *EE*, the phrase does not specifically speak about biological process such as gestation or labor (natural or caesarean), nor does it mark the exact moment of our creation (247).[7] Third, rather than speaking to a physiological fact, or a single moment in time, the phrase implies "a continuous process, itself continuous with processes that precede and follow it" (247).[8] In his construction, "the precise character of

---

6. Here, Kelsey is attuned to the problems associated with a doctrine of creation ex nihilo. See, for example, Keller, *Face of the Deep*; Waltke, *Creation and Chaos*.

7. One is not immediately convinced that he is being consistent on this point. Throughout his discussion on creation as 'having been born,' he continuously refers to the biological fact of birth. This is evidenced by the continuous references to physiological realities of human reproduction (Kelsey, *Eccentric Existence*, 245–80). Indeed, he defines birth as the process whereby a foetus is "delivered from its mother's body and able to live outside of her body" (Kelsey, *Eccentric Existence*, 247–48). While it is true that he cautions us to understand this statement as being "vague" since there is no "clear and fixed criteria by which to assess such an ability" (Kelsey, *Eccentric Existence*, 247), he is also clear that once the foetus is physically separate from the maternal womb (even if technological aids such as incubators are needed) the human being has effectively been born. His entire discussion of 'having been born' is wrapped up in physiological concepts. Even when he speaks of the non-physical processes of human reproduction—such as the complexity of culturally mediated relationships (Kelsey, *Eccentric Existence*, 247)—he is talking about the interactions of physical living bodies. Furthermore, throughout his discussion on 'having been born' he makes no reference to how it is that one can conceive of 'having been born' in non-physiological, metaphorically minded ways.

8. Again, one is not convinced that Kelsey is being true to his construction when he claims that there is no clear point at which one becomes an actual living body by 'having been born.' He is very clear that whatever exists in a pre-birth state, be that a zygote, embryo or foetus, is not an actual living body, while that which exists post-birth, that which is independent of the mother's womb—including pre-mature infants who require artificial environments—is an actual living human body (Kelsey, *Eccentric Existence*, 254). Although we can acknowledge his point that the processes that lead to the birth of a human being are themselves "not marked by breaks, gaps, and discontinuities"

any particular birthing procedure [is] not a punctiliar fact" (247), but rather a process that has begun in the past and is now completed (247).

> There is no single point that can be identified in the process from conception through gestation to birth at which potentialities for a new living human body become the actuality of a new living human body in its having been born. (254–55)

Kelsey contends, therefore, that the phrase 'having been born' is "vague" (255). It covers a wide range of processes and conditions, from natural childbirth to caesarean section, from the newborn baby who is independent of its mother's womb to the premature baby who requires an artificial environment. To Kelsey,

> "Created by God as an actual living human body through having been born" does not help to specify a moment of creation. It only specifies that "created by God" means "created as an actual living human body able to live apart from the body of its mother." (255)[9]

(Kelsey, *Eccentric Existence*, 254), when we consider his emphatic proposal that one must be born in order to have been created as an actual living body, are we not forced to claim that there is indeed a specific point or moment in time in which a potential living human personal body becomes an actual living human personal body? This moment in time has a name, a term, and we regularly record the date and time of its happening—even when this is assisted through caesarean section. This term is 'birth.'

9. It is apparent that Kelsey puts forward a very distinct doctrine of creation for our consideration, one that cannot be easily compared and contrasted to other conceptions of creation. Such a discussion would have little impact on the issue at hand: human actuality. We have therefore left it for others to discuss. There are numerous minor points which one can take issue with. One may question, for example, Kelsey's preference for Wisdom literature above the Genesis accounts—contrary to many other doctrines of creation—(see Kelsey, *Eccentric Existence*, chapters 4A, 4B; cf. Kelsey, "Wisdom Theological Anthropology," 44–51). Alternatively, one may question the genre of Job 10. Kelsey questions the narrative nature of the Genesis accounts, claiming that while they may be called narratives, they are very different types of narratives and in some cases are "fantastical narratives" (Kelsey, *Eccentric Existence*, 187). Such a critique is, according to Kelsey, a justification for rejecting them as foundational narratives of creation (Kelsey, *Eccentric Existence*, 186–88). Yet he does not question the narrative character of Job 10, which may be argued to be of a poetic genre rather than narrative. Even if one does accept that Job 10 is indeed narrative, one may question Kelsey's use of a narrative that is arguably "bent" (Kelsey, *Eccentric Existence*, 162, 176–89) by the narrative of reconciliation. Kelsey himself introduces his discussion on Job's narrative by claiming that Job is experiencing "spiritual suffering" and "bitterness about his life" (Kelsey, *Eccentric Existence*, 243) and is seeking a "face-to-face encounter with God" (Kelsey, *Eccentric Existence*, 245). Kelsey admits that, at least in Job's case, "while he [Job] has faultlessly kept faith with Creator God, his suffering shows that God has been faithless to God's commitment to creature Job" (Kelsey, *Eccentric Existence*, 271). One could argue, therefore, that Job's narrative of creation is itself 'bent' by the narrative of

We should note that the primary goal of chapter 6 of *EE* is to lay the groundwork for human dignity and value. This topic is then picked up again in Kelsey's understanding of human beings as *personal* and *unsubstitutable* identities in chapters 7 and 9 of *EE*.[10] This is the immediate context in which the notion of human actuality is discussed. In particular, his understanding of *actual* takes place within the narrow scope of a discussion on the dignity and value of pre-born beings.[11] He is particularly concerned with the distinctive ontological status of pre-birth and post-birth entities.

> I have found myself dissatisfied by much of the debate concerning medical ethics issues, especially in connection with abortion, because of what has seemed to me a failure to draw important distinctions between different types of what I can only call 'ontological' status. The distinctions are particularly challenging to make in regard to living creatures that are inherently 'developmental.' The distinctions are important at those junctions where assessment of a thing's 'ontological status' intersect with assessment of its 'value.' At any particular stage of an organism's maturation the organism is, I want to say, actually something and potentially something else into which it will, under the proper circumstances, 'develop.' It may be that what it is potentially and will develop into eventually will [sic], when actual, be of unqualified value; but in that regard it now only has the ontological status of 'potentially that' and 'actually this,' where the actual 'this' may be considered of value but not necessarily of unqualified value. Slippage of that sort seems to me often to plague debates about abortion.[12]

According to Kelsey, only *actual living human personal bodies* have absolute dignity and value. He, therefore, attempts[13] to specify what counts as an *actual living human personal body*. To do this, he engages in a discussion on the distinction between possibilities, potentialities and actualities as they apply to the human being:

---

reconciliation. Rather than addressing these issues, Kelsey takes it for granted that the reader will accept uncritically his "privileging" (Kelsey, *Eccentric Existence*, 161) of Job 10 over Genesis 1–3.

10. See chapters 6 and 7 of this project.

11. The importance of the potential-actual dynamic in abortion debates is well established. See Lizza, "Potentiality and Human Embryos"; Morgan, "Potentiality Principle"; Williams, "Abortion, Potential, and Value."

12. Kelsey, email to the author, January 14, 2013.

13. We say 'attempts' here because we shortly see that he does not specify this exactly.

> What God creates in creating humankind is actual living human bodies, not merely the physical possibilities of there being living human bodies, nor merely the transcendental existential-ontological 'conditions of the possibility' of human bodies' lives, nor the potentiality of living human bodies. (251)

This quotation needs further exploration. What does Kelsey mean when he distinguishes between 'possible,' 'potential' and 'actual?' To answer this question, we need to understand clearly how Kelsey defines possibilities, potentialities and actualities and how he relates them to each other.

According to Kelsey, a possibility "is a *determinate* actual reality, or determinate set of realities, that is defined by reference to a determinate actuality for which it is the possibility" (252). In other words, an actual state of affairs is reliant on a prior, yet different, state of affairs for its actuality. This prior state of affairs is known as a possibility (or state of the possibility) only in reference to the subsequent actuality. The realization of the subsequent state of affairs may be through accidental or deliberate agency.

To demonstrate the point, Kelsey uses the example of flour, yeast, salt and milk in a kitchen. These ingredients are the physical possibilities for a loaf of bread, but the presence of them does not guarantee that the loaf of bread will actually be made. If these possibilities are to become actualities, they are dependent on instrumental action (accidental or deliberate). In our example, the deliberate action of a baker is needed to turn these possibilities into a loaf of bread (252).

There are a number of conditions required for the existence of the possibility for a human being to be born. First, the existence of human beings is dependent on the physical context and processes needed to make life possible. For example, there needs to be distinctive DNA, itself reliant on natural physical laws (such as the presence and attraction of the required molecules necessary for DNA). Other physical conditions include nourishment, the correct temperature, water and all the physical elements necessary to initiate and sustain life (252–53).

Second, human beings are dependent on non-physical conditions. We are born into a multitude of organic relationships that are culturally and psychologically mediated (252). This is the proximate context of our existence and is a fundamental condition of our being, since "it is only in the context of such relationships that human living bodies are ever conceived and brought to birth" (252). We do not simply appear on the scene; we require the interaction between a range of "energy systems"[14] to emerge into actuality.

---

14. A phrase Kelsey uses frequently throughout his work. See Kelsey, *Eccentric Existence*, 145, 248–51, 264–66, 303–6.

Third, human beings have distinctive human experiences, which Kelsey claims are essential to the distinctive character of human beings and therefore essential for the possibility of human life to emerge. By analyzing the types of distinctive human experiences (such as consciousness, self-awareness, anxiety, courage, etc.) through a process of transcendental deduction, one may identify structures called 'existentials.' These are found universally to shape human experiences ('ontic' experiences) but are not themselves part of the content of this experience. These transcendental structures are, to Kelsey, "ontological rather than ontic in that they are the transcendental conditions of the possibility of human experience *being* what it actually is 'ontically' on any given occasion—namely, specifically human experience" (253). One example of a transcendental structure, according to Kelsey, is that of God's presence and creative relation toward human beings (252–53).

However, claiming that God's relating to us in creative blessing is the transcendental condition of human experience is more than simply claiming that God's creative relation is a condition of the possibility of human life (and in particular the possibility of the distinctive types of experiences humans have). Rather, what Kelsey claims is that God is immediately and intimately involved through his creative relating not only to the physical and non-physical conditions of human life, but also to the distinctive experiences of human life.[15]

While the conditions for human existence are necessary, their presence remains simply the state of the possibility of human experience and does not guarantee that they either have the potential to create human life nor that human life will actually emerge out of these conditions. In order to actualize the actuality of human existence, one not only needs the possibilities but also the potential.

Potentiality, as Kelsey uses the term, is

> A more or less complex dynamic system of some determinate kind that, given the right circumstances, will develop in definite, rule-governed ways into a dynamic system of a related but different kind. (253)

Kelsey explains that, given the right circumstances, a possibility becomes a potentiality that emerges into actuality. For example, under the right circumstances of nutrients in the soil, water and sunlight, an acorn

---

15. Kelsey's rooting of human existence in the broader context of physical, non-physical and transcendental experiences of human nature is picked up later in this chapter when we discuss the concept of 'complete reality' as highlighted by Aristotle's understanding of actuality.

will develop into an oak. A fertilized ovum, given the right circumstances, will develop into a fetus, which will eventually be born.

As far as human beings are concerned, God—immediately and freely—engages with all these necessary conditions to allow for the potentiality and the subsequent development into actuality of the human being. In this way, humanity is to be comprehended eccentrically. We emerge not out of ourselves, one individual coming from itself, but from the natural processes that require the necessary physical, non-physical and transcendental structures that form the possibility which, along with the right circumstances, becomes the potentiality that develops in rule-governed ways into the actuality of human existence. To Kelsey, human actuality is rooted entirely eccentrically in two ways. First, in the pre-existing, external created order. We, like much of the rest of creation, emerge into actuality through natural processes (themselves pre-existent, created and part of the created order). Second, our existence is embedded in God's relating to us in creative blessing. It is God who creates through our 'having been born.' This is the ultimate context, our basic identity, out of which we emerge into actuality.

In contradistinction to possibilities and potentialities, Kelsey argues that human beings who have been born are actual human beings, and it is only these types of living human bodies that have unqualified dignity and respect. His argument is that pre-birth realities may be actualities in other respects (they are an actual ovum, actual zygote and actual fetus[16]), yet "the logic of [Job's] story cuts against classification of human eggs and sperm, zygotes, foetuses, and embryos as actual living human bodies" (254).

Kelsey's construction poses many challenges, not least of which are questions surrounding the viability of the radical distinction between potentiality and actuality[17] that ultimately leads to particular conclusions in

---

16. Kelsey, *Eccentric Existence*, 254.

17. The relationship between potentiality and actuality is highly complex. We can note for example four minor challenges. First, defining the terms is problematic, especially when one considers their paradoxical relationship whereby what is actual must at all times have been potential, and simultaneously, what was not potentially so cannot be actually so. See Weiss, "Difference between Actuality and Possibility," 165–68. Second, there are potentials for potentials so that what counts as a 'genuine potential' is paradoxically the actuality itself. See Bechler, *Aristotle's Theory of Actuality*. Third, in the same way as a teacher's actualized potential to educate exists in a pupil, it is arguable that a person's actuality exists in another person altogether. See Golluber, "Aristotle," 371–81. However, most problematic for Kelsey's construction and anthropology generally is the relationship between potentiality and actuality in motion. The definition of this concept is a conundrum itself involving both potentiality and actuality in the same entity. See Aristotle, *Physics*, 3.2.201a11; 7.251a9; Brague, "Aristotle's Definition of Motion"; Chen, "Different Meanings," 59; Cohen, "Aristotle's Definition of Kinêsis:"; Kosman, "Aristotle's Definition of Motion"; Sachs, "Aristotle." Indeed, Aquinas notes that motion is the

the abortion debate.[18] However, these challenges are beyond the scope of the topic at hand. What is most problematic for us here is that Kelsey does not define actuality in any real sense.

Unlike his notions of possibility and potential, which each have clear definitions and examples, Kelsey simply notes that actuality is to be understood in contradistinction to possibilities and potentialities (251–55). When we consider the importance of actuality for human dignity; the substantive-relational debate; that the term is used throughout *EE*; and that it is incorporated into Kelsey's anthropological formula, the lack of clarification is problematic. Therefore, the question of his understanding of actuality was put to Kelsey directly. In his response, Kelsey states that he has drawn on a number of sources and in particular on Aristotle.[19] Kelsey, however, does not indicate which interpretation of Aristotle he is using. Recalling that *EE* invites us to use its proposals as springboards for further discussion and that our aims in this thesis are to constructively and critically reflect on these proposals, it is here proposed that we consider elements of Aristotle's sense of actuality that might be brought into constructive conversation with *EE*.[20] In particular, we note Aristotle's priority of actuality over potentiality and his two coinages: *energeia* and *entelecheia*. We shortly see that these two coinages, although synonymous, carry different connotations. These connotations illuminate the concept of actuality in two important ways: first, emphasizing the 'complete reality' of an actuality and second, holding static and dynamic notions of existence together.

---

state of being both a potentiality and an actuality at the same time. See Sachs, *Aristotle's Physics*, 22. It is arguable that, in *EE*, 'having been born' is the term of art for a human being's motion from potential to actual, and the dynamic nature of humanity speaks to the constant motion of human existence. Therefore, in light of the definitions of motion, is it really possible to establish such a radical ontological distinction between potentiality and actuality so as to imbue only actualities with unqualified dignity?

18. In this construction, pre-birth realities are not spoken of as having the same ontological status as *actual living human personal bodies* and therefore do not possess the same value and dignity. The consequence, although not blatantly stated, is that abortion, at any point until the foetus is able to live independently of its mother's womb, is not to be considered the assisted killing of an *actual living human personal body*.

19. Kelsey, email to the author, January 14, 2013.

20. It should be noted that Aristotle speaks about actuality in a range of different senses. The discussions that follow draw on those senses, which can illuminate Kelsey's construction. For more see Chen, "Different Meanings"; "Relation between the Terms."

Aristotle and Actuality

The Priority of Actuality

Let us consider the value Kelsey places on actual human beings in distinction to possible or potential human beings. Is this emphasis justified? To Aristotle, "it is obvious that actuality is prior to potentiality."[21] He contends that "to every potentiality of this kind actuality is prior, both in form and in substance; in time it is sometimes prior and sometimes not."[22] Charlotte Witt believes that the priority of actuality over potentiality is the "linchpin of Aristotle's hierarchical organisation of being,"[23] which is not a hierarchy of kinds of beings but of ways of being.[24] According to Witt, to be potential is in itself a form of being—although, hierarchically speaking, not a better way of being. This priority of being, according to Witt, is an ontological priority which is based on Aristotle's triadic approach to the priority of actuality: a) in definition, b) in being and c) in time. Let us deal briefly with each in turn, as expounded on by Witt.[25]

a) When Aristotle speaks about the priority of actuality in definition, he is pointing to the fact that we can only speak of the content of a given potentiality in relation to the actuality of which it is the potential for. In other words, one can only define a potentiality in terms of an actuality. Without some knowledge and understanding (definition) of the actuality, one cannot know and understand what the potentiality is potential for. This leads to the second way in which actuality is prior to potentiality.

b) Since one can speak of an actuality without a potentiality, and yet one cannot speak of a potentiality without an actuality, we are forced to say that a potentiality is ontologically dependent on an actuality, while an actuality is not ontologically dependent on a potentiality.[26] As P. F. Strawson would say, potentiality is predicated on actuality but not *vice versa*.[27] Witt

---

21. Aristotle, *Metaphysics*, 9.2049b2. See also Aristotle, *Metaphysics*, 9.1049b4–5. For more on Aristotle on priority, consider Bechler, *Aristotle's Theory of Actuality*, 25–26; Peramatzis, *Priority in Aristotle's Metaphysics*; Witt, *Ways of Being*, 75–96. It is interesting to note that Witt believes that Aristotle includes a hierarchy of value in his hierarchy of being in much the same way that Kelsey claims that what is potentiality does not obtain the same value and universal dignity as that which is actuality, as far as the human being is concerned. See Witt, *Ways of Being*, 14, 39, 75.

22. Aristotle, *Metaphysics*, 9.1049b10–11.
23. Witt, *Ways of Being*, 5.
24. See also Chen, "Different Meanings," 57.
25. Witt, *Ways of Being*, 3–9, 75–96.
26. For more on this concept, see Bechler, *Aristotle's Theory of Actuality*, 25–27.
27. Strawson, *Individuals*, 17.

refers to this as the "existential dependency of being potentially on being actually"[28] and expresses it as follows: "A is prior in being to B if A can exist without B but B cannot exist without A."[29]

Aristotle justifies this ontological priority by pointing to two factors: first, the absence of form in incomplete beings and its presence in complete beings, and second the teleological directedness of potentialities toward actualities.[30] In both senses, a potentiality may be temporally prior to its respective actuality, and yet at the same time the actuality may remain, in time, prior to the potentiality.

c) The priority in definition and being may be straightforward, but what does Aristotle mean when he claims that an actuality may be prior in time? Witt expounds on the complexity of this notion. Witt claims that, in one way, Aristotle believes that an actuality is always prior to a potentiality: "For from the potential being, the actual being is always produced by an actual being; man from man, musician by musician; there is always a first mover, and the mover already exists actually."[31]

From one perspective, the potentiality is always temporally prior. According to Aristotle, the seed, which produces the plant, is temporarily prior to the plant it produces. One should be careful on this point; such a priority is to be understood in terms of a particular potentiality in relation to its particular actuality. A particular seed is the potentiality for a particular plant. Yet one should keep in mind that, on the whole, plants (actualities) produce seeds (potentialities), which themselves become actualities that then produce potentialities.[32] In this latter sense, actuality is temporarily prior to potentiality.

In sum, in Aristotle's understanding one finds the conception that actuality—in definition, being and time—is ontologically primary. Let us now consider the terms Aristotle uses in his understanding of actuality and the connotations they bring.

---

28. Witt, *Ways of Being*, 77–78.
29. Witt, *Ways of Being*, 81.
30. Witt, *Ways of Being*, 83. See also Weiss, "Difference between Actuality and Possibility," 167–69.
31. Aristotle, *Metaphysics*, 9.1049b23–26.
32. Aristotle, *Metaphysics*, 9.1049b19–23.

Actuality as *Energeia* and *Entelecheia*

Aristotle coined two words to refer to the concept of actuality: *energeia* and *entelecheia*.[33] The correct English translation and meaning of each term has been so widely and fiercely debated that George Blair claims the debate is akin to a "minefield."[34] Within our short discussion, it is impossible to produce a definitive definition or explanation of each term. However, there is value in extrapolating some of the connotations of these terms that are important for our broader thesis. To do this, we consider each term in turn, their relation to each other and two important aspects of actuality they illuminate.

Defining Energeia

Energeia, from which we get the English word 'energy,' was coined by Aristotle early in his career.[35] This word, according to Joe Sachs, was formed from the word *ergono* (deed, work or action) with the adjective *energon* (activity, busy or being at work).[36] Sachs demonstrates how one may construct the word 'is-at-work-ness' using Anglo-Saxon roots. However, a simpler English translation would be 'being-at-work.' Using Latin roots, one may translate *energeia* as 'actuality,' but one should be careful with this translation.

The word 'actuality' is already present in the English language and sometimes carries no connotation of activity. Sachs notes that, "by the actuality of a thing, we [in English] mean not its being-in-action but its being what it is."[37] To demonstrate the point, Sachs uses the example of a fish that has the ability to camouflage itself to look like a rock as it sits on the ocean floor; "it looks like a rock but it is *actually* a fish."[38] In this example, when actuality is attributed to the fish, we are not speaking about an activity of the fish.

Aristotle, according to Blair,[39] wanted to include an aspect of activity in his understanding of actuality. In coining *energeia*, he was seeking a word

---

33. The debate surrounding the meaning and relation between these two terms is well known. See for example Blair, "Aristotle on Entelexeia"; Chen, "Different Meanings"; "Relation between the Terms"; Graham, "Etymology of Entelexeia"; Ritter, "Why Aristotle"; "Why Aristotle (Continued)."

34. Blair, "Aristotle on Entelexeia," 97. Blair has indeed written a book on this topic. See Blair, *Energeia and Entelecheia*.

35. Blair, "Aristotle on Entelexeia," 95.

36. See also Golluber, "Aristotle," 368.

37. Sachs, "Aristotle."

38. Sachs, "Aristotle."

39. Blair, "Aristotle on Entelexeia."

that would express what later became known as 'immanent activity,' which is characteristic of living beings. Immanent and internal activity speaks to the state in which living creatures find themselves. This is not a state of inactivity but a state of being (verb) whereby the living being is in a constant state of activity to remain what it is.

Blair concludes that Aristotle struggled to find a word that carried this connotation. According to Blair,[40] Aristotle considered a number of words and yet could not find one that meant 'being internally active.' He therefore coined *energeia*. Aristotle was sure to use the ending *-eia* instead of the more common, and perhaps more grammatically correct, *-ia* so as to distinguish it from the term *energos*, which means 'effectiveness.'

Energeia was not used by Aristotle to speak to a single idea or concept but rather to a range of meanings. Chung-Hwan Chen summarizes Aristotle's understanding of the term as having 10 meanings,[41] two of which are of interest to us. First, *energeia* in the meaning actuality. This is the most well-known meaning of the term and creates a correspondence between *energeia* and *dynamis* (potentiality). According to Chen, Aristotle held these two terms to be a pair of principles valid for the whole realm of being, representing two distinct ways of being.[42]

Second, *energeia* in the meaning of actualization or of being made perfect. These two concepts, 'being actualized' and 'being made perfect,' are very closely associated with the meaning of actuality in Aristotle. This is particularly evident in his understanding of matter and form. To Aristotle, matter has a natural tendency to be a certain way; that is to say, it has a determinative nature. In Chen's words, "this actual determination is its end."[43] When a thing reaches its end—according to Aristotle—it is perfect.[44] *Energeia* may be considered the 'being-at-work' at the end or perfect/complete state of a thing. Reaching this end does not mean that the being ceases to be active, but rather that it continues to work to retain and remain what has already been actualized.

It should be noted that it is not easy to distinguish clearly the meaning of 'actualized' from 'actuality.' The complexity of the problem becomes

---

40. Blair, "Aristotle on Entelexeia," 95.

41. Chen, "Different Meanings," 57–65; cf. Chen, "Relation between the Terms." While Chen claims ten meanings, his discussion is complex with a number of the meanings overlapping. A reader of this work is left questioning the exact number of meanings.

42. Chen, "Different Meanings," 57. This idea is picked up in Witt's work. See Witt, *Ways of Being*.

43. Chen, "Different Meanings," 58.

44. Chen, "Different Meanings," 58; Aristotle, *Metaphysics*, 9.1050a.

particularly evident when the terms are applied to living objects, which are the subject of the process of coming to be, such as in the case of the human being. For such realities, Chen expresses the complication of the actual/actualized dynamic as follows: "what is actual is that which has become actual, that is, which is actualized; and, conversely, what is actualized is actual."[45] In other words; the human being, as an actuality, has not only become actual but is and continues to be actualized. This actualization is its actuality and it continues to exist, as an actuality, through its actualization.

Defining Entelecheia

Aristotle coined the term *entelecheia* at around the same time the term *energeia* was beginning to change from denoting 'activity' to 'actuality.'[46] As shown directly below, there is general agreement that Aristotle sought a term that conveyed a more "static"[47] or persistent notion of actuality than the activity implied in his coinage *energeia*.[48] Yet the exact meaning of this second coinage remains in dispute. Some claim that Aristotle created a pun on Plato's *endelecheia* (persistence) by inserting *telos*.[49] Others contend that it stems from the phrase *enteles echein*, but translating this phrase has proven nearly impossible. Leibniz goes so far as to say that Ermolao Barbaro's Latin translation of the phrase into *perfectihabia* was such a great feat that it required the assistance of Lucifer himself.[50] The phrase is often translated with rather awkward English phrases, such as to 'have completeness' (Diels) or 'have an end in itself' (Von Fritz)[51] or 'being fully real.'[52] However, even these English translations are in much dispute as to what they themselves mean.[53]

While it may be argued that *entelecheia* is a poorly formed Greek word, as it appears to be formed from the word *entelechis* (a word which

---

45. Chen, "Different Meanings," 58.
46. Graham, "Etymology of Entelexeia," 79–80.
47. Blair, "Aristotle on Entelexeia," 93.
48. Blair, "Aristotle on Entelexeia," 93; Graham, "Etymology of Entelexeia," 79.
49. Sachs, *Aristotle's Physics*, 245; Graham, "Etymology of Entelexeia," 74.
50. Leibniz quoted in Graham, "Etymology of Entelexeia," 74.
51. See as examples of these disputes Graham, "Etymology of Entelexeia," 73–75; Blair, "Aristotle on Entelexeia"; Sachs, "Aristotle."
52. Bradshaw, *Aristotle East and West*, 13.
53. Blair, "Aristotle on Entelexeia," 94–95.

does not exist),[54] Blair, in opposition to Graham,[55] contends that Aristotle was very careful in his formation of neologisms. According to Blair, Aristotle found no word in the Greek language that fully expressed the notion of 'possessing the end' without having misleading implications.[56] Aristotle, therefore, had to invent one. To do this he combined the word *en* (as in 'internal'), which links analogously with the *en* in *energeia*, with the word *telos* (end) and *echein* (to have) and included the noun ending *-eia* in much the same way as he added the same ending to *energeia*.[57] In this way, Blair contends that Aristotle included all these notions (*internal, activity, to have* and *end/goal*) into one term.

Although Blair's interpretation has been widely accepted, recently Sachs has proposed a slightly different view. He argues that the term *entelecheia* represents the fusion of the idea of completeness with that of continuity or persistence. Sachs claims that Aristotle combined the word *enteles* (meaning complete or full-grown) with the word *echein*, which Sachs understands as containing the connotation of being a certain way through a continued and sustained effort of holding on to a certain condition. *Entelecheia*, claims Sachs, is a pun on *endelecheai* (persistence), with the word *telos* (completion) as its root. It is "a three-ring circus of a word"[58] that has the power to carry the meaning of each of the three subsidiary words used by Aristotle to coin this term. To Sachs, translating the word as 'being-at-an-end' or 'having the end within,' as Blair would prefer,[59] "misses the point entirely,"[60] as it fails to grasp the implied persistence.

Although it may indeed have the connotation of actuality, the English term 'actuality,' according to Sachs, is often used to refer to "anything,

---

54. Blair, "Aristotle on Entelexeia," 92.

55. Graham is rather critical of Aristotle's formation and use of neologisms and claims that his lack of systematic distinction between *energeia* and *entelecheia* "is just one of many indications of a lack of terminological discipline" (Graham, "Etymology of Entelexeia," 80). This view may be supported by Kostman, who claims that Aristotle uses the term *entelecheia* outside of his etymological purpose (Kostman, "Aristotle's Definition of Change," 5). However, it must be noted that Kostman believes Aristotle is free to use a word (which he coined) as he sees fit, and that it is possible Aristotle struggled to express himself as well as certain concepts clearly. See Kostman, "Aristotle's Definition of Change," 7.

56. Blair, "Aristotle on Entelexeia," 95.

57. Blair, "Aristotle on Entelexeia," 96. Blair's translation is supported by a number of thinkers. See, for example, Kostman, "Aristotle's Definition of Change," 5n10.

58. Sachs, *Aristotle's Physics*, 245.

59. Blair, "Aristotle on Entelexeia," 96.

60. Sachs, *Aristotle's Physics*, 245.

however trivial, incidental, transient, or static, that happens to be the case,"[61] and therefore the true meaning of Aristotle's understanding of actuality is often lost in translation. The best way to translate *entelecheia*, according to Sachs, is "being-at-work-staying-itself."[62]

The Relation between Energeia *and* Entelecheia

As we have seen above, there are no universally accepted English translations and definitions of *energeia* or *entelecheia*. All we have done is briefly highlight some of the key concepts and notions entailed in Aristotle's coinages. It is important, at this point, to note that these two terms speak to different aspects of actuality. One may therefore wonder why, in seeking an understanding of actuality, Aristotle felt he needed two terms to express one concept.

Although there is some disagreement as to how these two words are related, many authors believe that while the terms have different meanings, they function in Aristotle's corpus synonymously.[63] This does not mean, however, that the words carry the exact same connotations. Words are not only related to each other in meaning but in history and connotation.[64] Chen has written an in-depth article on the historical development of each of these terms and how they are related to each other.[65] He demonstrates that the two terms developed along different roots; the term *energeia* originally had a kinetic element to it, that is, a sense of movement, motion or activity, while *entelecheia* originally emphasized a static, persistent state of having arrived at the end.[66] These connotations are important to the one concept of human actuality. Let us explore each in turn.

---

61. Sachs, *Aristotle's Physics*, 245.

62. Sachs, *Aristotle's Physics*, 245.

63. Blair, "Aristotle on Entelexeia," 96–97; Bradshaw, *Aristotle East and West*, 13; Golluber, "Aristotle," 368; Graham, "Etymology of Entelexeia," 75; Ritter, "Why Aristotle," 378; Sachs, "Aristotle"; Witt, *Ways of Being*, 12–13.

64. Chen, "Relation between the Terms," 14.

65. Chen, "Relation between the Terms."

66. See Chen, "Relation between the Terms," 14n1; "Different Meanings," 57–65.

Two Important Connotations

'Complete Reality'

Wm E. Ritter[67] illuminates Aristotle's understanding of *entelecheia* by providing a unique analysis of the meaning and connotation of *telos*, as it forms part of the root of *entelecheia*. To Ritter, *telos* brings the meaning of *entelecheia* into an arena which cannot be grasped fully by *energeia*. He begins by warning us of the dangers of simply attaching an English equivalent to *telos*, such as 'end.' Ritter highlights how 'end,' in the original Greek context, does not have the connotation of end as in the end of a stick or the end of a road. Rather it implies the idea of completion, or wholeness.[68]

Referencing Burnet's introduction to his own translation of *The Nichomachean Ethics*, Ritter argues that Aristotle's understanding of *telos* is more akin with 'compete wholeness' than with the English equivalent 'end.' According to Burnet, Aristotle understood that no animal continues to grow indefinitely; all animals reach a point where they are 'complete' or 'fully grown.'[69] This 'fully grown' or 'complete' state is the *telos* of the animal. It is not the *telos* in the sense that the animal ceases to be, but rather that the animal reaches the intended end state of being.

Furthermore, Aristotle's understanding of *telos* as it relates to *entelecheia* has to do with the sum of an actuality's parts and with their relationship to each other. According to Aristotle, all the parts of an actuality must be present before an *entelecheia* may be considered whole. We read, for example in Aristotle's *Metaphysics*:

> To come from the combination of matter and form (as the parts come from the whole, and the verse from the Iliad, and the stones from the house); for the shape is an end, and that is a complete thing which has attained its end.[70]

In the quotation above, the end of a house is its shape, and when it has obtained this shape it is considered complete. Ritter, relying on Butcher, expands on the relationship between the concepts of wholeness and

---

67. We are aware that Ritter's work is slightly dated, first published in 1932. However, the work is widely cited. See, as examples, Golluber, "Aristotle," 368n21; Graham, "Etymology of Entelexeia," 75n9, 80n21.

68. Ritter, "Why Aristotle," 380–83. For a discussion of Aristotelian writings that highlight the kindred nature between *telos* and *entelecheia* see Ritter, "Why Aristotle," 380–81.

69. Ritter, "Why Aristotle," 380.

70. Aristotle, *Metaphysics*, 9.1023a.

completeness within the concept of *telos*.[71] He demonstrates that these two concepts are not synonymous. According to Ritter, whatever is complete must also be whole, since it must "all be there" (381). Yet it is possible for every part to be present and for the actuality in question not to be complete. Ritter uses the example of a salamander which has had one of its own legs removed and grafted on to its back. In Aristotelian thinking, such a salamander would be a whole salamander, in that every part of it is present, and yet it would not be considered a complete salamander since it would not be in the ordinary end state of salamanders. In other words, it would not have reached the *telos* of being a salamander.[72]

When Aristotle speaks of actuality as *entelecheia*, he has in mind this understanding of the end or *telos* of an actuality. It is not that the actuality has ceased or that the actuality has reached some ultimate purpose.[73] What is being expressed is that the actuality has reached its end in that it is composed of all the necessary parts for it to be considered whole, and these parts are "structurally related so that none can be removed, [and] none transposed, without disturbing the organism."[74] After considering the implications of such an understanding of telos within *entelecheia*, Ritter concludes that what Aristotle means by actuality is the "complete reality"[75] of a thing.

Describing the human being as a 'complete reality' (an *entelecheia*) requires that we take into consideration the numerous features (parts) that are necessary components of human existence. The various aspects of human existence are taken up in Aristotle's understanding of actuality and included in the 'complete reality' of human existence.[76] Whatever aspect there is of human being that cannot be separated from human existence is incorporated in Aristotle's understanding of *entelecheia*. This includes not only the end-state of humanity and the sum of his or her parts (body, mind, spirit, etc.), but also the processes by which these parts become the human being.

Active and Static Actuality

As we have noted, the terms *energeia* and *entelecheia* derive from roots that bring both active and static connotations: active in the sense of energy, work and activity incorporated in the original meaning of *energeia*, and static in

71. Ritter, "Why Aristotle," 381.
72. Ritter, "Why Aristotle," 381–82.
73. See Ritter, "Why Aristotle," 382–84.
74. Butcher quoted in Ritter, "Why Aristotle," 381.
75. Ritter, "Why Aristotle," 389–401. See also Ritter, "Why Aristotle (Continued)," 4.
76. Ritter, "Why Aristotle," 401.

the sense of being, or arriving at a completed/whole state implied in the root terms of *entelecheia*. Yet we have also noted that the two words act as synonyms for the concept of actuality. The question we need to ask ourselves is: How is it that these two notions are held together in one concept? How is it that a being may be at work, in activity, and yet remain the same?

L. A. Kosman has written much on this topic.[77] He explains that Greek philosophy had very little difficulty with this seeming contradiction:

> The temptation for the Greeks to put true reality with movement was much greater than the temptation to put it with rest. . . . Actuality is de-motionalized being not by virtue of having been brought to quiescence, but by virtue of having become *entelic*, having become its own end.[78]

We ought to pay special attention to the subtleties of Kosman's claim. What he postulates is that a being is considered an actuality not by virtue of the fact that it has reached some ultimate goal or state of perfection and thereby ceases to be actualized. Rather, the actuality of a being is in its 'having become its own end,' which conveys a state of being by which an actuality is continually actualized as it works to remain what it is. As maintenance speaks to an active process of working to retain what is already actual, so actuality speaks of the entity "being-at-work-staying-itself."[79]

Aristotle explains that this 'being-at-work' is an action and that this "act is an end."[80] Since *energeia* stems from the word *energon* (work), and since this work or act is an end itself, it follows that *energeia* extends to the "being-at-an-end [*enteletchia*]."[81] The actuality of a thing, therefore, in Aristotle's construction, lies in its acting or working to be what it already is: an end, a complete and whole being. In Kosman's words, "Aristotle finds at the heart of all being that which is unmoved, but not inactive."[82] As such, actuality speaks to the state of being where one is in motion and at the same time remains as one is.

It is for this reason, explains Kosman, that circular motion, where each part is as much a part of the end as any other, is the closest analogy for the concept of 'complete reality.' Plato's analogy of a spinning top in Book IV of *The Republic* is a prime example of this type of being. The immovable

77. Kosman, "Aristotle's Definition of Motion."
78. Kosman, "Aristotle's Definition of Motion," 59.
79. Sachs, *Aristotle's Physics*, 245.
80. Aristotle, *Metaphysics*, 9.1050a21–23. See also Sachs, "Aristotle."
81. Aristotle, *Metaphysics*, 9.1050a21–23. See also Sachs, "Aristotle."
82. Kosman, "Aristotle's Definition of Motion," 60.

peg which sits at the center of the spinning top brings to mind the picture of a calm and ordered soul that is at the center of activity.[83] This center holds together the entire spinning top, preserving the integrity of the whole in symbiotic union with the rest. To Kosman, this simple analogy can be used to speak of God's activity in the cosmos: "Aristotle's unmoved mover, as much at the circumference as at the center of the cosmos, descends from that more ancient god, the great encircling Okeanos, forever flowing and nourishing, yet un-changed."[84]

It is a beautiful picture that combines both active and static notions into one 'complete reality.' Being is the activity of manifesting what something is: "For the activity is the end, and the actuality is the activity; hence the term "actuality" [*energeia*] is derived from "activity," and tends to have the meaning of "complete reality" [*entelecheia*]."[85]

Actuality is not something stationary but is an on-going reality. This applies to both biological and non-biological beings alike. Even a rock, seemingly stationary on the ground, is in a state of activity. The rock is in motion, yet it is constrained by the earth. It is at work maintaining its place against the counter-tendency of the earth to displace it.[86]

In biological beings, the dual nature of existing in both static and active states at the same time is explained in concepts such as metabolism.[87] The natural functioning of living beings like birds, fish and cattle is constant change. As actualities, they are in a continual state of motion. Their bodies are continually at work maintaining their being. Respiration, metabolism and the continual process of creating new cells to replace old cells speaks to the activity necessary to remain what one is.

Elaborating on Human Actuality

We have noted Kelsey's unique and eccentric doctrine of creation, which is the context of human value and dignity in *EE*. We have further noted important elements of Aristotle's understanding of actuality: the ontological priority of actuality over potentiality, the 'complete reality' of an actuality and how actuality speaks to both static and dynamic concepts of existence. Let us turn our attention now to a constructive interpretation of Kelsey's notion of actuality in light of these discussions.

    83. Kosman, "Aristotle's Definition of Motion," 59.
    84. Kosman, "Aristotle's Definition of Motion," 60.
    85. Aristotle, *Metaphysics*, 9.1050a21–23.
    86. Sachs, "Aristotle."
    87. Sachs, *Aristotle's Physics*, 244.

First, we can begin by noting the manner in which actuality is being used. In relational understandings, the distinction between potential and actual is far more pronounced than in substantive thinking. Here, human beings have the potential to develop an appropriate relationship to God. If they reach this potential, they image (verb) God. If they fail to reach this potential, they remain merely potential images of God. In substantive thinking, humans actually possess certain qualities, and their possession makes them the actual images of God.[88]

In regard to the potential-actual dynamic, Kelsey's position is more substantive than relational. Although Kelsey makes allowances for potential human beings prior to their creation, in their being created they no longer display an aspect of the potential-actual dynamic in terms of their humanity. To Kelsey, once a human is created (born), one cannot speak of their potentiality *qua* humanity. All created human beings simply are *actual living human personal bodies*.

Kelsey's construction acknowledges the primacy—in definition, being and time—of actuality over potentiality. That is to say, actuality is, in hierarchical terms, ontologically a better way of being than being in potentiality. Those that exist as only potential human beings exist in a manner that is ontologically inferior to those who are actual human beings. It follows that their dignity and value is negatively impacted. Thus, considering the central role the *imago Dei* plays in humanity, there is sympathy for the substantive concern to establish human beings as actually being images of God. Indeed, we noted in chapter 1 of this thesis the problematic ethical results of the relational camps dichotomizing human beings into potential and actual images of God. Kelsey's argument, that all human beings—by virtue of being created—are actual human beings, takes cognizance of the priority of actuality and furthermore establishes humanity, ontologically, as an actuality.

Second, we should note where human actuality is located. In substantive understandings, humans are actual images of God in their possession of certain characteristics such as rationality. In relational thinking, humans become actual images of God if they obtain or develop a particular relationality. In both cases, humans actually image God in a single or limited set of features that is located in the human beings themselves. In order to understand where Kelsey locates human actuality, it is fruitful for us to reinterpret *EE* in light of our discussions on Aristotle.

Kelsey makes mention of the numerous different aspects of human creation in his discussions in chapter 6 of *EE*. These include the physical,

---

88. In chapter 1 of this project we noted the limitation of this apparent universality in terms of humans who fail to actually possess these characteristics.

non-physical and transcendental properties of human existence. He does not, however, go into great detail as to the relationship between these different aspects as far as human actuality is concerned. These aspects are noted as the possibilities and potentialities for human beings to be what they actually are. A key question is: Do these factors act as catalysts in a reaction, allowing for the presence of a reaction while not themselves being incorporated into the final reaction, or are these factors more fundamental to human existence, themselves taken up as part of that existence? To understand the relationship between possibilities, potentialities and actualities, it is helpful to call on Kosman's discussion on this very topic.

Kosman, in clarifying Aristotle's definition of motion, speaks to the relationship between potentiality and actuality. He argues that a potentiality may be related to its actuality in one of two ways. First, it can be related through the process of 'deprivative perfection,' whereby the potentiality is destroyed so as to create the actuality.[89] Such is the case of someone who suffers from a speech impediment but has the potential to improve their speech. In order for the potential to be realized (proper speech), the prior state of affairs (the stutter) must be destroyed. Second, it can be related through the process of 'constitutive perfection,' whereby the prior state of affairs is perfected to become the actuality.[90] For example, when the potential for bricks and stones to be a house has been reached, they continue to exist as bricks and stones within the actuality of the house.

Turning back to Kelsey, we must ask ourselves: Is human actuality the result of constitutive or deprivative perfection? On the one hand, in Kelsey's terminology, we feed off of energy systems (248–50), destroying them to make way for our actuality. Such is the case of the possibility of plants and animals to nourish us. The plants and animals which we feed off of are destroyed so that we may sustain our beings and in so doing actualize our actuality. In this sense, human actuality is the result of deprivative perfection. On the other hand, drawing on Kelsey for support, one may claim that we are the actualities of prior potentialities. Using Kelsey's examples, we may say that the infant is the actuality of the fetus (253). In being born, the fetus is incorporated, not destroyed, by the process of actualization. In this sense, Kelsey can be interpreted as stating that possibilities and potentialities are drawn into human actuality through a process of constitutive perfection.

As the product of both deprivation and constitutive perfection, Kelsey locates human actuality in the distinctive features of human being which can be extended exponentially beyond a single or even limited set of

---

89. Kosman, "Aristotle's Definition of Motion," 48–50.
90. Kosman, "Aristotle's Definition of Motion," 46–50.

definitive features. To Aristotle, this is the 'complete reality' of the human being. So numerous are the features that make us this 'complete reality' that it is impossible to produce an inventory of its contents.[91]

Furthermore, Kelsey's particular doctrine of creation locates human actuality eccentrically. First, in his appeal to the natural process of human reproduction, he argues that human beings—as ordinary parts of creation—emerge into actuality as the consequence of pre-existing processes and realities (physical, non-physical and transcendental) that are integrated, amalgamated and incorporated into the 'complete reality' of human being. Second, God is immediately and freely engaged both directly (it is he who creates us) and indirectly (he creates us through the natural and ordinary process of human reproduction) in this process.

Third, although all human beings are actual human beings, we can interpret EE as taking relational concerns seriously. There are parallels between Aristotle's notion of actuality and Kelsey's understanding of the gift and vocation of human existence expounded on in chapter 5 of this thesis (1045). In that chapter, we note that Kelsey conceives of God's creative blessing as an "odd" (213) gift. It is God's gift of human creatureliness that is our basic identity. What the human being is is gifted to it through God's free and immediate relating through the natural process of human reproduction. It is the gift of human being itself, the gift of our 'complete reality' and our basic identity. Since it is God's gift of human being, it is persistently and statically present in all human beings everywhere. Simply by being born, by being given our humanity as an *actual living human personal body*, one images the image of God.

At the same time, Kelsey's doctrine of creation emphasizes our quotidian identity as an important feature of the 'complete reality' of human actuality. Through the process of deprivative and constitutive perfection, the quotidian context is incorporated into our very actuality. This speaks to our vocation to respond appropriately to God's relating. As an actuality, the human being is called to act in ways that are appropriate responses to God's relating in creative blessing. This brings the human beings' quotidian identity into congruence with its basic identity and in so doing becomes—in the proximate context— what it already is in the ultimate context. In this manner of understanding human actuality, the human being continues to be in motion and yet remains the same. It is, so to speak 'being-at-work-staying-itself.'

Kelsey's understanding of the human being as an actuality, interpreted against the backdrop of Aristotle, offers a way to speak about the *imago Dei* that is open to both substantive and relational thinkers. We exist as actual

---

91. Ritter, "Why Aristotle," 401.

living human bodies who image the image of God by continually working to remain what we are. As actualities we *are* images of the image of God yet, at the same time, are called to *become* images of the image of God. This aspect of our reality mirrors the ultimate reality of God, who is in continual activity remaining what He was and is and is to come (Revelations 4:8). Kosman states it as such:

> Beings therefore imitate divinity in being, acting out, what they are; *imitation Dei* consists in striving not to be God, but to be one's self, to emulate that being who is totally active, i.e., who totally is what he is.[92]

---

92. Kosman, "Aristotle's Definition of Motion," 60. Kosman here touches on God as *actus purus* (pure act). Our interpretation of Kelsey and the *imago Dei*, however, touches on the role of potentiality as an intimate part of actuality, the two being very closely related. If we image God in the way we have interpreted Kelsey (thereby including some form of potentiality), this raises questions about potentiality within God. Kelsey does not develop a systematic doctrine of God and so we are not able to draw out his understanding of God as omnipotent (here 'omni' negates the implied 'potency') *actus purus*. It is possible that our interpretation of Kelsey may be departing from the more traditional understanding of God as *actus purus*. If so, more deliberations are necessary. However, we will leave these deliberations for others to pick up. For more, see Jüngel, *God's Being Is in Becoming*, pt. 3.

Living Human Body

IN OUR PREVIOUS CHAPTER, we considered Kelsey's understanding of human actuality. Recall how it is that Kelsey casts his doctrine of creation within the context of 'having been born.' This doctrine construes human beings as arising from the 'utterly ordinary' processes of human reproduction. In all cases we are familiar with, human reproduction leads to a human living body. In other words, human actuality—at least within EE—implies that humans have a living body. This is one reason that Kelsey includes the descriptive sub-phrase *living body* in his anthropological formula. Yet this is not the only reason.

Kelsey's reference in the anthropological formula to human embodiment follows a growing consensus among theological anthropologists that human bodiliness is of major importance to the subject.[1] Although pre-modern theological anthropology tended toward a dualism that distinguished between the body and spirit/soul (29–31),[2] there has been a shift in recent times to emphasize the unity of the human being as an embodied creature, thereby linking human embodiment directly with the *imago Dei*. For example, Zizioulas exclaims: "The body is an *inseparable aspect of the human Person* and for this reason it is regarded as partaking of the *imago Dei*."[3]

Kelsey's accommodation of this recent move to include human embodiment within the doctrine of the image of God raises two questions. First, considering that much of our Christian heritage is dualistic, that is to say, emphasizes the distinction between the body and the spirit, why does

---

1. Kelsey, "Human Creature," 127. See also Berkouwer, *Man*, 74–81; Huyssteen van, "When Were We Persons?"; Lewis, *Self and Immortality*, 115–39; McFadyen, *Call to Personhood*, 86–90; Ricoeur, *Oneself as Other*, 33–35.

2. The traditional tendency toward a body/soul dualism is well established throughout the literature. For a discussion on the dualism explicit in historical authors such as Augustine, Aquinas and Calvin, see Cooper, *Body, Soul, and Life Everlasting*, 10–16. For an overview of numerous writers who hold dualistic and non-dualistic positions see Berkouwer, *Man*, 74–81; Cairns, *Image of God in Man*, 22–23.

3. Zizioulas, "Human Capacity and Human Incapacity," 423. See also Moltmann-Wendel and Moltmann, *Humanity in God*, 103–4; Hall, *Imaging God*.

Kelsey follow this recent shift? What is his underlying concern with the inclusion of *living body* in the context of recent anthropology? Our next section considers this question and in particular Kelsey's concern to avoid value anthropocentricism and at the same time be hospitable to contemporary understandings of anthropology.

Second, in the context of Christian particularism, if we are to argue that human embodiment is fundamental to human being, what of the Christian question of bodily death and the possibility of post-mortem life? Is the reality of physical mortality and the hope of post-mortem life incongruent with necessary embodiment? How is it that human embodiment is not only essential for human beings as *imago Dei* pre-mortem, but that it continues post-mortem? We will shortly see that these issues have serious implications for the eschatological continuity question. This latter question occupies the majority of this chapter.

Before we begin, it is important to remember that questions of post-mortem continuity are inevitably speculative. There is little empirical data upon which to base proposals; indeed, Kelsey himself notes that one is not even sure what would count as empirical data (553).[4] Although speculation itself is important and necessary to provide a framework for conceiving of answers to important theological questions such as those of post-mortem continuity, it is important that we recognize that our proposals are speculative in nature and therefore place limits on our conjectures. Therefore, this chapter does not attempt to solve the problems with post-mortem continuity entirely, but rather is limited to what is relevant for Kelsey's anthropological formula and the substantive-relational debate.

Having said all this, let us begin by considering the driving force behind recent shifts in theological anthropology toward necessary embodiment.

The Driving Force

There are two reasons behind the recent shift toward emphasizing human embodiment. The first, evidenced in the recent rise of eco-theologies, is an awareness over the past few decades of what many consider to be a negative

---

4. There are attempts within the natural sciences to provide such empirical data. For example, a team of researchers at University of Southampton under the guidance of Dr. Sam Parnia considered 2,060 cases of people whose hearts had stopped for an extended period. They concluded that 40 percent had some form of awareness after being pronounced clinically dead. See Flanagan, "Scientists Have Finally Proven." Others have proposed theories that argue for the continuation of human consciousness after physical death in a 'spiritual' quantum field. See Fröböse, "Scientists Find Hints." As these experiments and theories are beyond the scope of this project, we refrain from critically engaging them here.

emphasis on the non-physical at the expense of the physical. We have noted these concerns in chapter 1 of our project, and it is therefore not necessary to revisit that discussion here. The reader recalls that a number of authors have argued against traditional body-soul dualisms, a theology that has occupied the church for centuries. This theology has at times led to the devaluing, and consequently abuse of, the physical (both the environment and human bodies). Contemporary theology attempts to respond to this heritage and provide a holistic approach by encapsulating both the physical and the non-physical within theological anthropology.[5]

Yet there is evidence that this recent shift is driven first and foremost not by the negative effects of past Christian doctrine, but by the rise of what Wesley Wildman calls the Modern Secular Interpretation of Humanity (MSIH). Largely dependent on recent empirical scientific research—most notably in evolutionary biology, human physiology and the natural sciences—MSIH emphasizes the material nature of reality.[6] Such an interpretation of humanity has elevated the importance of human embodiment to such lofty heights that it now stands on a pedestal matched only by the pre-modern Christian emphasis of the human soul. As theological anthropology, and with it Kelsey, seeks to be "hospitable to scientifically warranted secular anthropological claims,"[7] it has tended to emphasize the importance of human embodiment.[8]

This second shift is most evident in theological and philosophical discussions on personal identity. Stanley Rudman, for example, argues that human embodiment is "one of the most essential features of a person."[9] He claims that the reason for this insistence is quite clear: "the persons we are most familiar with, other human agents, are, without exception, embodied."[10] In Hille Haker's construction, "physical immediacy"[11] is essential for personal identity. It is through the physically immediate body

---

5. Many have noted this, including Kelsey. See our discussions in chapter 3; cf. Kelsey, *Eccentric Existence*, 29–31, 39, 272; Anderson, *On Being Human*, 71. Hall's work is a prime example of this. See Hall, *Imaging God*.

6. Kelsey, "Wisdom Theological Anthropology"; Wildman, "Theological Challenge."

7. Kelsey, "Wisdom Theological Anthropology," 44, 51.

8. This is evidenced in many recent articles and books on theological anthropology. For example see Cooper, *Body, Soul, and Life Everlasting*; Gregersen, et al., *Human Person*; Huyssteen van, "When Were We Persons?"; Rudman, *Concepts of Persons*, 145–51.

9. Rudman, *Concepts of Persons*, 148.

10. Rudman, *Concepts of Persons*, 148.

11. Haker, "Narrative and Moral Identity," 59–60.

that the self is able to treat itself (and others) as objects of consideration. This physical immediacy is the necessary reference point for reflection on the self and its body. It is only through this physically present body that one may reflect on the distinction between one's personal identity and every other identity. Indeed, in many cases, the continuation of this physical immediacy is the ground upon which a personal identity is able to claim that it has remained the self-same identity over time.[12] According to Dorothy Emmet, this is simply taken for granted. Emmet notes that "we are unlikely to say, 'Here am I, and I have brought my body with me.'"[13]

Therefore, in ordinary and philosophical discourse the concept of embodiment is of utmost importance. It allows for the localization in a single spatiotemporal schema needed for the process of personal identification. It is, in Paul Ricoeur's view, no less primitive than the notion of person itself: "possessing bodies is precisely what persons do indeed do, or rather what they actually are."[14]

Kelsey is both aware of and responsive to these two shifts. In the first instance, very early in his project, Kelsey actively objects to value anthropocentrism, arguing that such "'value anthropocentrism' is problematic because it can yield no theological resistance to the conflation of human stewardship with human self-interested exploitation and devastation of fellow creatures" (30, see also 29–31, 255–57).

So concerned is he about avoiding such a problematic value anthropocentrism that he adds two desiderata to his theological anthropology: 1) the human creature must be understood as being embodied, and 2) any method for identifying what the human being is must not rely on "invidious comparison and contrast either with other, allegedly lesser creatures, or between human creatures' 'physical' and 'mental' capacities" (31). His position on this point is so strong that his anthropology has been used as the basis for eco-theologies.[15]

Secondly, Kelsey is very conscious that his anthropology should be "hospitable"[16] to the MSIH. Not only is this concern rooted in borrowing from his host culture, what he refers to as theology's contemporary equiva-

---

12. Haker, "Narrative and Moral Identity," 59–60.

13. Whitehead quoted in Emmet, "Could God Be a Person?," 5.

14. Ricoeur, *Oneself as Other*, 33. Many of these authors—including Ricoeur and Kelsey—draw on Strawson's theory of M- and P-predicates: Kelsey, *Eccentric Existence*, 287–88; "Biblical Narrative and Theological Anthropology," 124; "Personal Bodies," 149–51; Ricoeur, *Oneself as Other*, 30–39.

15. Marais, "Eccentric Existence?"

16. Kelsey, "Wisdom Theological Anthropology," 44, 51. See also Kelsey, "Human Creature," 128; "Spiritual Machines," 7.

lent of the Israelites despoiling the Egyptians during the exodus,[17] but it also causes him to emphasize the natural sciences as a key dialogue partner with theological anthropology. For example, in his article "Spiritual Machines, Personal Bodies, and God: Theological Education and Theological Anthropology" (2002), Kelsey uses Christology to demonstrate that God relates to human beings through the embodied Jesus, and it is this embodied Jesus that speaks most aptly to the inner life of God. To Kelsey, the theological consequence is that God relates in especially close ways to complex organic life.[18] He concludes that if the *theos* in theological anthropology delights and rejoices in complex organic life, then our account of the *anthropos* in theological anthropology needs to "privilege and not fear all the wisdom we can borrow from the natural and human sciences that illuminate human bodiliness."[19]

At this point, it is beneficial to pause briefly to clarify Kelsey's engagement with non-theological dialogue partners such as the natural sciences. Kelsey's desire to be hospitable to the MSIH and the natural sciences appears in contradiction to his postliberal approach of offering proposals from the stance of Christian particularism. That is to say, according to Kelsey, *EE* is first and foremost concerned with how its proposals function within the Christian community, not external epistemological endeavors. Yet he makes allowance for his proposals to be of interest to "those people who are for any reason interested in what Christians propose as answers to anthropological questions" (3; cf. 7). Here Kelsey is following a typical postliberal methodology of engaging with external dialogue partners on an *ad hoc* basis. Postliberals contend that the attempt to systematically demonstrate the meaningfulness of Christianity to non-Christian dialogue partners is misplaced, even "self-defeating,"[20] unless it is done in an *ad hoc* fashion. In the words of Mark Wallace, the postliberal

> borrows from other disciplines concepts and expressions for articulating the unique witness of the church.... This process of borrowing, then, is thoroughly specific to the concrete situations in which Christian witnesses needs intelligible and defensible explanation; in turn, it seeks to avoid the temptation to allow the other disciplines to control materially, rather than aid formally, the exposition of theology's subject matter.[21]

---

17. Kelsey, "Spiritual Machines," 6–7.
18. Kelsey, "Spiritual Machines," 6.
19. Kelsey, "Spiritual Machines," 7.
20. Frei, *Identity of Jesus Christ*, xii; Michener, *Postliberal Theology*, 104.
21. Wallace, *Second Naiveté*, 95–96. In this regard, Lindbeck has noted the isolation

Yet Wallace immediately goes on to say that: "Understandably, this temptation is difficult to avoid."[22] Indeed, postliberal theology is quick to point out "how extratheological conceptualities have often functioned as Trojan horses in the camp of the church."[23] Indeed, there are dangers associated with Kelsey's urge to make theological anthropology hospitable to the MSIH by despoiling the knowledge natural and human sciences have to offer. In the words of Russell Aldwinckle, the 'wisdom' of the human sciences "of necessity can admit only body and never more than body."[24] There is support for Aldwinckle's claim. Consider for example the Nobel Prize-winning scientist Francis Crick's "astonishing hypothesis"[25] that the human being is "in fact no more than the behaviour of a vast assembly of nerve cells and their associated molecules."[26] Such material reductionism argues that belief in a non-physical reality is a myth that experimental evidence has begun to, and will continue to, eradicate.[27]

Some of the consequences of material reductionism are startling. Richard Dawkins, for example, in his work *The Extended Phenotype: The Gene as the Unit of Selection* (1982),[28] argues for the notion of a "skinless organism" (248).[29] Dawkins contends that although zoology usually considers the organism the basic unit, it is the gene-replicator (the optimon)

---

of theology from other intellectual discourse as tending "to ghettoize theology and deprives it of the vitality that comes from close association with the best in nontheolgoical thinking" (Lindbeck, *Nature of Doctrine*, 25). However, Lindbeck goes on to argue that engagement with nontheolgoical thinking is best done on an *ad hoc* basis. See Lindbeck, *Nature of Doctrine*, 128–34. For more on the *ad hoc* nature of postliberalism, see Michener, *Postliberal Theology*, 104–7; van den Toren, *Christian Apologetics*, 51–56; Wallace, *Second Naiveté*, 89–96. It has not gone unnoticed that such *ad hoc* apologetics presuppose some form of commensurability between the Christian community and non-Christian dialogue partners. See Crane, "Postliberals"; Michener, *Postliberal Theology*, 107–8; van den Toren, *Christian Apologetics*, 51–53.

22. Wallace, *Second Naiveté*, 96.
23. Wallace, *Second Naiveté*, 96.
24. Aldwinckle, *Death in the Secular City*, 68.
25. Crick, *Astonishing Hypothesis*, 3.
26. Crick, *Astonishing Hypothesis*, 3.
27. Crick, *Astonishing Hypothesis*, 3–11. Crick does support the emergence theory as long as it is firmly based in materialism. It should also be noted that Crick is aware of the limitations of the reductionist approach, the possibility of the veracity of traditional dualistic approaches and the prospect that he may be "deceiving" himself. Yet he nevertheless is adamant that some prejudice is necessary and only scientific research, not philosophy or theology, is the grounds for anthropology. Crick, *Astonishing Hypothesis*, 3–11 (cf. 262–63).
28. Dawkins, *Extended Phenotype*.
29. See also Schloss, "From Evolution to Eschatology," 64–66.

that is the basic unit of life instead. The organism is simply a vehicle used to transport the optimon. Some vehicles are better suited than others to ensuring the survival of their replicator genes and as such are selected above others. It is our genes, not the human body, that are the basic fundamental unit of life. The body, as a vehicle, is only there to transport these replicator genes, which are simply using the human being as a tool for their own survival and reproduction.[30] Dawkins imagines a pair of glasses that show only the replicator genes. Using these glasses, he sees a world in which replicator genes glow in non-random constellations (human bodies) separated by vast cavernous space: "A million billion pinpricks move in unison with each other."[31]

In the latter chapters of his book, Dawkins expounds on some of the implications of his theory. Extending the phenotypical effect of the gene beyond the human body, he argues for the 'skinless' organism. Not only do genes affect the body in which they are transported, but the gene's phenotype reaches "unimpeded through individual body walls as though those walls were transparent, interacting with the world and with each other without regard to organismal boundaries."[32] As an example he contends that in forcing a robin to feed a cuckoo chick, the replicator genes transported in the cuckoo manipulate the robin, turning the robin into a tool for their own survival and transmission. As such, it is the robin that becomes part of the phenotypical effects of the replicator genes carried in the cuckoo. In simple terms, the robin is as much part of the same organism as the cuckoo.[33]

The consequence of Dawkins's reductionism is the elimination of human beings themselves. Human beings become nothing more than the vehicle used by replicator genes for transportation and replication. The human being is a clever illusion, a shell whose sole purpose is to transport the optimon. Indeed, the human being may lose all control of their own body and may even become the vehicle (body) for replicator genes residing in another's body. Ultimately, personal identity is distilled to the identity of replicator genes. The human being's identity is stripped of its personhood and subjectivity. Even if it retains some semblance of personal identity, its location is ambiguous and fluid, extending beyond its body to the bodies and environment that are the phenotypical features of replicator genes housed in multiple bodies. Schloss, considering Dawkins's theory, concludes that:

---

30. Dawkins, *Extended Phenotype*, 81–117.
31. Dawkins, *Extended Phenotype*, 250 (cf. 81–117).
32. Dawkins, *Extended Phenotype*, 250.
33. Dawkins, *Extended Phenotype*, 54, 55, 226–27.

> Organismal identity becomes fluid, and there is thus ambiguity over 'whose' body a body is. . . . What the current controversy points to is a relativity, or at the very least an unavoidable ambiguity, in the fundamental biological ontology of the living body or organismal identity.[34]

It may be argued that Dawkins's far-reaching extended phenotypical conclusions are an extreme consequence of material reductionism. If one does not hold to such an extreme conclusion, MSIH's emphasis on human embodiment may not be detrimental to personal identity, at least as far as pre-mortem personal identity is understood. As already noted, we are unfamiliar with non-embodied pre-mortem persons.[35] In describing human beings, it is possible to argue that one need only identify the physical distinctive features of this subset of living bodies that sets it apart from other living bodies. At first, this appears to be a relatively simple process.

One could, for example, use a distinctive set of DNA as the marker of human embodiment. Indeed, Kelsey's reference to *human* in *living human body* is just such a reference. In answering the question: to whom/what theological anthropological proposals refer, Kelsey seeks an identification marker that is anthropologically universally present. Considering other candidates such as 'rational animal,' 'conscious being' or 'language user,' Kelsey argues that these identifiers are not universally present in every human being. According to Kelsey, there is only one viable candidate and therefore, within *EE*, distinctive DNA is the "marker by which to identify to whom theological anthropological claims refer" (258).

It is important to understand Kelsey clearly on this point. Kelsey's inclusion of *human* in a description of human beings does not create a circular referential. The necessity for using the term *human* arises from the possibility that other entities may be described using the same terms used in Kelsey's anthropological formula. For example, it is possible to claim that artificially intelligent robots, extra-terrestrial aliens or angels have basic unsubstitutable personal identities. However, Kelsey argues that the fact that his claims apply to other beings does not say anything specifically within the locus of theological anthropology *per se*.[36] Rather, Kelsey states that when he makes theological anthropological claims, those claims are made about beings who share a distinctive set of DNA.

34. Schloss, "From Evolution to Eschatology," 65.

35. Of course, there are debates as to whether or not God is such a person. For an overview of these debates, see Emmet, "Could God Be a Person?"; Harrison, "Embodiment of Mind," 54–55; Penelhum, *Survival and Disembodied Existence*, 103–8; Swinburne, *Coherence of Theism*, 99–124.

36. For more see Kelsey, *Eccentric Existence*, 252–59; "Personal Bodies," 155.

Kelsey applies this marker directly to the concept of human embodiment: "A given living body either has human DNA and counts as a human living body or it does not" (261). Although Kelsey would like us to believe that the point is as simple as he puts it, one is not immediately convinced. First, the mathematical extrapolation of DNA distinctions is hardly straightforward. For example, Katherine Pollard's research has demonstrated that human beings share 99 percent of their DNA with chimpanzees. Of the remaining 1 percent, or 15 million letters, only a small portion, known as High Acceleration Regions, are responsible for the major distinctions.[37] In other words, only a tiny proportion of our DNA is distinctive. Yet even this tiny proportion may not be universally present in all human beings. There are genetic illnesses which affect DNA in these High Acceleration Regions. Is Kelsey saying that the entire distinctive set of DNA is to be present? Or, in light of specifically human genetic illnesses, is he saying that a proportion of this distinctive DNA is to be present? In which case, what proportion, or perhaps which genes, are necessary?

Furthermore, considering progressions in the field of genetic manipulation in the last few decades, it is conceivable that eventually we may be able to modify chimpanzee DNA so that it includes this tiny proportion of DNA that is distinctive to the human being. Were we to do this, would Kelsey contend that the remarks made in *EE* would refer to this particular *living body*, a living body that was not born (actually) a *human living body* but now has distinctive DNA? These questions are left unexplored by Kelsey, and it is for this reason that one is left questioning both his reliance on distinctive DNA as the categorical marker of humanity and his concern that "theological claims about the body are coherent with understandings of the human body warranted by the life and human sciences for which it is the central subject of research."[38]

Considering all this, one wonders if Kelsey has completely avoided the temptation to allow his non-Christian dialogue partners to control his theological proposals. In light of scientific conclusions such as those of Dawkins and Crick, is the drive to make theological anthropology hospitable to the MSIH not fraught with devastating results? Is it perhaps more prudent to turn the question around and ask if natural sciences are coherent with understandings of humanity gleaned not only from theology but from other epistemological endeavors such as philosophy? After all, the search for an understanding of humanity is, contrary to Crick's insistence, not the sole

---

37. Pollard, "What Makes Us Human?" See also Huyssteen van, "When Were We Persons?," 330–31.
38. Kelsey, "Human Creature," 128.

prerogative of experimental science.³⁹ Let us turn now to just such a non-experimental epistemological endeavor: philosophical theology.

The Challenge to Human Embodiment: Resurrected Persons

Although natural and life sciences are almost[40] entirely concerned with pre-mortem human beings, the notion of life after death throws a spanner in the works. Not only is this one of the central tenets of the Christian faith, but belief in a post-mortem existence has been, and continues to be, a central part of the vast majority of human beings.[41] It is no wonder, therefore, that it is on this point that the major battles in the debate surrounding human embodiment are pitched, fought, won and lost. Considering the third strand in Kelsey's triple helix construction, eschatological consummation, it is only natural that Kelsey's discussions on human embodiment take place within the context of questions about post-mortem life and particularly question of the continuity of the pre- and post-Easter Jesus.[42] Before discussing his views, it is important that we clarify exactly the problems associated with human embodiment in the context of life after death.

Post-mortem life raises a number of questions about human embodiment, two of which are important for our purposes here: Does it involve a physical, embodied resurrection? If it is not physical, how do we identify the post-mortem being with the pre-mortem being? To answer these questions let us consider the two broad opposing views about survival after death: 1) embodied resurrection and 2) disembodied resurrection. Terence Penelhum has argued that these two positions are so powerful that it is impossible to consider the personal continuity of pre- and post-mortem identities without picking one or the other.[43]

---

39. Crick, *Astonishing Hypothesis*, 262–63.

40. We say 'almost' here because there is evidence of limited interest in post-mortem continuation. See footnote 4 of this chapter.

41. Lewis, *Self and Immortality*, 141; Penelhum, *Survival and Disembodied Existence*, 2.

42. Kelsey, *Eccentric Existence*, 35–39, 248–50, 543–49, 947–51, 1016–23.

43. Penelhum, *Survival and Disembodied Existence*, 13–14. Penelhum comes down firmly on the side of physical continuity.

Embodied Resurrection

The central concern in post-mortem existence is that of continuity. How would one claim that the pre-mortem being is the same as the post-mortem being? A belief in a bodily resurrection can solve this problem. In the words of Penelhum, "One can wonder whether beings without bodies can intelligibly be said to remain identical through time in their disembodied state. And one can wonder whether they can be identified with pre-mortem, embodied, persons."[44] Perhaps it is for this reason that belief in a bodily resurrection has been a central Christian teaching for centuries.[45] Hundreds of millions of Christians around the world, reciting the Apostles' Creed, proclaim their belief in 'the resurrection of the body.' What exactly that means is still open to debate. If it is the exact same body that continues post-mortem, then the issue of the continuation of personal identity is easily resolved. Yet common sense strongly suggests that it cannot be the exact same body. Not only does the body radically change throughout pre-mortem life, but bodily decay usually follows bodily death. More than this, there is good reason to speculate that the eschatological ecology is radically different from ecologies we are familiar with.[46] A body made for one ecology would struggle to survive in the other. Walker Bynum is, therefore, right to highlight the paradox of a body that is demolished, dismembered and dissolved, only to be raised again, transformed, glorified and yet be identified as the same personal identity throughout.[47]

The questions as to how to solve the obvious problems of bodily decay or redundant bodily elements (such as genitals or teeth) has been widely debated. From the first century (epitomized in 1 Cor 15) (947–51), through the early church fathers, the Middle Ages[48] and right up to the present, myriad

---

44. Penelhum, *Survival and Disembodied Existence*, 13.

45. Zizioulas, "Human Capacity and Human Incapacity," 423.

46. We recognize that there are grounds to argue for similarity between the two ecologies. After all, Jesus has a body that one can touch (John 20:17). However, it is here argued that the case for dissimilarity is greater. Jesus is able to vanish without trace (Luke 24:31) and pass through walls (John 20:19). Indeed, the picture of a 'new order' (2 Pet 3:10, Rev 21:1) indicates a distinctly different reality than the one with which we are acquainted. The biblical narratives talk about the eschaton as a radical transformation. For example, death is no more (Isa 25:8, 1 Cor 15:53, Rev 21:4), there is no hunger or thirst (Rev 7:16), no need for predation (Isa 11:6) and no decay (Rom 8:21). Whatever physicality remains in heaven it is here argued that it must be an entirely different physicality than the one with which we are familiar.

47. Walker Bynum, *Resurrection of the Body*, 40–43.

48. For an overview of the history of the resurrection of the body in Western Christianity from 200 to 336, see Walker Bynum, *Resurrection of the Body*.

conjectures have been put forward. Considering the challenges alluded to directly above, some have argued for a nuanced version of bodily resurrection. Dahl and Wiener,[49] for example, argue for a 'somatically identical' bodily resurrection, which does not entail materially identical bodies. They argue that one should think of the body not as one thinks of the body of a stone, but of a flame.[50] It is constantly in fluctuation: "'Somatic identity' describes that continuous bodily identity which we recognize our friends as possessing, despite the fact that their constituent parts are in a continuous state of flux."[51] It may be argued that this resonates with Aquinas's position. Aquinas argued that the precise particle formation of the body is its accident and not its substance, which is restored at the resurrection. In Aquinas's view, the identity of the body is "specific, not numerical."[52] The nuanced approaches of such theologians as Dahl, Wiener, and Aquinas make it coherent to consider a post-mortem material body that is not necessarily numerically identical with the pre-mortem body. In Paul Badham's words:

49. Dahl and Wiener in Badham, *Christian Beliefs*, 65–67; Hick, *Death and Eternal Life*, 281–83.
50. A similar notion may be deduced from Harrison's distinction between standard and non-standard bodies. See Harrison, "Embodiment of Mind," 43.
51. Badham, *Christian Beliefs*, 66. One may draw to mind Scotus's notion of Haecceity from *Ordinatio* in Scotus, *Early Oxford Lecture*.
52. Aquinas, *ST* 1.79.1–2; cf. Badham, *Christian Beliefs*, 66. Here Aquinas differs slightly from his understanding of angels as non-corporeal beings without a material body. Although one may contend that Aquinas thought of angels as having a body, this is only a comparable body: "the incorporeal substances are midway between God and corporeal things, and the point midway between extremes appears extreme with respect to either; the tepid, compared with the hot, seems cold. Hence angels might be called material and bodily as compared with God, without implying that they are so intrinsically." Aquinas, *ST* 1.50.1.1. It is possible to argue that Aquinas sees this comparable body as some form of 'body' in that angels exist in a composition of both potency and actuality—as opposed to God who is pure actuality—and as such they may assume bodies for humans' sake (Aquinas, *ST* 1.51.2), have location and locomotion (Aquinas, *ST* 1.51–52) and gain knowledge (Aquinas, *ST* 1.54). However, there is much in Aquinas to contend with this reading, not least of which is his insistence that body is not an essential part to being (Aquinas, *ST* 1.51.1). Moreover, he understands that angels are intellectual beings and "intellection cannot be the act of a body or of bodily energies" and later "the activity of understanding is wholly non-material" and further still "every intellectual being is wholly non-material" (Aquinas, *ST* 1.50.1–2). Although it is true that Aquinas considers human beings intellectual beings, he contends that they are inferior intellectual beings to angels, and it is for this reason that human beings require a body: "So it is with the human soul: its natural aptitude for union with a body is due to its low degree of intellectuality, to the fact that as intellect it begins in a state of potency, not possessing by nature all the knowledge of which it is capable" (Aquinas, *ST* 1.51.1). Furthermore, Aquinas contends that angels are composed of only form and not matter: They subsist in form without any matter (Aquinas, *ST* 1.50.2.3) and therefore do not have any material body (Aquinas, *ST* 1.50.2). For more, see Aquinas, *ST* 1.50–64.

> If God were to create a 'replica' of a dead person, then as long as this divinely created 'replica' possessed the same 'somatic' identity (Dahl), or the same 'seminal principle or form' (Origen), or the same 'substance' (in Aquinas's use of the word), or the same 'organizing principle' (Ramsey), or the same 'code' (Wiener), it would be the same person though possessing no material continuity with the deceased.[53]

However, these theories of embodied resurrection are not without challenges themselves. Concepts such as 'form,' 'organizing principle' or 'code,' while rooted in—or emergent from—material realities are not physical themselves. It may, therefore, be argued that such theories, in their appeal to non-physical attributes, are similar to past body-soul dualistic approaches.

Furthermore, the question of continuity in such theories is highly problematic. Penelhum summarizes the problem eloquently:

> If resurrected persons have bodies like ours, there seems to be no great difficulty in . . . understanding how they can retain their personal identity in the future state. These questions only became seriously difficult if the proponents of the doctrine of resurrection put inordinate weight upon the extent to which the resurrected person exists in a *transformed* state radically unlike this present one. The greater the transformation, the greater the difficulty of understanding the description of this state.[54]

Considering the core notions of eschatological consummation—that is, of radical transformation, or a change to a 'new order'—surely we must acknowledge a substantial transformation? Not only is this warranted, as we have seen, by the notion that the eschatological reality is radically different from our present reality, but philosophically and scientifically in the claim that such a reality is beyond the spatiotemporal realm with which we are acquainted. If there is no time or space, how can there be a body that is anything like the one we currently possess?

Clearly the notion of embodied resurrection has much explaining to do as far as the question of eschatological continuation of personal identity is concerned, but does the appeal to a disembodied resurrection fare any better?

---

53. Badham, *Christian Beliefs*, 67.
54. Penelhum, *Survival and Disembodied Existence*, 12–13 (cf. 93–102).

Disembodied Resurrection

Considering the problems associated with personal identity and embodiment, is it even possible to be a disembodied person? Many have considered the possibility of disembodied personhood.[55] Some, for example, have argued that one can appeal to the perseveration and continuity of a set of psychological characteristics, most notably memory, as the basis of continued identity.[56] Hume, for example, argues that "personal identity is a matter of similarity of memory and character."[57] If a post-mortem being remembers existing in a pre-mortem state and has all the associated memories of that state, would we not claim that these two beings are one and the same?

Yet an appeal to memory, or psychological characteristics, has its challenges, not least of which is that modern neuroscience—based on an enormous amount of empirical data—argues that psychological characteristics are fundamentally dependent on the physical brain.[58] More than this, memory—and with it character—are inherently fickle. Not only is it common for people to lose their memory (either partially or fully), or for someone to remember past experiences incorrectly, but in some cases memories may be passed on to others who then absorb them as their own. For example, when a parent tells a historical story to a child, the child may reflect or dream about these stories, often absorbing parts of them into their own memory bank as if they were their own memories.[59]

Furthermore, the test for the accuracy of such memories is available only through bodily identification. To say that someone remembers a past event is to say that they have special knowledge of that event only available to one who was physically present. Considering all this, Penelhum concludes that "an intelligible account of the identity of a disembodied person in terms of memory alone is doomed to failure."[60]

If memory or personal characteristics are unable to solve the continuity question, does this mean that a disembodied personal resurrection is impossible?

---

55. See, as examples, Harrison, "Embodiment of Mind"; Swinburne, "Structure of the Soul"; cf. Swinburne, *Coherence of Theism*; Emmet, "Could God Be a Person?"

56. See Harrison, "Embodiment of Mind," 48–51; Lewis, *Self and Immortality*, 71–92; Linke, "God Gives the Memory," 185; Swinburne, *Coherence of Theism*, 109–25.

57. Hume quoted in Swinburne, *Coherence of Theism*, 111.

58. Linke, "God Gives the Memory." See also Crick, *Astonishing Hypothesis*, 6–7.

59. Penelhum, *Survival and Disembodied Existence*, 54–67.

60. Penelhum, *Survival and Disembodied Existence*, 67. See also Penelhum, *Survival and Disembodied Existence*, 54–67.

Consider the existence of God. Does this being's existence not suggest the possibility of a disembodied existence? After all, as Richard Swinburne notes: "That God is a person, yet one without a body, seems the most elementary claim of theism."[61] Yet an appeal to God as a disembodied person does not solve the problem of continuity and identification. Penelhum argues that without a spatiotemporal reference point, one is unable to distinguish between different disembodied persons.[62] His conclusion is that either there are no disembodied persons or there is only one such being who is self-referent.[63] If Penelhum's arguments are correct, then the notion that God is a disembodied personal identity does not entail that other disembodied personal identities exist. On the contrary, it may well prove that others are impossible.

Setting all this aside, most problematic of all is the implied dualism entailed in a disembodied state. Jonathan Harrison,[64] for example, considers these implications in his thought experiment. He begins by establishing embodiment on the personal experience of an object (body) in five ways: 1) sensations such as pain, 2) a vestibular sense of bodily orientation,[65] 3) the ability to move itself in a primary sense, 4) the vantage point from which to observe the world and 5) experiencing the effects of stimuli on the body. Through his thought experiment, he argues that it is possible to have one or more of these experiences in relation to more than one object (body). Reflecting on his thought experiment he concludes:

> That people may change from having one body at one time to having a numerically different body at a later time; that two people may have the same body; that one person may have more than one body at the same time; and that people may have different kinds of body from the kind we and the people we know have.[66]

Swinburne's discussions, based on Harrison, contend that a person may not experience all five of Harrison's requirements for embodiment either at the same time or to the same degree. The repercussion is that embodiment is an attribute that admits degrees. One may be more or less embodied. For example, if one loses some of one's senses, they would be embodied only in four of the five ways. Such a person would be a partially embodied personal

---

61. Swinburne, *Coherence of Theism*, 99.
62. Penelhum, *Survival and Disembodied Existence*, 108.
63. Penelhum, *Survival and Disembodied Existence*, 108.
64. Harrison, "Embodiment of Mind."
65. Harrison does not use this word but it is what he is referring to in his second requirement for embodiment.
66. Harrison, "Embodiment of Mind," 36.

identity.⁶⁷ When both Swinburne and Harrison consider that God is immediately aware of the material universe and is able to move it in a primary sense, they come to the same conclusion: "though it may be possible that there should be persons who not only do not have bodies, but are not embodied in any way whatsoever, God is not one of these."⁶⁸ In other words, God is an embodied person and the universe is that body. Although many have argued for the embodiment of God—most notably in the debates surrounding the *Logos asarkos/ensarkos*—Swinburne and Harrison's arguments come dangerously close to pantheism.⁶⁹

If the human being, as Harrison theorizes, can have one body, no body or many bodies at the same time, is Harrison not allowing for the possibility of an omnipresent human body? Let us explain further. Harrison's thought experiment sees his disembodied spirit transition through a number of states, ultimately ending with him as a disembodied spirit haunting a philosopher's house. A question that can be raised is as follows: Without a body, why is it that he is left hunting a particular house at a particular time? What constrains his non-physical personal identity to a spatiotemporal location? Surely being purely non-physical breaches all the confines of a material spatiotemporal body? Is it not more plausible to argue that it cannot be located at all? After all, is location not just a measure of chronological and geographical relativity? Postulating a being without a body is to postulate an ever-present, or perhaps ever-absent, being. If such a being cannot be located either geographically, chronologically or characteristically, how can the continuation question be answered?⁷⁰

Herein lies the problem: both an embodied and disembodied resurrection cannot stand as the final solution to the continuity question. Embodied resurrection either implies the numeric continuity of the material body—which has been shown to be difficult to conceive—or a radical transformation by which some non-physical attribute is responsible for the continuation of personal identity. The latter option tends toward non-physical continuity entailed in notions such as 'form,' 'organization,' etc., thereby creating a duality that historically has been negative. Such negative dualism can result not only

---

67. Swinburne, *Coherence of Theism*, 102–4; cf. Rudman's discussion of Swinburne's position in Rudman, *Concepts of Persons*, 145–51.

68. Harrison, "Embodiment of Mind," 55; cf. Swinburne, *Coherence of Theism*, 103–4.

69. Rudman, *Concepts of Persons*, 147–48.

70. It is possible here to appeal to Aquinas's discussion on the locomotion of angels, in which he argues that non-embodied angels do indeed move between locations. See Aquinas, *ST* 1.53. However, his understanding of angels as purely intellectual beings differs quite substantially from the MSIH of intellectual beings. See Aquinas, *ST* 1.50.1.

in the devaluation of the material body but the possibility of a human being having one body, no body or many bodies at the same time.

A Third Proposal

It is against these searching questions that we must read Kelsey's notion of *living human body*. In *EE* and his wider work, Kelsey considers two attempts to solve the problem with resurrected bodies highlighted directly above. With regard to the problems associated with physical resurrection, he considers Nancy Murphy's theory of "nonreductive physicalism" (541).[71] Murphy wrestles with modern scientific discoveries, particularly in neuroscience, that establish the material basis of human being. Materialism sometimes leads to a form of ontological reductionism: the belief that higher-level entities can be explained entirely in terms of lower-level units. In other words, higher-level entities are reducible to the sum of their lower-level parts. The consequence of such reductionism is the belief that only lower-level entities are *real*, and all higher-level entities are nothing more than the composites of sub-atomic particles. As we have noted, Dawkins uses this form of reductionism. Against reductionism, Murphy argues for 'nonreductive physicalism;' the notion that organisms and wholes are genuinely significant and not simply aggregates of elementary particles.[72]

Kelsey argues that Murphy poses a "maxim [that] must be honoured: no physical brain and nervous-system processes, no mental acts, events, or processes" (541; cf. 1021), or as Kelsey elsewhere rephrases it, "no brain, never mind" (1021). Murphy's particular take on the emergence theory is used by Kelsey to argue that what the human being is, while not reducible to physicalism, must be rooted in it. Thus, Kelsey's inclusion of *living human body* indicates that "all human capacities and powers are in some way rooted in human bodies."[73] Elsewhere, he claims: "'Mind' has its own 'reality' distinct from, but not separable from, the brain."[74]

On the other hand, Kelsey is also very much aware of John Cooper's challenge posed by resurrected bodies.[75] In his work *Body, Soul and Life Everlasting* (1989), Cooper considers, from a biblical point of view, the

71. Kelsey, "Human Creature," 128; "Spiritual Machines," 7; Murphy, "Nonreductive Physicalism," 127–48.

72. Murphy, "Nonreductive Physicalism," 131. It is interesting to note that Cooper uses Murphy to support a dualistic view. See Cooper, *Body, Soul, and Life Everlasting*, xxvi.

73. Kelsey, "Spiritual Machines," 7.

74. Kelsey, "Human Creature," 128.

75. Kelsey, "Human Creature," 128.

monism-dualism debate. Although Cooper affirms the resurrection of the body, he argues that there are three possible options to conceive of this resurrection: first, that one is immediately bodily resurrected upon death; second, that there is a period of non-existence (Extinction-Re-creation theory); and third, that there is an intermediate state of non-bodily existence between death and resurrection. Cooper's in-depth analysis of the biblical narratives forces him to reject the first two options.[76] He argues that the biblical narratives speak of a single and general resurrection in which all are included and that there are texts that talk of the existence of the dead prior to this general resurrection. Thus, Cooper concludes that there must be an intermediate state between death and bodily resurrection in which the human being exists without a body.[77] Cooper is aware of the practical, scientific, theological and philosophical objections to pure dualism.[78] He also argues that the biblical picture portrays a "psychosomatic unity"[79] of the human being. The only viable option, according to Cooper, is a form of "holistic dualism,"[80] which argues for the constitution of the human being to be such that it affirms the psychosomatic unity of the human being and simultaneously allows for "enough of a duality in human nature so that God can sustain Moses, Paul and my mother in fellowship with him even though they are currently without their earthly bodies."[81]

Kelsey affirms that Cooper's challenge to anthropology to include a conceptual resource to explain human continuity beyond death is "obviously important."[82] He proceeds to say that "its near absence in theologian's debates about the 'emergence' thesis raises a major issue for that approach."[83] Yet he is not convinced that Cooper's holistic dualism is developed enough to engage effectively with the anthropological implications of life sciences.[84]

Having considered Murphy and Cooper earlier in his project, in *EE*'s second Coda Kelsey contends for an alternate proposal to either physicalism or dualism, one that he argues is hospitable to both the MSIH and

---

76. Cooper, *Body, Soul, and Life Everlasting*, 110–57.

77. Cooper is not unique in his contention for an intermediary state. Indeed, Calvin defended this position quite fervently. See Calvin, "Psychopannychia."

78. Cooper, *Body, Soul, and Life Everlasting*, chaps. 6–10.

79. Cooper, *Body, Soul, and Life Everlasting*, 91; cf. chap 2, 3, 4.

80. Cooper, *Body, Soul, and Life Everlasting*, xxvii–xxviii.

81. Cooper, *Body, Soul, and Life Everlasting*, xvi.

82. Kelsey, "Human Creature," 128.

83. Kelsey, "Human Creature," 128.

84. Kelsey, "Human Creature," 128. Indeed there is reason to argue that Cooper's 'holistic dualism' is simply a reformulated pure dualism. See Cooper, *Body, Soul, and Life Everlasting*, xxvii–xxviii.

the biblical witness (922–1007). To support this proposal, he utilizes a particular reading of Paul's reference to 'spiritual' and 'physical' bodies in 1 Corinthians 15 (947–51). In this text, Paul defends the centrality of resurrection for both Jesus and the Christian faith. Kelsey's particular interpretation of this text concludes that in answering the question: 'What type of body do resurrected Christians have?' Paul references different types of 'human bodies': physical and spiritual. Yet Kelsey reads Paul as stating that both are specifically human bodies and not qualifiers or identifiers of different kinds of body. Rather, "these are two modes of *living human body*: quotidian and glorified" (1018).[85]

Kelsey uses this particular interpretation of Paul so as to argue that one needs to talk about *living body* in a manner that covers both quotidian and glorified bodies. In other words, if one wants to answer the continuity question, one must be able to speak about living bodies in ways that are applicable to both pre- and post-mortem living human bodies. The only way to accomplish this, according to Kelsey, is to find a common denominator between these two states. He argues that it is possible to identify this common denominator by removing

> from the concept of a living human body those properties that make it impossible for a body in the quotidian mode to do what a body in the glorified mode may coherently be said to do, on the grounds that they are not properties that are essential to bodily life as such. (1019–20)

To identify what is 'essential to bodily life' Kelsey turns to Jeffery Schloss (248–50; cf. 1020). Since this is so important to Kelsey's concept of *living human body*, let us pause to consider Schloss's argument.

Schloss's article "From Evolution to Eschatology" (2002), considers the questions raised by science in light of Christianity's doctrine of the resurrection. Schloss argues that if we believe God has given life to mortal bodies not just as machinery for the soul, then it is pertinent to address the question of those living human bodies. Having considered Dawkins's notion of skinless organisms,[86] Schloss demonstrates that the Darwinian account of humanity still proposes a form of dualism. Rather than a body-soul dualism, Schloss deduces a genotype-phenotype or germline-soma dualism.[87] The reasons

---

85. There are issues with Kelsey's interpretation of Paul that we will not explore further. Paul's discussion in 1 Cor 15 is complex, compounded by the context of a growing Gnostic heresy that ultimately led the church against the background of the Marcion controversies to affirm physical resurrection in the early creeds.
86. Schloss, "From Evolution to Eschatology," 64–66.
87. Schloss, "From Evolution to Eschatology," 66.

behind these dualisms are linear, one-sided notions of either materialism or dualism. In dualism, it is the soul that impacts the body, while in materialism it is the genome/replicator gene that impacts the body/organism. Very little allowance is made for the reverse relationship. To counter this linear tendency, Schloss argues for a relationally conceived notion of biology. Contrary to material reductionism, which seeks to keep the matter while throwing away the organization (organism), relational biology keeps the organization, treating it as a *thing* in itself. Using such a relational biology, Schloss argues that living organisms are relationally open at two ends as they seek out information and energy that is used to resist decay.

This openness is circular: "the possession of one being instrumental to the acquisition of the other."[88] The attainment of knowledge is used to gain energy, which is then used to obtain further knowledge and so on and so forth. In asserting itself against the non-organic world, a living organism maintains its structural integrity against entropic deterioration, "and it is both this process [seeking information and energy], and this structural organization itself, which may be viewed as the essence of life."[89]

Schloss contends that the upshot of this view is twofold. First, it rehabilitates the concept of a living soul, not in a dualistic way, but in the Aristotelian sense of a functional *telos*: form being substance. The consequence is that the means to retain homeostasis becomes the end in itself. As one may achieve this end/means to a greater or lesser extent, "livingness may be understood to admit itself in degrees."[90] Second, the body—being not only the means to obtain the end (homeostasis)—becomes part of the end itself: "it is the singular manifestation of it."[91] At death, the material matter is exchanged, yet the form/organization of the organism (the process of information and energy obtainment for the purpose of resisting entropic forces)—the resurrected body—is retained in post-mortem existence.

There are a number of implications of Schloss's account. First, there are no physiological or thermodynamic reasons why death must occur. Schloss notes that there are creatures that do not grow old and die (bristlecone pine, for example, can be 5,000 years old).[92] The necessity of death, according to Schloss, is an adaptation built into an organism "enhancing

---

88. Lorenz quoted in Schloss, "From Evolution to Eschatology," 67; cf. Kelsey, *Eccentric Existence*, 248–49.

89. Schloss, "From Evolution to Eschatology," 67.

90. Schloss, "From Evolution to Eschatology," 68; cf. Kelsey, *Eccentric Existence*, 249.

91. Schloss, "From Evolution to Eschatology," 69.

92. Schloss, "From Evolution to Eschatology," 83.

fitness by 'making room' for progeny."[93] Furthermore, if the eschatological ecology is not conceived of as the same material ecology with which we are familiar, it is conceivable that energy may be obtained without the need for predation. In an ecology that has unlimited resources, neither death nor predation are necessary.[94]

While death itself may not be necessary, Schloss notes that the possibility of it is. Since his definition of living body revolves around entropic forces, the possibility of thermodynamic decay must exist for life to exist. If there is no entropy, there is no need for sets of energy systems to actively maintain homeostasis so as to resist entropic forces.

Second, in Schloss's account one may deduce a "soulish organism,"[95] in the sense that the organism is more than simply the sum of its material parts. It is the dynamic interaction of the organism as it seeks out information in order to obtain energy that it uses to resist entropic forces. This process/organization is a substance in its own right, and it is this substance that one may call the "essence of life"[96] or the "soul."[97]

Schloss's definition of a living body is brought into Kelsey's discussions on the anthropological formula in the first part of his anthropology. Discussing Job's telling of his creation as one who has been born (chapters 6 and 7 of *EE*), Kelsey understands this to partly imply that what God creates in human beings having been born are actual human living bodies (248).[98] To clarify the notion of *living body*, Kelsey relies on Schloss's construction. Kelsey makes "three broad generalizations about the structure and dynamics of every living body that arise from modern life sciences" (248): first, that a living body must be set into an ecology;[99] second, that a living body is a set of energy systems that resists entropic forces; and third, that there are generalizations one can make about death, predation and evolutionary processes for living bodies.[100] In his second generalization a description of

---

93. Schloss, "From Evolution to Eschatology," 83.

94. Schloss, "From Evolution to Eschatology," 83–84; cf. Kelsey, *Eccentric Existence*, 249. To provide biblical support for this view, Schloss and Kelsey both reference biblical pictures (such as Isa 11:6; 65:25) in which the lion lies down with the lamb (Kelsey, *Eccentric Existence*, 1022). See also Schloss, "From Evolution to Eschatology," 57–58.

95. Schloss, "From Evolution to Eschatology," 66–69.

96. Schloss, "From Evolution to Eschatology," 67.

97. Schloss, "From Evolution to Eschatology," 66–71.

98. See chapter 8 of this project.

99. It is here that he references Dawkins's notion of the extended phenotype (Kelsey, *Eccentric Existence*, 248).

100. During this third generalization, Kelsey speaks of the mortality of eschatological

what Kelsey means by *living body* comes to the fore: "Living bodies are self-regulating sets of energy systems that seek to preserve internal homeostasis, a relatively persisting, self-organizing structure that does not dissipate the equilibrium of its various internal energy systems and resists entropy or thermodynamic decay" (248).

The Eschatological Continuity Question

Having clarified what he means by *human living body* relatively early in his project, Kelsey re-introduces the concept in later sections as he considers what he terms the "eschatological continuity question" (560): Can a human being remain what it was created to be and yet be glorified? This is not a question of 'How does God raise the dead?' but of 'What is the raised human being?' (35–39). In eschatological blessing, God transforms personal bodies and their contexts so radically that it is referred to as a new creation (Revelations 21:1–8). Yet, God's blessing also implies a strong continuity:

> If an eschatologically transfigured personal body is simply discontinuous with its pretransfigured distorted condition, then it is difficult to see how it is the same personal body transfigured, in contradistinction to an ontologically altogether distinct personal body. And if it is not strictly speaking the same personal body, it is difficult to see how it is accountable for another personal body's orientations. (560)

Kelsey's model for answering this continuity question is to make use of Jesus as the paradigmatic example of "continuity-in-discontinuity" (543) of resurrected personal bodies (543–49).[101] In particular, he uses Jesus' post-Easter pre-ascension state to clarify what a resurrected body is (543–49; cf. 1016–23). Using the phrase, "It is the material body of the crucified Jesus" (545), Kelsey expands on both the continuity and the radical discontinuity.

When Kelsey speaks of continuity, he emphasizes that the term "needs to be parsed carefully in relation to the use of 'body' in canonical accounts of encounters with the risen Jesus" (544). The post-Easter Jesus is able to abruptly vanish (Luke 24:31), appear in a closed and locked room (John 20:19–20) and be ultimately carried up into heaven (Luke 24:51) (544,

---

beings, stating that even eschatological "life is essentially finite in the sense that it is capable of disintegrating and, absent God's creative relating to it, will disintegrate" (Kelsey, *Eccentric Existence*, 1022). However, God faithfully sustains eschatological life. Therefore, while disintegration may be a potential, it is never an actuality.

101. Kelsey is not alone in this model. See, as examples, Hick, *Death and Eternal Life*, 171–74; Frei, *Identity of Jesus Christ*, 104–6, 174–83.

1018): "These are not movements in space of which physically living bodies are capable" (544). Kelsey therefore argues that there must be some way of speaking of the continuity-in-discontinuity of this Jesus without appealing to the physical matter of his body. To do this, Kelsey notes that "whenever traditional Jews said 'body,' they meant not just the tangible, physical parts but rather the entire person" (544 [quoting Lampe]).[102] Thus, when the narratives speak of *soma* (usually translated as 'body'), Kelsey argues that it is best translated as "actual living human personal body" (544) and not merely 'physical body.' Therefore, while Jesus' identity is continuous, Kelsey goes to great pains to show that the matter, or formed matter that constituted the pre-Easter body, does not continue as one might naturally assume. Affirmation of Jesus' bodily resurrection is affirmation of numerical identity—used here in reference to personal identity—and not necessarily affirmation of physical identity.[103]

Reference to the crucified Jesus highlights the decisive discontinuity. The *living human body* in question was crucified, dead and buried. Yet it is this same body that is now risen and able to do things that no physical body can do (not even its own physical counterpart). On the one hand, it has a tangible feel (Thomas is able to put his hands directly into it), it can eat and drink. On the other hand, it can pass through walls and vanish abruptly. The biblical narratives move back and forth between stressing continuity and discontinuity with the pre- and post-Easter Jesus. This stress is almost always placed on Jesus' body. It is therefore necessary, argues Kelsey, to grasp an "adequately broad concept of 'human body'" (548).

> One conceptual consequence of this analysis is that if 'body' is used in primary and secondary Christian theology as it is in canonical accounts of encounters with the resurrected Jesus to indicate the continuity between the post- and pre-Easter Jesus, it must be explained in a way that can indicate the continuity between the biochemistry with which we are acquainted, but does not make it essential to the concept of a living human body. (545)

As we have noted, Kelsey makes use of Schloss to speak of the body in just such a manner. Jesus' resurrected living human body is not a resuscitated body. The body that was crucified and buried is not just revived (546).

---

102. Cf. Cooper, *Body, Soul, and Life Everlasting*, chaps. 2, 3.

103. It is arguable that Kelsey has not taken seriously the empty tomb, that is, the physically resurrected body. The fact that the tomb is empty indicates that the material body of Jesus of Nazareth is an important part of the resurrected Christ. Much work has been done to emphasize the empty tomb in theology. For a recent example, see Novakovic, *Resurrection*.

Rather, it is a transformed body that is both continuous and discontinuous with the pre-Easter Jesus. It continues to be the same set of energy systems that maintained homeostasis and resisted entropic forces as the pre-Easter body, while not necessarily consisting of the same matter. Since God respects the creaturely integrity of Jesus' humanity, he does not simply ignore the disintegration of the physical body. Rather, consummation should be viewed as a "gift upon gift" (1017); it is grace that does not violate creation. Kelsey argues that "the new creation arises *ex vetere*, as the redeemed transformation of the old creation, and not as a second, totally new, creation *ex nihilo*" (1017 [quoting Polkinghorne]). The continuity is grounded in the self-same God who relates in creative and eschatological blessing, while the discontinuity is grounded in the different narrative logics of creation and eschatological blessing:

> Correlatively, the continuity for Jesus lies in the fact that his living human body remains the self-same creature, radically dependent on God for his being and value, the discontinuity lies in the fact that, as we may put it, he is one living personal body in two different modes of bodiliness: quotidian and glorified. (1017)

Kelsey adds a caveat to his understanding of *living human body*. In regard to the physicality of his construction, he notes that while we are unfamiliar with energy systems that are not integrated into physical energy systems, this does not mean that all energy systems are epiphenomena of physical systems. He contends that "on this account of the organisation and functions of anything that can count as a living body, a physical energy system is not, as such, an essential property of life" (1020). In this regard, he does not follow Murphy's maxim of "no brain, never mind" (541; cf. 1021) and affirms a continuity of identity even in the face of physical decay.[104]

Kelsey does note, however, that speculation as to what exactly it means to be an energy system not rooted in physical biochemistry "invites theologians to invent thought experiments that may sometimes approximate theological science fiction, but more often count as theological science fantasy" (1021).[105] Kelsey argues that it cannot be stressed enough that "what eschatologically fully consummated living human personal bodies are is highly formal. It has no empirical content. Indeed, it is difficult to

---

104. Wood has briefly questioned Kelsey on this point noting that it is possible to have a Christianly understood consummation without experienced survival of the physical death. See Wood, "Response to Eccentric Existence," 28–29.

105. Indeed, it may be argued that Harrison is doing just this. See Harrison, "Embodiment of Mind."

know what would count as empirical content in regard to bodies that are not physical" (553).

Thus, his project cannot "pretend to be informative or to have any explanatory power whatever" (1021) in regard to what non-physical energy systems may comprise. Although not speaking to the question of non-physical energy systems, Kelsey's construction does have implications for the doctrine of the *imago Dei*.

The *Imago Dei* as Non-dualistic Non-materialistic Living Human Body

In his final coda, Kelsey expounds on his understanding of *living human body* for his construction of the *imago Dei*. The second aspect of the answer to the anthropological 'What?' question, according to Kelsey, is that

> Human beings image the image of God simply by living on borrowed time—that is, simply by being drawn (passive tense) to an eschatological consummation that is ultimately actualized in the glorification of their human bodies in the new creation of God's eschatological rule. (1016)

As Jesus images God in different ways in both his pre- and post-Easter body, marked by discontinuities within continuities, human beings—whose bodies are drawn to eschatological consummation—image the image of God. The *living human body* that is eschatologically glorified is the self-same body that, in the pre-mortem state, sought to resist entropic forces albeit, not necessarily the self-same physical matter.

The goal of Kelsey's proposal is to draw human embodiment into the doctrine of the image of God in ways that have not been done before. Here he offers a unique way of speaking about living human bodies in pre- and post-mortem modes without relying on reductive materialism or metaphysical dualism. As we noted in the introduction to this chapter, Kelsey is speculating about what a glorified body may look like, he is offering a conceptual framework within which we can conceive of our future glorified state as human beings and consequently as the image of God. Let us critically reflect on this goal.

First, there is ambiguity regarding the consistency of his non-physicalist description.[106] The most important for our purposes is the role played by

---

106. Kelsey, "Spiritual Machines," 7. For example, his insistence on non-perfected glorified bodies. Kelsey argues that there are no theological grounds for rejecting the claim that glorified bodies continue to have imperfections and disabilities that were constitutive properties of their pre-mortem bodies (Kelsey, *Eccentric Existence*, 540; cf.

human DNA. If post-mortem bodies are non-materialistic energy systems, can we really contend that they continue to retain distinctive human DNA? And if they do not, then by Kelsey's own measure, his anthropological claims cannot be distinguished between claims made about humans and other beings (such as extra-terrestrials or artificially intelligent beings). In other words, without reference to distinctive human DNA, what exactly is anthropological about his anthropological claims? This is a topic we pick up in further detail in the concluding chapter of our project.

Second, contrary to his commitment to avoid negative dualism, it may be argued that Kelsey's construction is far more dualist than he may admit. Kelsey notes that the phrase *living human body*

> expresses the integral 'psycho-somatic unity of human beings.' . . . Since the root of the idea of 'soul' is 'principle of life in a living being,' the word 'living' points to what theories of soul speculate about, without commitment to any particular metaphysical view.[107]

Yet one is unconvinced that he is not committing himself to just such a metaphysical view.[108] Indeed, it may be argued that his construction is a scientifically hospitable dynamic equivalent of doctrines of the soul. His construction is harmonious with other dualistic positions such as Dahl's notion of 'somatic identity,' Aquinas's notion of specific rather than numeric continuity or Origen's theory of the continuity of form rather than matter.[109] All these authors, like Kelsey, distil human embodiment to its most basic notion that can transcend material death. Is a non-physical set of energy systems that resists entropic forces not just the soul by another name?

Kelsey is aware of some of these "loose ends" (562–66), as he calls them. He argues that they are purposely and legitimately left open on the basis that the questions, out of which they arise, are open. Answers to questions such as those raised immediately above are, in his opinion, beyond the scope of his theological anthropology (541, 560–61). Indeed, he argues that in many cases, to answer such questions is to engage in "theological science

---

1019). Yet this appears incompatible with his notion of a non-physical resurrected body or that the body is not the basis of the continuity of personal identity (Kelsey, *Eccentric Existence*, 560–61). The notion of glorified yet disabled seems entirely contradictory, especially if not materially founded. For more, see Kelsey, *Eccentric Existence*, 537–41 (cf. 548–49, 1018–19).

107. Kelsey, "Personal Bodies," 155.

108. Metaphysical here refers to the traditional view of human beings as body and soul/spirit.

109. Badham, *Christian Beliefs*, 65–67.

fantasy" (1021, see also 552–53) and he therefore cautions "a certain pious agnosticism" (541) to further deliberation.

Although we can appreciate Kelsey's recognition of the limits of theological anthropology, it may be argued that what he calls 'theological science fantasy' is a legitimate attempt to provide a conceptual framework within which to conceive of important anthropological questions. Indeed, his description of *living body* is just such an attempt at speculating about human glorified existence. Such speculation is an important part of theology as it enables human beings to coherently conceive of themselves and their context. The speculative aspect (or 'fantasy'—as Kelsey calls it) is not necessarily detrimental to the endeavor as long as humans are aware that their proposals in this regard are attempts (that is, approximations rather than exact representations) at conceiving what is difficult to conceive.

It is not necessary in our discussions here to ensure that our proposals are accurate reflections that stand unchallenged in all contexts. On the contrary, we are exploring Kelsey's speculations to ask if his conjectures can provide a framework to coherently conceive of human beings in both pre- and post-mortem existence. Considering this purpose, it is not an option to leave the questions we have raised above unanswered. The implied possible inconsistencies for his notion of human embodiment are too problematic for our aim here. As such, we have only two options available to us. The first is to simply remove the notion of *living human body* from the anthropological formula altogether. The second is to nuance Kelsey's construction in such a way that it remains faithful to his overall project while avoiding some of these inconsistencies. Considering the importance of human embodiment in both MSIH and theological anthropology, as outlined in the beginning of this chapter, the latter option is the only viable way forward. As such, two modifications are proposed here.

First, let us consider the second and third claim of Kelsey's core theological claims that must be applicable to any answer to the eschatological continuity question (560): "What is continuous is personal identity" (560) and "the eschatologically transformed personal body must be the same 'what' as the creaturely personal body" (560). Recalling our discussions on personal identity in chapter 6 of this project, it is intriguing that Kelsey does not argue for the answer to the eschatological continuity question, in light of personal identity, to be rooted in the continuation of God's personal relation. Such an approach allows one to establish personal continuity without appealing to either a physicalist or non-physicalist dualist foundation while remaining faithful to Kelsey's broader thesis.

Second, although Kelsey has concerns about non-physical dualism, and in particular in answer to the 'What?' question raised directly above, it should be noted that he is not fundamentally opposed to this position. Indeed, he himself claims that proposed answers to the eschatological continuity question "would probably have to rely on additional, probably metaphysical, claims" (561). Kelsey is clear that "*EE* does not claim 'neutrality concerning ontology,' much less a 'metaphysics-free ontology.'"[110] Appeals to a non-physical basis of human continuation can be coherent with *EE* if one is sure to avoid the limitations of 'traditional' body-soul dualism.

Kelsey's objection to 'traditional' body-soul dualism is twofold: First, he objects to "value anthropomorphism" (29–30), and second, non-physical ontologies are often not hospitable to the MSIH.[111] Yet, in the first instance, rejecting a non-physical answer is akin to throwing the baby out with the bath water. Although it is true that in the past some have used non-physical ontologies as the basis for the devaluation of the physical, there is nothing innate in the appeal to non-physical aspects that necessitates such a response. Some contemporary non-physicalists have argued for the value of the material context.[112]

In the second instance, one must not conflate hospitability and the borrowing of concepts from the host culture with uncritical adoption. Kelsey himself insists that we bend borrowed concepts from the MSIH for our theological purposes.[113] Thus, using Kelsey's own argument, our hospitality does not automatically force us to abandon the Christian dualistic heritage. It simply encourages us to wrestle with the problem of physicality and human embodiment.

In light of these modifications, we may argue that human embodiment is an important part of the answer to the questions surrounding the image of God. Yet this does not commit us to materialism or monism. Pre-mortem bodies are entirely rooted in the material, while post-mortem bodies are not necessarily equally limited. There is discontinuity within continuity. Kelsey and Schloss have provided us with a coherent framework in which to conceive of resurrected bodies. Embodiment can be spoken of in terms of self-organizing, self-regulating and self-directing (1020) sets of energy systems that resist entropic forces. Human beings retain embodiment in their glorified state, and yet the continuation of this embodiment does not imply the continuation of the material matter or the continuation of personal identity. The process of obtaining information and energy that enables

---

110. Kelsey, "Response to the Symposium," 78.

111. Kelsey, "Wisdom Theological Anthropology," 44, 51. See also Kelsey, "Human Creature," 128.

112. Cooper's notion of holistic dualism is just one example (Cooper, *Body, Soul, and Life Everlasting*). See also Visala, "Imago Dei," 110–13.

113. Kelsey, "Personal Bodies," 155–56.

a living human body to resist entropic forces is the 'essence of life,' with life understood here as an embodied state.

Using this constructive critical interpretation enables us to draw out some conclusions for the central problem of the project at hand. We can begin by noting that Kelsey's notion of embodiment incorporates both substantive and relational elements. Recall Schloss's argument that a living body is open at two ends (to obtain information and energy) and that the means by which it achieves its goal (resisting thermodynamic decay) becomes the end itself.[114] This definition requires both a substantive and relational understanding of embodiment. First, it has elements of substantive thinking in that the process of maintaining homeostasis requires a feature of the human being that cannot be distilled further. It is a substantive process, that is, a structural part of the being itself. It is part of the very 'essence' of the being, the 'life essence,' one may say. To remove this organismal organization from the human being would be tantamount to destroying the human being.

Such a description addresses the substantive concern for universality. All human beings may be described as sets of energy systems that resist entropic forces, and they may be described as such at every point in their existence. It does not matter at what stage they are in their development—if they are old or young or mentally and physically fit or unwell—or whether they display certain aspects such as rational or moral powers. As such, it is not possible to say that there is a single human being to which this description would not apply.

On the other hand, this process requires relational interaction between the living body and the ecology (which includes other living bodies), and as such it is relational. This relationality is not accidental but fundamental to the organismal organization. Without relational interaction, neither information nor energy may be exchanged and obtained. This interaction is highly dynamic. A living body cannot remain stationary; it must continually seek both information and energy to resist entropic forces. As such, this description of living bodies addresses a key relational concern: that of the dynamic nature of human life. During the course of its life (both pre- and post-mortem) as a living body, the human being is compelled to a dynamic existence. It is compelled to develop, grow, change and work toward maintaining its homeostasis. To be static is to cease to exist. Furthermore, our modification of Kelsey's construction advances relational concerns. In this regard, the eschatological continuity question is a relational question: God continues to personally relate to the post-mortem living body in the same way as He did the pre-mortem living body.

114. Schloss, "From Evolution to Eschatology," 66–69.

Finally, we should note that this description goes to the heart of the problem associated with the substantive-relational debate. In chapter 1 of our project, we noted that (with a few exceptions), on the whole, substantive and relational thinkers do not incorporate human embodiment into their descriptions of human beings as images of God. As a result, we noted that a common limitation in both substantive and relational anthropology is that of negative reductionism that leads to negative dualism and consequently 'value anthropocentricism.' In their attempt to distil the essential nature of human being to a single feature within the human being that distinguishes them from the rest of creation, both relational and substantive thinkers appeal, more often than not, to a non-physical principle that leads to the devaluation of the human body.

Our interpretation of Kelsey, however, does not commit us to identifying a single feature within the human being that distinguishes it from the rest of creation. Kelsey's notion of embodiment is dependent on the organismal organization and obtainment of information and energy, neither of which may be said to comprise a single feature within the human being itself nor distinguish the human being from the rest of creation. Both energy and information are obtained externally, and all living creatures display the same organismal organization. Kelsey is able to speak about human beings, as images of the image of God, in a distinctly unique way: incorporating human embodiment (in both pre- and post-mortem existence) into the very heart of the image of God. This is decidedly different to either substantive or relational thinkers. It offers us a way of speaking about the image of God hitherto unknown.

Conclusion

RECALL HOW WE BEGAN this enquiry: an affirmation that Christian anthropological questions are intertwined with the notion of the *imago Dei*. More often than not, such answers are presented within the context of a counterfeit choice between two mutually exclusive, opposing views: the substantive and relational. The primary concern for substantive thinkers is to establish an aspect within every human being that is universally present. The substantive position argues that all human beings, because they are made in God's image, belong to a single category whose membership imparts unqualified dignity and value. To establish this universality, substantive thinkers contend that all human beings are the image (noun) of God because of an attribute that is inherently present in every single human being. It cannot be removed or destroyed. It is a structural part of humanity.

In contradistinction to the substantive view, relational thinkers are primarily concerned with dynamic relationality. To these theologians, the image of God speaks to a potential within the human being for relationship and, in particular, the relationship between God and human beings. There is no universally present capacity or attribute that is structurally part of the human being as the image of God. Rather, human beings image (verb) God as they develop and grow the relevant relationality.

Both views offer positive contributions to the debate. The substantive concern for universality is a concern for the universal basis of human dignity and value, while the relational view draws our attention to the dynamic nature of human being: a nature that can grow and develop as relationships deepen. Yet, as we have demonstrated in chapter 1, both approaches are vulnerable to common limitations. It is arguable that the reason behind their susceptibility to these limitations lies in their similar approach to the doctrine of the *imago Dei*. Both substantive and relational thinkers appeal to a single or limited set of features residing within the human being that sets it apart from the rest of creation (895). In this common approach, they pose questions that are similarly shaped and, as a consequence, offer comparable answers.

Considering that *EE* is being met with critical acclaim and that it is complex, idiosyncratic and creative, the primary focus of our discussions has been to critically and constructively analyze Kelsey's contribution to the doctrine of the *imago Dei* in light of the substantive-relational debate. Having laid out some of the background context of our central question, including considering Kelsey's postliberal heritage and tracing key 'buoys' for *EE*, we homed in on Kelsey's anthropological formula. This formula, which emerges primarily out of part 1 of *EE* (within the context of the doctrine of creation), is Kelsey's description of human beings in the image of God. It is for this reason that it occupied our interest for the majority of this project. We have spent considerable time on the formulaic sub-terms— *basic and actual*, *personal*, *unsubstitutable*, *actual* and *living body*—ending our respective chapters with observations of how Kelsey's anthropological formula relates to the substantive-relational debate. It is not necessary to rehash these conclusions here. In this discussion we move past these sub-terms to speak of the broader implications of Kelsey's description of humanity and the image of God.

What Is Offered

We have seen that Kelsey's postliberal approach yields interesting and unique perspectives on the notion of the *imago Dei*. His approach to systematic theology, and in particular to theological anthropology, is narratively shaped and guided by a community-orientated, pragmatic epistemology. That is to say, his interest does not lie in definitions, foundational statements or doctrines, which are universally true and valid. He is far more interested in the way 'truth statements' are used within Christian communities in primary and secondary theology. Since *EE* is a project in secondary theology within the Christian community (most notably the Western protestant community), his anthropological proposals do not "assert conversation-stopper pronouncements of what Christians must say on a given topic" (9).

In a very real sense, Kelsey is offering a new way of theologizing. His project is laid out in a unique manner: physically in the shaping of his chapters—making use of A and B chapters (in different fonts), dedicating six chapters to the introduction and providing three extended codas—but also theologically in the manner in which he engages with secondary literature, sparsely referencing his sources and engaging in 'one-sided conversations' (e.g., chapter 4B).[1] As chapter 2 of our project notes, *EE* is an important

---

1. It should be noted that some have critiqued his manner of referencing secondary literature. Indeed, Ford goes so far as to say that Kelsey rarely considers the current

example of postliberal theologizing: uniquely systematically unsystematic.[2] Such an approach, although systematic, moves the conversation away from strict definitions toward descriptions of a community's understanding of the way truth functions within a particular context. In this way, doctrinal statements and anthropological proposals made in *EE* are not to be understood as unqualified definitions of human beings or humanity in general. Rather, Kelsey seeks a description, one of many, that may describe human beings as *imago Dei*. This very subtle shift from definitions to descriptions enables Kelsey to actively question common or 'traditional' approaches to theological anthropology and to offer unique ways of speaking about doctrines such as the doctrine of the *imago Dei* (897–900).

Kelsey's aversion to 'traditional' approaches to anthropology is evident throughout *EE*. An important example of this aversion is Kelsey's approach to the questions surrounding the image of God. Kelsey's project does not follow the approach, which we have argued is taken by both substantive and relational thinkers. Early in *EE*, Kelsey sets out a number of theological *desiderata*, the first of which deals with the very problem outlined above and in chapter 1 of our project. He acknowledges that many anthropologies attempt to answer the question 'What are human beings?' by appealing to a secondary question phrased as "In what ways are human beings like other creatures and in what ways are they distinguished from and superior to all other creatures?" (29; cf. 895). Kelsey argues that this secondary question relies on an "invidious comparison and contrast either with other, allegedly lesser creatures, or between human creatures' 'physical' and 'mental' capacities" (31). He is clear that his anthropology is an attempt to avoid such comparisons and contrasts (31).

During our discussions we have highlighted many of the instances where Kelsey reshapes these secondary questions. For example, in chapter 5 we noted that Kelsey does not ask 'What is personal identity?' but rather "How can one describe the subject of a 'Who?' question?" (334, see also 385–87). A similar move was noted in chapter 7, as we discussed Kelsey's understanding of *unsubstitutable individuality*, in which he seeks not to define individuality but to describe *unsubstitutability*.

Kelsey's reshaping of the questions is particularly evident in his reshaping of the doctrine of the *imago Dei*. As we have discussed in chapter 4, Kelsey

---

theological scene and that his explicit references in *EE* to theology of the past 50 years is very limited and "almost totally North American and European" (Ford, "What, How, and Who," 47). However, it should be noted that Ford finds Kelsey's explanation—Kelsey's desire to avoid contrastive discussions and advocate his own proposals—"persuasive." See Ford, "Humanity Before God," 42n16; cf. Kelsey, "Response to the Symposium," 81.

2. See chapter 3 of our project, footnote 12.

contends that the *imago Dei* does not define a single feature within the human being in general and Jesus Christ in particular. Rather, it is a description of who, what and how Jesus of Nazareth is as the paradigmatic human being. This description is given in the format of an anthropological formula that is applied to Jesus as a human being, who is the image of God and at the same time images God. It is then applied subsequently to human beings in general as they image the image of God. As such, rather than seeking to answer the question 'What is a human being?' and by extension 'How do we define humanity?' Kelsey instead asks, 'How do we describe Jesus of Nazareth in his humanity?' and by extension 'How do we describe human beings in general?' Within this context, the image of God plays the role of a summary description of human beings rather than a definition. Kelsey expands this summary description into the anthropological formula—itself a summary of anthropological proposals made in *EE*. The move away from definitions and toward descriptions enables Kelsey to offer answers to the questions surrounding the image of God that are unique in three key ways.

First, Kelsey's description of human beings does not rely on a single feature or on a limited set of features. Our analysis of the anthropological formula has demonstrated that in many cases Kelsey extends the descriptive features of humanity well past any limited set. For example, chapter 5 of our project has highlighted Kelsey's understanding of the highly complex nature of human identity. The human being is describable in its quotidian context (the basis for its quotidian identity), which includes both physical, non-physical and transcendental features. Using this description, one may say that human *quotidian identity* comprises myriad features—both external and internal to human beings—that are formative for who and what the human being is. Such complexity is further expanded, as we saw in chapter 8, in Kelsey's notion of actuality. Seen through our critical constructive analysis of Kelsey's understanding of actuality, the human being—as an actual human being—is to be described in terms of physical, non-physical and transcendental features. These features comprise the 'complete reality' of the actual human being and drawn into human identity through the process of constitutive and deprivative perfection.

Thus, to distil humanity down to either a single or limited set of features is impossible. It is doomed to failure because an adequate description of human beings that appeals to the necessary features incorporated in humanity would be inexhaustibly long. Indeed, if we consider our discussions in chapter 7 on *individuality* and *unsubstitutability*, Kelsey urges us not to even attempt such a description.

Second, appeals to invidious contrasts between the human being itself and the rest of creation are fraught with difficulties. We have noted in chapter

1, along with Kelsey, that previous attempts to establish human distinction often lead to 'value anthropocentrism' (29–31). As a consequence, Kelsey prefers to describe human beings as one with the created order.[3] This was most evident in our discussion in chapter 8 on actuality. Kelsey contends that human actuality in 'having been born' implies that human beings are in many respects "utterly ordinary" (246). They are created (born) through the process of human reproduction, a process that is in many ways shared by other members of the created order. They do not appear *ex nihilo*. To Kelsey—as far as God's immediacy and free relating is concerned—human beings are "on a par with all other creatures" (255).

Third, unlike previous attempts to define human beings by appealing to features in human beings themselves, Kelsey proposes an entirely eccentric description of human beings. As we have seen in chapter 3, this is the central theme of his project and has been noted in many of our discussions. His understanding of identity (basic, quotidian, personal and unsubstitutable) is entirely eccentric. As we noted in chapters 5 and 6, human beings' ultimate context is the personal identity that results from God's relating in creative blessing, eschatological consummation and reconciliation. It is in God that their identities are rooted and in the quotidian context that they are expressed and shaped.

As actualities, they are unsubstitutable (chapter 7) as they emerge from the natural processes of birth, dependent on physical, non-physical and transcendental properties to become the beloved of God. God's beloved is always described in terms of, among other things, a *living body* (chapter 9), itself reliant on externally obtained energy and information to resist entropic forces. In these ways, all that the human being is may be described only in reference to an eccentric existence: an existence whose very basis is rooted externally.

Not only does Kelsey's reshaping of the questions allow unique descriptions of human beings, but it enables paradoxical positions to sit side by side. For our purposes, the paradox expressed in the notions of gift and vocation is of key interest. As we saw in chapter 5, the human being has a basic identity that cannot be changed, destroyed or taken away. Yet this basic identity is expressed, and lived out, within the quotidian context, giving

---

3. Clough has contended this point. Although he acknowledges that Kelsey conducts his anthropology without taking bearings from human/non-human difference (what he calls the first type of 'not-animal' methodology), he contends that Kelsey is in danger of viewing human beings as God's only creatures. His argument is that "an alien unfamiliar with life on earth would gain the impression from most of the thousand-plus pages of *Eccentric Existence* that human beings were the only species on earth" (Clough, "Not a Not-Animal," 10). Our analysis of Kelsey during the course of this project has, however, demonstrated the error of Clough's contention.

rise to a quotidian identity. Not only is it possible, but it is very common for quotidian identities to be lived at cross grain to basic identities. The human being may become what it is not. Kelsey describes this as "bondage in living death" (385, 194).[4]

Kelsey understands the relationship between the basic and quotidian identities as an interplay between the gift and vocation of human being. This dual emphasis speaks to the paradox of being: One becomes what one already is, or more perturbingly, one risks becoming what one is not. This paradox mirrors the positions of the substantive-relational debate. We are (universally) the image of God (gift—used here as a noun), and yet we must grow and develop into this image (vocation—used here as a verb). Kelsey's position enables the paradoxical descriptions of gift and vocation to sit side by side and, as a result, allows both substantive and relational concerns to co-exist in one description.

This gift-vocation, noun-verb, static-dynamic inter-play within Kelsey's construction is most aptly seen in our proposed constructive reinterpretation of his understanding of actuality in light of Aristotle. Recall chapter 8's discussions of Aristotle's dual understanding of actuality as both *energeia* and *entelecheia*. In that chapter, we described the actuality of human existence as a dynamic state of remaining the same: a 'being-at-work-staying-itself.' Human actuality speaks of both substantive and relational qualities of human being, incorporating the paradox of gift and vocation into the description of human existence.

Considering all that has been said of Kelsey's approach, what of the five common limitations laid out against the substantive-relational positions? Is Kelsey himself susceptible to these limitations? Let us deal with each in turn.

Kelsey and the Limitations of the Substantive-Relational Debate

First, relational thinkers accuse substantive thinking of being 'baptized' in contemporary culture, whereby attributes held in high regard by respective cultures are used as the defining characteristic of the image of God. Although relational thinkers argue for the detrimental effect of this practice, Kelsey does not share their concern. On the contrary, he encourages the practice. He is quite clear that his work seeks to be hospitable to the Modern

---

4. The concept is explored throughout Kelsey's anthropology, see Kelsey, *Eccentric Existence*, chap. 11, 17, 25.

Secular Interpretation of Humanity (MSIH).[5] While relational thinkers may argue that such baptizing distorts the original meaning of the biblical narratives, Kelsey contends, in a very postliberal fashion, that such baptizing is not only inevitable but important for secondary theology. It is through cultural baptism that the Christian faith is spoken, and it is in this context that the grammar of faith grows and develops. Therefore, although Kelsey is indeed susceptible to this first limitation, it is arguable whether he would find this problematic in any real sense.

Second, substantive and relation theologians—although they attempt to—fail to identify universally shared human characteristics. Unlike their proposals, Kelsey's anthropological universality is not established by appealing to a single or limited set of features within the human being. His eccentric rooting of humanity in God's creative blessing, eschatological consummation and reconciliation is a viable means of establishing anthropological universality. His construction does not rely on the human being itself and as such is not reliant on the possession or development of certain features that are necessary for beings to be included in the category of *anthropos*. The infant, the mentally and physically challenged, the homicidal psychopath, the elderly and all those who lie between are incorporated into the category of humanity simply because God has related to them in the same manner.

Third, substantive and relational thinking is based on negative reductionism: distilling the essential attributes of humanity into a single or limited set of features, which are negatively elevated above other attributes. More often than not these features are non-physical, such as in the case of classically conceived body-soul dualism in which the body is seen as merely the dispensable physical container of the indispensable non-physical human soul.

It is arguable that Kelsey's construction relies, at least in part, on a non-physical duality. To be sure, as our discussions in chapter 9 on *living body* have demonstrated, Kelsey's understanding of the relationship between the physical and non-physical aspects of humanity is complex. On the one hand, he appears to be against the notion that the essential human feature is non-physical: It is for this reason that he considers Murphy's theory of 'nonreductive physicalism' and ultimately relies on Schloss's definition of the living body. On the other hand, even Kelsey admits that some appeal to non-physical attributes is necessary (391, 1021). As such, Kelsey's answer to the eschatological continuity question is, on some level, based on

---

5. Kelsey, "Wisdom Theological Anthropology," 44, 51; "Human Creature," 128; "Spiritual Machines," 7.

non-physical attributes. However, unlike substantive and relational thinkers, Kelsey does not elevate these non-physical attributes at the expense of the physical—quite the contrary. Not only does he emphasize that human living bodies are only one aspect of his description of human beings as the image of God, but he appeals to physical elements as being essential to a description of human beings. This is most evidenced in our discussions in chapter 8 on the importance of our quotidian identity that incorporates physical, non-physical and transcendental elements—through the process of constitutive and deprivative perfection—into human actuality. As such, it is difficult to argue that Kelsey distils the human creature down into a single or limited set of features or that he elevates the non-physical at the expense of the physical.

Fourth, substantive and relational thinkers—in their reliance on negative reductionism—risk a value anthropocentricism (setting human beings against creation). Kelsey goes to great length to avoid such anthropocentrism, affirming at many points that humanity is "utterly ordinary" (246). Chapter 9 of our project has argued that he goes so far as to make it difficult to distinguish the human being from the rest of creation—a topic we shortly discuss. Indeed, as we have seen, Kelsey's construction is so eco-friendly that it has formed the basis of recent eco-theologies.[6] Not only does he affirm the quotidian context as fundamental for human existence, going so far as to argue that it is part of our very identity (see chapter 5 of our project), but he goes so far as to affirm the necessity for an ecology even in the *eschaton* (249, 1022). Kelsey is quite clear that the human being is a creature not only in terms of being a part of the created order, but in terms of arising from it and, even in the *eschaton*, remaining a creature reliant on the created order. In sum, one is hard-pressed to contend that *EE* presents a 'value anthropocentrism.'

Fifth, it is arguable that substantive and relational thinkers perceive of human beings as a *vestigium Dei*. That is to say, by considering the human being, knowledge of God may be gained independently of God's specific revelation. Kelsey's insistence on an eccentric rooting to humanity avoids almost entirely the setting up of human beings as a *vestigium Dei*. Since the human being is eccentrically rooted, it is impossible to gain knowledge of the divine substance by consideration of the *humanum* independently. To consider the human is to consider God, for—in Kelsey's eccentric construction—one cannot consider the human being without considering God first and foremost. Without knowledge of God, one can have no knowledge of the human being.

6. Marais, "Eccentric Existence?"

Therefore, we must conclude that Kelsey's construction does indeed offer much to the debate surrounding the image of God. Our discussions above have shown that his reshaping of the questions furnishes answers that are less susceptible to the limitations laid against both substantive and relational positions while still addressing their respective concerns. All this goes to emphasize the uniqueness and distinctiveness of Kelsey's position.

It should be noted, however, that our conclusion here is not that every aspect of Kelsey's construction is new. Quite the contrary, many have argued, for example, that Jesus Christ is the *imago Dei par excellence*,[7] that humanity is in some sense an 'is' and 'is not',[8] or that we need to look to God first and foremost before we can have knowledge of human beings.[9] The uniqueness of *EE* lies in the manner in which many of these conceptions are drawn into Kelsey's doctrine of the *imago Dei*. What is unique is his systematically unsystematic approach that provides descriptions of Jesus Christ as the image of God and human beings who image the image of God through the use of an anthropological formula.

The use of an anthropological formula is particularly distinctive. Although there is little evidence that Kelsey has made a methodological choice to set out and use an anthropological formula, the formula is more than simply stylistic. It emerges naturally out of discussions in part 1 of *EE* and, along with its derivatives, is applied through his work to describe human beings and Jesus of Nazareth. As the *EE* progresses, this formulaic description is impressed upon the reader's mind in such a way that it becomes central to understanding many of Kelsey's proposals. This is demonstrable in parts 2 and 3, as Kelsey discusses the narratives of eschatological consummation and reconciliation, but is most evident in the codas, particularly his final coda. As Kelsey summarizes all that he has done within the framework of the *imago Dei*, the formula becomes a central aspect. It is directly applicable to the anthropological 'What?' question within the context of God relating in creative blessing. Here human beings are describable as the image of God by making use of this formula.

The move toward a formulaic description of human beings as the image of God is an important move in both *EE* and theological anthropology as a whole. It urges us to extend our view of the image of God beyond the usual approaches that attempt to abstract and elevate limited

7. Berkouwer, *Man*, 107; Brunner, "Christian Understanding of Man," 58–59; Grenz, "Jesus as the Imago Dei"; Pittenger, *Christian Understanding of Human Nature*, 31.

8. Indeed, we have noted that McFadyen contends that identity—as it relates to the *imago Dei*—"is both an 'is' and an 'ought.'" See McFadyen, *Call to Personhood*, 17.

9. See Torrance, *Persons in Communion*, 125.

features from the human being as a whole. This draws our attention to the immense complexity of human beings as images of God. At the same time, in its formulaic shape—that is, as it acts as a placeholder for complex theological and philosophical concepts—it is a manageable summary of wider theological discussions.

Yet there is still another important question to ask: Does Kelsey radically change this debate or simply add one more perspective?

A New Approach to the *Imago Dei*?

We have seen that both substantive and relational views have value and at the same time limitation. One could, therefore, argue that the substantive-relational debate has a certain sense of equilibrium about it. Like a seesaw to-ing and fro-ing, the substantive-relational debate is kept in check by its dialogue partners. As each partner acknowledges the value and counters the limitations of the other, one finds a certain equilibrium in the to-ing and fro-ing between substantive and relational thinkers. Is Kelsey simply another seesaw partner, countering the limitations of the substantive-relational debate while himself needing to be countered by either that same debate or another conversation partner?

It is possible to argue that the partners of the substantive-relational debate can act as counterweights on the basis of their similarities, which we have expounded on in chapter 1 of this project. Their approach to the questions surrounding the *imago Dei* are grounded in a comparable secondary question, with the result that their answers are similarly shaped and open to common limitations. As such, it makes sense that one counters the other, as it itself needs to be countered by the other.

Kelsey, however, makes use of an entirely different approach and as such presents a non-comparable answer in the form of his anthropological formula. Although appreciating the value brought by both substantive and relational thinkers, he departs from the underlying structure of their arguments. Kelsey's point of departure and direction is entirely different. The substantive-relational debate urges us to seek out definitions, to look for single or limited sets of features that are internal to humanity and to locate the human being in contradistinction to the created order. Kelsey calls us to descriptions, to vast arrays of features and to looking outward and upward as we see ourselves as part of the created order.

Yet this is not to say that Kelsey has somehow put forward the final solution. On the contrary, his proposals raise serious questions that need further exploration. Setting aside the many critiques we have raised during the course of our discussions, there is a theme that needs to be addressed following our critical constructive interpretation of the anthropological formula: What is anthropological about the anthropological formula? Put another way: What is distinctive about human beings that grants them the unqualified dignity and value other creatures do not have?

As we noted in chapter 1, historically the image of God has played an important role in theological anthropology. Used with classificatory and evaluative force, it has acted as the anthropologically distinctive feature and as such has been the foundation of human dignity and value. That is to say, it is the defining characteristic of human beings that they image God. As such, they belong to a distinctive class whose membership has unqualified dignity and value. According to Visala, this is the presupposition of all competing theories of the image of God.[10] Yet in *EE*, the path taken is slightly different.

Kelsey begins his project by asking questions that have traditionally fallen under the remit of the doctrine of the *imago Dei*, that is, specifically anthropological questions. These are questions of "ultimate concern" (1). Kelsey sub-divides these questions into the 'What?,' 'How?,' and 'Who?' He poses the first question as follows:

> What are we? Is there a human essence? Is there a set of attributes exhibited by all human persons no matter how different their location by race, gender, ethnicity, culture, and history? Is there a set of attributes that are singly necessary and collectively sufficient for any individual who exhibits them to count as a 'human being? If so, what is it? (1–2)

Traditionally these sets of questions were answered in reference to the image of God. Indeed, chapter 1 of our project noted how it is that substantive and relational thinkers have attempted to answer this 'What?' question by appealing to an attribute, or limited set of attributes, exhibited by all human beings that is sufficient to define humanity. In seeking to answer questions of 'ultimate concern' and, in particular, 'What is the human being?' Kelsey begins his project with the same concerns as those addressed by the doctrine of the image of God.

This question occupies part 1 of his project with a particular focus on the narrative of creation. Within this context, he develops an anthropological formula that exhibits a set of attributes that is collectively sufficient to describe human beings. Later, he applies this same question and the narrative of creation within the framework of the doctrine of the *imago Dei* to state that human beings, simply by being what they are—that is, simply

10. Visala, "Imago Dei," 118.

by being basic unsubstitutable identities of actual living human personal bodies—are the image of the image of God. It was for this reason that our project has focused primarily on part 1 and on the narrative of creation as it applies to the 'What?' question in the final coda of *EE*.

Yet as we have also noted during our discussions, Kelsey deviates from the approaches of substantive and relational thinkers in a number of ways, three of which have consequences for the doctrine of the *imago Dei* and human distinction. The first is his postliberal move way from definitions toward descriptions. Historically, theological anthropologists have attempted to answer the 'What?' question by providing a definition of the distinctive human feature, that is, the image of God. The argument is as follows: If we can define what the image of God is, then we can define what the human being is. Kelsey's move toward description does not help to clarify and simplify the debate. On the contrary, it complicates and blurs the issues.

Definitions aid in clarifying and specifying what exactly we are talking about. They help create a mutually agreed-upon understanding of the issue at hand. Descriptions, on the other hand, do not necessarily produce this same clarification. This is particularly true when they are used in a postliberal manner, that is to say, when one understands descriptions as 'truth claims' that are communally mediated. Postliberal descriptions of human beings are only applicable in certain contexts. Indeed, Kelsey is quite clear that his description of humanity as *imago Dei* is intended primarily within the context of Christian particularism and only secondarily within the context of inter-cultural dialogue (6–7).

If humanity, as *imago Dei*, is to be universally applied so as to establish human distinction as well as universal unqualified dignity and value—as Christians have historically argued—how can Kelsey's proposals be applied usefully beyond the language of the Christian faith? In other words: Does *EE* say something about human beings generally or simply about what Christianity says about human beings?[11] If *EE* is only applicable within the context of the Christian community, then we need to conclude that Kelsey has so radically changed the doctrine of the *imago Dei* that it can no longer be used in the 'traditional' sense of establishing human distinction and value. This conclusion would seriously limit the wider ethical and practical implications of both Kelsey's anthropological proposals and our constructive critical interpretation.[12]

---

11. Or more accurately, what some Christians say. We have raised this question in chapter 2 of our project. See particularly footnote 152 of that chapter.

12. Kelsey does explore some of these. See Kelsey, *Eccentric Existence*, chap. 8, 9A, 14, 15A, 21A, 22. However, if his descriptions only apply to certain contexts, then surely the practice must as well. As one can imagine, this opens up an entire minefield for further debate as to what applies where and when.

Second (as noted in chapter 1 of our project), historically, theological anthropology has focused on a set of features in human beings themselves. That is to say, the image of God has been seen as a fundamental characteristic of the human being. Human beings were part of a class of beings because they possessed (substantive) or exhibited (relational) certain characteristics and features, which are taken to be definitive of what it means to image God. Yet within *EE*, human beings are eccentric. Their entire being is rooted externally in God's triadic relations.

In light of this construction, Catherine Pickstock criticizes Kelsey's "radical eccentricity."[13] She argues that Kelsey promotes a "radical relationality,"[14] which presents us with "a picture of extrinsic bullying into being by an interventionist God."[15] Although it is arguable that Pickstock goes too far in her critique, and Kelsey is able to defend his proposals,[16] one is nevertheless left wondering if there is anything native in the human being. Is everything foreign, received externally, with nothing innate and internal? Is the human being a *thing* in its own right, or is it simply that which God relates to as a human being? If all that we are is that which God relates to in a specific manner, then what God relates to in this self-same manner, even if this is not us *per se*, must be all that we are. Of course, the likelihood of God relating to another being in the exact same manner as He relates to human beings is improbable. Nevertheless, the possibility of it creates some confusion as to what exactly the human being is.

Third, in *EE*, human beings image the image of God simply by being what they are, that is, simply by being the basic unsubstitutable identities of actual living human personal bodies.[17] Yet we have noted in chapter 9 that Kelsey is open to the possibility that almost all of his anthropological claims may be applicable to non-human beings such as artificially intelligent beings, angels or extra-terrestrials (258–59). His argument is that *EE* speaks primarily to those living bodies who have human DNA. However, we noted the limitations of making DNA the categorical marker in chapter 9 of our project.[18] Since Kelsey's description of human beings as the image

13. Pickstock, "One Story," 31.

14. Pickstock, "One Story," 31.

15. Pickstock, "One Story," 31. McAnnally-Linz has considered Pickstock's 'extrinsicism' critique of Kelsey in quite some depth and ultimately concludes that it cannot be "brushed off as mere Protestant extrinsicism" as Pickstock would contend. See McAnnally-Linz, "Extrinsic Grace and Eccentric Existence," 186–94.

16. Kelsey, "Response to the Symposium," 77–80.

17. See chapter 4 of our project.

18. In previous discussions we have noted that we share almost all of our DNA with other creatures, that it is possible to have DNA and yet not be a living body, and that glorified human beings do not retain their distinctive DNA.

of God may apply equally to non-human beings, one is left questioning both the role of the *imago Dei* and the anthropological formula for his theological anthropology.

The question we are asking here is has to do with human distinction. What is it that makes human beings different from any other being? More than that, is human distinction superficial or fundamental? For example, cats are different from dogs in that they have retractable claws, 30 teeth rather than 42 and belong to the genus *felis* rather than *canis*. Yet both have claws and teeth and belong to the class *Mammalia*. In many ways, they are equally valued and to a very large extent are substitutable;[19] many will substitute a dog or cat for a family pet. Like cats and dogs, human beings have claws and teeth and belong to the class *Mammalia*. The differences between their claws and teeth is superficial. Yet it seems self-evident that a dog or cat could never take the place of a human. Although cats, dogs and humans are all animals, there is a fundamental difference between humans and other animals.

What that difference is exactly is difficult to establish using Kelsey's description of human beings as the image of God. If all the terms of Kelsey's anthropological formula may be equally applied to aliens, angels or artificially intelligent beings, are the distinctive human features fundamentally distinct?

Questioning the fundamental distinction of human beings as a class of beings is to question the innate value and dignity of every human being. How is it possible to claim that this particular creature has a status so fundamentally different from many other creatures, and yet its distinctions are merely superficial? Such a conclusion is far removed from the historical use of the doctrine of the *imago Dei*, which seeks to demonstrate that humanity is different from other creatures in such a radical way that it innately processes inalienable, unqualified dignity and value. One is left wondering if Kelsey's use of the image of God as a framework to bring his discussions into a wholeness-in-complexity really does hold together. Surely, in light of its limited Christian communal orientation, its eccentric construction and its application to a wide range of other beings, Kelsey's doctrine of the *imago Dei* can no longer carry the weight traditionally assigned to this doctrine. No longer does the image of God refer to that which is distinctive about human beings or to established human dignity and value, but rather to a broad range of proposals that are applied to numerous creatures discovered

---

19. Naturally there are those who would argue that dogs are 'better' than cats, but even here these arguments are superficial, based on energy, size, intelligence, suitable pet, etc.

and undiscovered. If this is the case, does Kelsey's anthropological formula offer any anthropological value?

Although it is arguable that his formula questions human distinction and that this is a significant limitation, it is also possible to argue that this is a great strength. Indeed, David Clough has noted that:

> Kelsey's account makes clear that nothing is lost and much is gained by a theological anthropology that turns its face away from an account based on differentiation from other animals and defines human identity outside the competitive logic that establishes human attributes through denying them to other animals.[20]

One cannot help but wonder if recent shifts in the MSIH require a shift in our doctrine of the *imago Dei*. Such shifts have challenged the perception of human distinctiveness. Traditionally, biological species classification was based on essential properties of classes of organisms. Classifications sought the 'essence of a thing,' that is to say, the properties that an object must necessarily possess in order to be what it is. This view, however, has come into question. Consider John Dupré's assessment:

> What has become increasingly clear to post-Darwinian biologists is that there can be no necessary and sufficient condition for being an organism of a certain species, and the characteristic properties of members of a species are, first, almost always typical rather than universal in the species and, second, to be explained in various different ways rather than by appeal to any simple or homogeneous underlying property.[21]

Here Dupré questions the notion of classification by essence. Within contemporary biological sciences, the distinctive lines between species are imprecise. In many cases, to belong to a specific species is a question of belonging to a historical population rather than having a universally present set of characteristics.[22]

Yet the challenges do not only come from biology. Other theories based on reductive materialism pose serious challenges. The result of the 'astonishing hypothesis' (to use Francis Crick's words) that underlies reductive materialism is the demise of human distinction. Human beings are to be perceived of as a particular type of animal, but an animal nonetheless. The consequence is either the elevation of animals, as is the case of Sandra the

20. Clough, "Not a Not-Animal," 16.
21. Dupré quoted in Visala, "Imago Dei," 114.
22. Visala, "Imago Dei," 114–17.

orangutan,[23] or the devaluation of human beings, as is the case of Dawkins's 'skinless organism.'[24]

The MSIH is compounded by recent technological developments. In particular, one can note the rise of artificial intelligence (perceivable in the next decade[25]), and cosmological and astrological discoveries—such as the discovery of exoplanets and liquid water—that have reinvigorated the search for extra-terrestrial life.[26] These developments raise expectations of the presence of other sentient beings hitherto unknown. This increases the possibility that other entities may be described using descriptions previously only ascribed to human beings as the image of God. The MSIH challenges *imago Dei* theories that argue for a strong qualitative distinction between human beings (as carriers of the *imago Dei*) and non-human beings.[27]

Recognizing these challenges, Kelsey builds into his doctrine of the *imago Dei* a flexibility that enables us to take the doctrine of the *imago Dei* beyond its 'traditional' use (258–59).[28] Unlike historical uses of this doctrine, whose emphasis was on the human boundary question—that is to say, defining the distinction between human beings and the rest of creation—Kelsey's proposals shift the emphasis elsewhere. Here the emphasis is not on human beings as a distinct species but on the individual as unsubstitutable. As our discussions in chapter 7 have noted, every individual instance of *Homo sapiens* is the beloved of God and as such images the image of God. In this move, Kelsey gives to his doctrine of the image of God a flexibility that allows a range of entities to image God, yet at the same time distinguishes between all of them. As every human being is the beloved of God, we may also claim that no human being is the beloved of God as I am. In like fashion, while other entities may image the image of God (humans, artificially intelligent beings, extra-terrestrials, angels, etc.) no other being images the image of God as I do.

---

23. See chapter 6 of this project
24. See chapter 9 of this project
25. See "Computers Could Develop Consciousness."
26. Wootten, "Yuri Milner and Stephen Hawking."
27. Visala, "Imago Dei," 114–15.
28. One is aware of the argument that the Second Person of the Trinity becomes a human being and in so doing establishes human uniqueness. However, there is nothing to say that the incarnation has to be purely anthropological and that it is not possible for the Second Person of the Trinity to become/have become a member of an extra-terrestrial species. Furthermore, issues of the *imago Dei*, at least within Kelsey's construction, have more to do with the narrative of creation than reconciliation.

Bibliography

Aldwinckle, Russell. *Death in the Secular City: A Study of the Notion of Life After Death in Contemporary Theology and Philosophy*. London: George Allen & Unwin, 1972.
Anderson, Ray S. *On Being Human: Essays in Theological Anthropology*. Grand Rapids: Eerdmans, 1982.
Aquinas, Thomas. *Summa Theologica*. Translated by Fathers of the English Dominican Province. Westminster, MD: Christian Classics, 1911.
Aristotle. *Metaphysics*. Translated by G. Cyril Armstrong. London: W. Heinemann, 1933. http://www.perseus.tufts.edu/hopper/text?doc=urn:cts:greekLit:tlg0086.tlg025.perseus-eng1.
———. *Physics: Books III–IV*. Translated by Edward Hussey. Oxford: Clarendon, 1983.
———. *Physics: Book VIII*. Translated by Daniel W. Graham. Oxford: Clarendon, 1999.
Augustine. *On the Trinity*. Vol. 3.1. of *A Select Library of Nicene and Post-Nicene Fathers of the Christian Church*. Edited by Philip Schaff. Translated by Arthur West Haddan. Grand Rapids: Eerdmans, 1956.
Badham, Paul. *Christian Beliefs About Life After Death*. London: Macmillan, 1976.
Baker, William H. *In the Image of God: A Biblical View of Humanity*. Chicago: Moody, 1991.
Barth, Karl. *Christ and Adam: Man and Humanity in Romans 5*. Translated by T. A. Smail. Eugene, OR: Wipf and Stock, 2004.
———. *Church Dogmatics*. Translated by G. W. Bromiley and T. F. Torrance. 4 vols. Edinburgh: T & T Clark, 1956–1975.
Bauman, Zygmunt. *The Individualized Society*. Cambridge: Polity, 2001.
Bawden, Tom. "Orangutan Inside Argentina Zoo Granted 'Non-Human Person Rights' in Landmark Ruling." *Independent*, December 22, 2014. http://www.independent.co.uk/news/world/americas/sandra-the-orangutan-inside-argentina-zoo-granted-human-rights-in-landmark-ruling-9940202.html.
Bechler, Zev. *Aristotle's Theory of Actuality*. New York: State University of New York Press, 1995.
Berkhof, Hendrikus. *Christian Faith: An Introduction to the Study of the Faith*. Grand Rapids: Eerdmans, 1979.
Berkhof, Louis. *Systematic Theology*. Edinburgh: Banner of Truth Trust, 1984.
Berkouwer, G. C. *Man: The Image of God*. Studies in Dogmatics. Grand Rapids: Eerdmans, 1962.
———. *The Person of Christ*. Studies in Dogmatics. Grand Rapids: Eerdmans, 1954.
Black, Max. "A Translation of Frege's Ueber Sinn Und Bedeutung." *The Philosophical Review* 57.3 (1948) 209–30.
Blackshaw, Tony. *Key Concepts in Community Studies*. London: SAGE, 2010.

Blair, George A. "Aristotle on Entelexeia: A Reply to Daniel Graham." *American Journal of Philology* 114.1 (1993) 91–97.

———. *Energeia and Entelecheia: "Act" in Aristotle*. Ottawa: University of Ottawa Press, 1992.

Bradshaw, David. *Aristotle East and West: Metaphysics and the Division of Christendom*. Cambridge: Cambridge University Press, 2004.

Brague, Remi. "Aristotle's Definition of Motion and Its Ontological Implications." *Graduate Faculty Philosophy Journal* 13.2 (1990) 1–22.

Bridger, F. W. "Humanity." In *New Dictionary of Christian Ethics and Pastoral Theology*, edited by David Atkinson and David Field, 21–27. Leicester: InterVarsity, 1995.

Brown, David. "Trinitarian Personhood and Individuality." In *Trinity, Incarnation and Atonement: Philosophical and Theological Essays*, edited by Ronald J. Fenstra and Cornelius Jr. Plantinga, 48–78. Notre Dame: University of Notre Dame Press, 1989.

Brown, Warren S. "Cognitive Contributions to Soul." In *Whatever Happened to the Soul*, edited by Warren S. Brown, et al., 99–125. Theology and the Sciences. Minneapolis: Fortress, 1998.

Brümmer, Vincent. "Religious Belief and Personal Identity." *Neue Zeitschrift Für Systematische Theologie Und Religions Philosophie* 38.2 (1996) 155–65.

Brunner, Emil. "The Christian Understanding of Man." In *The Christian Understanding of Man*, edited by T. E. Jessop and R. L. Calhoun, 139–78. London: George Allen & Unwin, 1938.

———. *Dogmatics: Christian Doctrine of Creation and Redemption*. Vol. 2. London: Lutterworth, 1952.

Buber, Martin. *I and Thou*. Translated by Walter Arnold Kaufmann. New York: T & T Clark, 1970.

Buckley, James J. "Buoys for Eccentric Existence." *Modern Theology* 27.1 (2011) 14–25.

Bühler, Pierre. "Christian Identity: Between Objectivity and Subjectivity." In *Christian Identity*, edited by Christian Duquoc and Casiano Floristán, 17–27. Edinburgh: T & T Clark, 1988.

Cahill, Lisa Sowle. "Toward a Christian Theory of Human Rights." *Journal of Religious Ethics* 8.2 (1980) 277–301.

Cairns, David. *The Image of God in Man*. London: SCM, 1953.

Calvin, John. *Institutes of the Christian Religion*. Edited by John T. McNeill. Translated by Ford Lewis Battles. Vol. 20. Library of Christian Classics. London: SCM, 1960.

———. "Psychopannychia: A Refutation of the Error Entertained by Some Unskilful Persons Who Ignorantly Imagine That in the Interval Between Death and the Judgement the Soul Sleeps. Together with an Explanation of the Condition and Life of the Soul After This Present Life." In *Tracts Relating to the Reformation*, edited by Robert Pitcairn, 3:413–90. Translated by Henry Beveridge. Edinburgh: Calvin Translation Society, 1844. https://archive.org/details/tractsrelatingto3calv.

Carbine, R. "Review of Eccentric Existence: A Theological Anthropology." *Theological Studies* 72.3 (2011) 663–65.

Carey, George. *I Believe in Man*. Sevenoaks: Hodder and Stoughton, 1980.

Chen, Chung-Hwan. "Different Meanings of the Term Energeia in the Philosophy of Aristotle." *Philosophy and Phenomenological Research* 17.1 (1956) 56–65.

———. "The Relation between the Terms Ἐνέργεια and Ἐντελέχεια in the Philosophy of Aristotle." *The Classical Quarterly* 8.1/2 (1958) 12–17.

Clines, D. J. A. "The Image of God in Man." *Tyndale Bulletin* 19 (1968) 53–103.
Clough, David. "Not a Not-Animal: The Vocation to Be a Human Animal Creature." *Studies in Christian Ethics* 26.1 (2013) 4–17.
Cohen, S. Marc. "Aristotle's Definition of Kinêsis: Physics III.1." Lecture delivered at the University of Washington, February 12, 2008. https://faculty.washington.edu/smcohen/433/KinesisLecture.pdf.
Colijn, Brenda B. "Paul's Use of the 'In Christ' Formula." *Ashland Theological Journal* 23 (1991) 9–26.
"Computers Could Develop Consciousness and May Need 'Human' Rights, Says Oxford Professor." *Telegraph*, May 29, 2016. http://www.telegraph.co.uk/science/2016/05/29/computers-could-develop-consciousness-and-may-need-human-rights.
Comstock, Gary L. "Two Types of Narrative Theology." *Journal of the American Academy of Religion* 55.4 (1987) 687–717.
Cooper, John W. *Body, Soul, and Life Everlasting: Biblical Anthropology and the Monism-Dualism Debate*. 2nd ed. Grand Rapids: Eerdmans, 2000.
Craigo-Snell, Shannon. "From Narrative to Performance." In *The Theological Anthropology of David Kelsey: Responses to Eccentric Existence*, edited by Gene Outka, 147–71. Grand Rapids: Eerdmans, 2016.
Crane, Richard. "Postliberals, Truth, Ad Hoc Apologetics, and (Something Like) General Revelation." *Perspectives in Religious Studies* 30.1 (2003) 29–53.
Crawford, Janet, and Michael Kinnamon. *In God's Image: Reflections on Identity, Human Wholeness and the Authority of Scripture*. Geneva: World Council of Churches, 1983.
Crawford, Nathan. "Review of Eccentric Existence: A Theological Anthropology." *Anglican Theological Review* 94.2 (2012) 355–56.
Crick, Francis. *The Astonishing Hypothesis: The Scientific Search for the Soul*. New York: Scribner's Sons, 1994.
Crisp, Oliver D. *Divinity and Humanity: Thee Incarnation Reconsidered*. Cambridge: Cambridge University Press, 2007.
Cross, Richard. "Medieval Theories of Haecceity." *Stanford Encyclopedia of Philosophy*, May 12, 2014. http://plato.stanford.edu/entries/medieval-haecceity.
Culver, Robert Duncan. *Systematic Theology: Biblical and Historical*. Fearn: Christian Focus, 2008.
Davis, Richard Brian. "Haecceities, Individuation, and the Trinity: A Reply to Keith Yandell." *Religious Studies* 38.2 (2002) 201–13.
Dawber, Alistair. "Human Rights for Cats and Dogs: Spanish Town Council Votes Overwhelmingly in Favour of Defining Pets as 'Non-Human Residents.'" *Independent*, July 22, 2015. http://www.independent.co.uk/news/world/europe/human-rights-for-cats-and-dogs-spanish-town-council-votes-overwhelmingly-in-favour-of-defining-pets-10408546.html.
Dawkins, Richard. *The Extended Phenotype: The Gene as the Unit of Selection*. Oxford: Oxford University Press, 1982.
DeHart, Paul J. *The Trial of the Witnesses: The Rise and Decline of Postliberal Theology*. Oxford: Blackwell, 2006.
Emmet, Dorothy Mary. "Could God Be a Person?" *Modern Believing* 37.1 (1996) 3–10.
Engelhardt, H. Tristram. "Beginnings of Personhood: Philosophical Considerations." *Perkins Journal* 27.1 (1973) 20–27.

Erickson, Millard. *Christian Theology*. 2nd ed. Grand Rapids: Baker, 1998.

———. *Introducing Christian Theology*. 2nd ed. Grand Rapids: Baker, 2001.

Erikson, Erik Homburger. *Identity: Youth and Crisis*. London: Faber & Faber, 1968.

Fackre, Gabriel J. "Narrative Theology: An Overview." *Interpretation* 37.4 (1983) 340–52.

Fang, Wan-Chuan. "Hume on Identity." *Hume Studies* 10.1 (1984) 59–68.

Feinberg, Charles Lee. "Image of God." *Bibliotheca Sacra* 129.515 (1972) 235–46.

Fergusson, David. "Humans Created According to the Imago Dei: An Alternative Proposal." *Zygon* 48.2 (2013) 439–53.

Flanagan, Pat. "Scientists Have Finally Proven That There Is Life After Death but We Might Not Be Going to Heaven." *Mirror*, May 17, 2016. http://www.msn.com/en-ie/news/world/scientists-have-finally-proven-that-there-is-life-after-death-but-we-might-not-be-going-to-heaven/ar-BBt9LAx?ocid=spartandhp.

Ford, David F. "Humanity Before God: Thinking Through Scripture." In *The Theological Anthropology of David Kelsey: Responses to Eccentric Existence*, edited by Gene Outka, 31–52. Grand Rapids: Eerdmans, 2016.

———. "The What, How, and Who of Humanity Before God: Theological Anthropology and the Bible in the Twenty-First Century." *Modern Theology* 27.1 (2011) 41–54.

Frame, John M. "Uses of Scripture in Recent Theology—Review Article." *Westminster Theological Journal* 39.2 (1977) 328–53.

Frege, Gottlob. "Über Sinn Und Bedeutung." *Zeitschrift Für Philosophie Und Philosophische Kritik* 100 (1892) 25–50.

Frei, Hans W. *The Eclipse of Biblical Narrative: A Study in Eighteenth and Nineteenth-Century Hermeneutics*. New Haven: Yale University Press, 1974.

———. *The Identity of Jesus Christ: The Hermeneutical Bases of Dogmatic Theology*. Eugene, OR: Wipf and Stock, 1997.

———. "The 'Literal Reading' of Biblical Narrative in the Christian Tradition: Does It Stretch or Will It Break?" In *The Bible and the Narrative Tradition*, edited by Frank McConnell, 36–77. Oxford: Oxford University Press, 1986.

———. "The 'Literal Reading' of Biblical Narrative in the Christian Tradition: Does It Stretch or Will It Break?" In *The Return to Scripture in Judaism and Christianity: Essays in Postcritical Scriptural Interpretation*, edited by Kathryn Tanner and Peter Ochs, 55–82. New York: Paulist, 1993.

———. "Theological Reflections on the Accounts of Jesus' Death and Resurrection." *Christian Scholar* 49.4 (1966) 263–315.

———. "Theological Reflections on the Accounts of Jesus' Death and Resurrection." In *Theology and Narrative: Selected Essays*, edited by George Hunsinger and William C. Placher, 45–93. Oxford: Oxford University Press, 1993.

———. *Types of Christian Theology*. New Haven: Yale University Press, 1992.

Froböse, Rolf. "Scientists Find Hints for the Immortality of the Soul." *Huffington Post*, August 16, 2014. http://www.huffingtonpost.co.uk/rolf-froboese/scientists-find-hints-for-the-immortality-of-the-soul_b_5499969.html.

Gabriel, Andrew. "A Trinitarian Doctrine of Creation? Considering Barth as a Guide." *McMaster Journal of Theology and Ministry* 6 (2003) 36–48.

Goh, Jeffrey C. K. *Christian Tradition Today: A Postliberal Vision of Church and World*. Leuven, Belgium: Eerdmans, 2000.

Goldberg, Michael. *Theology and Narrative: A Critical Introduction*. Nashville: Abingdon, 1982.

Golluber, Michael. "Aristotle on How One Becomes What One Is." *Review of Metaphysics* 53.2 (1999) 363–82.
Graham, Daniel W. "The Etymology of Entelexeia." *American Journal of Philology* 110.1 (1989) 73–80.
Grant, David. "Personal and Impersonal Concepts of God: A Tension Within Contemporary Christian Theology." *Encounter* 49.2 (1988) 79–91.
Green, Garrett, ed. *Scriptural Authority and Narrative Interpretation*. Philadelphia: Fortress, 1987.
Gregersen, Neils Henrik, et al., eds. *The Human Person in Science and Theology*. Edinburgh: T & T Clark, 2000.
Greggs, Tom. "David Kelsey, Eccentric Existence: A Theological Anthropology." *Scottish Journal of Theology* 65.4 (2012) 449–63.
Grenz, Stanley J. "Jesus as the Imago Dei: Image-of-God Christology and the Non-Linear Linearity of Theology." *Journal of the Evangelical Theological Society* 47.4 (2004) 617–28.
———. *The Social God and the Relational Self: A Trinitarian Theology of the Imago Dei*. Louisville: Westminster John Knox, 2007.
Grudem, Wayne. *Systematic Theology: An Introduction to Biblical Doctrine*. Grand Rapids: Zondervan, 1994.
Gunton, Colin E. *Christ and Creation*. Exeter: Paternoster, 1992.
———. *The One, the Three, and the Many: God, Creation, and the Culture of Modernity*. The Bampton Lectures 1992. Cambridge: Cambridge University Press, 1993.
Haker, Hille. "Narrative and Moral Identity in Paul Ricoeur." In *Creating Identity*, edited by Hermann Häring, et al., 59–68. London: SCM, 2000.
Hall, Douglas John. *Imaging God: Dominion as Stewardship*. Grand Rapids: Eerdmans, 1986.
Harink, Douglas. *Paul Among the Postliberals: Pauline Theology Beyond Christendom and Modernity*. Grand Rapids: Brazos, 2003.
Harris, Harriet A. "Should We Say That Personhood Is Relational." *Scottish Journal of Theology* 51.2 (1998) 214–34.
Harrison, Jonathan. "The Embodiment of Mind or What Use Is Having a Body?" *Proceedings of the Aristotelian Society, New Series* 74 (1973) 35–55.
Hasel, Gerhard F. "The Relationship Between Biblical Theology and Systematic Theology." *Trinity* 5.2 (1984) 113–27.
Hauerwas, Stanley. "The Politics of Justice: Why Justice Is a Bad Idea for Christians." In *After Christendom?*, 45–68. Nashville: Abingdon, 1991.
Hauerwas, Stanley, and L. Gregory Jones, eds. *Why Narrative? Readings in Narrative Theology*. Eugene, OR: Wipf and Stock, 1997.
Hause, Jeffrey. "John Duns Scotus (1266-1308)." *Internet Encyclopedia of Philosophy (IEP)*. http://www.iep.utm.edu/scotus.
Heidegger, Martin. *Being and Time: A Translation of Sein Und Zeit*. Translated by Joan Stambaugh. New York: State University of New York Press, 1996.
Hellegers, Andre E. "The Beginnings of Personhood: Medical Considerations." *Perkins Journal* 27.1 (1973) 11–15.
Henry, Carl F. H. "Theology and Biblical Authority: A Review Article of the Uses of Scripture in Recent Theology by D. H. Kelsey." *Journal of the Evangelical Theological Society* 19.4 (1976) 315–23.
Hick, John. *Death and Eternal Life*. London: Collins, 1976.

Hill, Edmund. *Being Human: A Biblical Perspective*. London: Geoffrey Chapman, 1984.
Hill, Wesley. "Divine Persons and Their 'Reduction' to Relations: A Plea for Conceptual Clarity." *Journal of Systematic Theology* 14.2 (2012) 148–60.
Hodge, Charles. *Systematic Theology*. New York: Scribner & Co., 1971.
Hoekema, A. *Created in God's Image*. Grand Rapids: Eerdmans, 1986.
Holmer, Paul L. *The Grammar of Faith*. San Francisco: Harper & Row, 1978.
Horst, Friedrich. "Face to Face: The Biblical Doctrine of the Image of God." *Interpretation* 4.3 (1950) 259–79.
Hudson, Rosalie. "Dementia and Personhood: A Living Death or Alive in God?" *Colloquium* 36.2 (2004) 123–42.
Hughes, Philip Edgecumbe. *The True Image: The Origin and Destiny of Man in Christ*. Grand Rapids: Eerdmans and InterVarsity, 1989.
Hume, David. *A Treatise of Human Nature*. Edited by Lewis Selby-Bigge and P. H. Nidditch. 2nd ed. Oxford: Oxford University Press, 1985.
Hunsinger, George. *How to Read Karl Barth: The Shape of His Theology*. Oxford: Oxford University Press, 1991.
Hütter, Reinhard. "Worth Discussing: Two Books by David Kelsey." *Currents in Theology and Mission* 22.1 (1995) 49–80.
Huyssteen van, J. Wentzel. "When Were We Persons? Why Huminid Evolution Holds the Key to Embodied Personhood." *Neue Zeitschrift Für Systematische Theologie Und Religions Philosophie* 52.4 (2010) 329–49.
Jacobson, Rolf. "We Are Our Stories: Narrative Dimensions of Human Identity and Its Implications for Christian Faith Formation." *Word & World* 34.2 (2014) 123–30.
Jenson, Robert W. "Once More the Logos Asarkos." *International Journal of Systematic Theology* 13.2 (2011) 130–33.
Jewett, Paul King, and Marguerite Shuster. *God, Creation, and Revelation: A Neo-Evangelical Theology*. Grand Rapids: Eerdmans, 1991.
John Paul II. "Catechism of the Catholic Church." Vatican City: Libreria Editrice Vaticana, 1993. http://www.vatican.va/archive/ENG0015/_INDEX.HTM.
———. "Homily for the Mass at Bourget (June 1, 1980)." In *Documentation Catholique* 1788 (1980) 584–86.
Jones, Ivor. "Narrative Theology, Postmodernism, and History." *Epworth Review* 23.1 (1996) 33–41.
Jüngel, Eberhard. *God's Being Is in Becoming: The Trinitarian Being of God in the Theology of Karl Barth: A Paraphrase*. Translated by John Webster. 2nd ed. Edinburgh: T & T Clark, 2001.
Kamitsuka, David G. *Theology and Contemporary Culture: Liberation, Postliberal, and Revisionary Perspectives*. Cambridge: Cambridge University Press, 1999.
Keller, Katherine. *The Face of the Deep: A Theology of Becoming*. London: Routledge, 2003.
Kelsey, David H. "Appeals to Scripture in Theology." *Journal of Religion* 48.1 (1968) 1–21.
———. *Between Athens and Berlin: The Theological Education Debate*. Grand Rapids: Eerdmans, 1993.
———. "The Bible and Christian Theology." *Journal of the American Academy of Religion* 48.3 (1980) 385–402.

———. "Biblical Narrative and Theological Anthropology." In *Scriptural Authority and Narrative Interpretation*, edited by Garrett Green, 121–43. Philadelphia: Fortress, 1987.

———. *Eccentric Existence: A Theological Anthropology*. Louisville: Westminster John Knox, 2009.

———. *The Fabric of Paul Tillich's Theology*. New Haven: Yale University Press, 1967.

———. "God and Teleology: Must God Have Only One 'Eternal Purpose'?" *Neue Zeitschrift Für Systematische Theologie Und Religions Philosophie* 54.4 (2012) 361–76.

———. "God's Power and Human Flourishing: A Theocentric Perspective." Paper presented at the Yale Center for Faith and Culture's Consultation on God's Power and Human Flourishing, New Haven, CT, May 23–24, 2008. http://faith.yale.edu/sites/default/files/david_kelsey_-_gods_power_and_human_flourishing_0.pdf#overlay-context=resources/god-and-human-flourishing-resources.

———. "Human Being." In *Christian Theology: An Introduction to Its Traditions and Tasks*, edited by Peter C. Hodgson and Robert H. King, 167–93. Philadelphia: Fortress, 1982.

———. "The Human Creature." In *The Oxford Handbook of Systematic Theology*, edited by John Webster, et al., 121–39. Oxford: Oxford University Press, 2007.

———. *Imagining Redemption*. London: Westminster John Knox, 2005.

———. "Personal Bodies: A Theological Anthropological Proposal." In *Personal Identity in Theological Perspective*, edited by Richard Lints, et al., 139–58. Grand Rapids: Eerdmans, 2006.

———. "Redeeming Sam: The Difference Jesus Makes." *Christian Century* 122.13 (2005) 22–27.

———. "Reforming Theological Anthropology: After the Philosophical Turn to Relationality by F. LeRon Shults." *Interpretation* 59.4 (2005) 424.

———. "Response to the Symposium on Eccentric Existence." *Modern Theology* 27.1 (2011) 72–86.

———. "Spiritual Machines, Personal Bodies, Theological Education, and Anthropology." *Teaching Theology and Religion* 5.1 (2002) 2–9.

———. *To Understand God Truly: What's Theological about a Theological School*. Louisville: John Knox, 1992.

———. "Two Theologies of Death: Anthropological Gleanings." *Modern Theology* 13.3 (1997) 647–70.

———. *The Uses of Scripture in Recent Theology*. London: SCM, 1975.

———. "Wisdom Theological Anthropology and Modern Secular Interpretation of Humanity." In *God's Life in Trinity*, edited by Miroslav Volf and Michael Welker, 44–60. Minneapolis: Fortress, 2006.

King, Robert H. *The Meaning of God*. London: SCM, 1974.

Knox, John. *The Humanity and Divinity of Christ: A Study of Pattern in Christology*. Cambridge: Cambridge University Press, 1967.

Kosman, L. A. "Aristotle's Definition of Motion." *Phronesis* 14.1 (1969) 40–62.

Kostman, James. "Aristotle's Definition of Change." *History of Philosophy Quarterly* 4.1 (1987) 3–16.

Kruger, Jaco. "Christian Identity in an Age of Difference." In *Christian Identity*, edited by Eduardus van der Borght, 16:119–32. Studies in Reformed Theology. Boston: Brill, 2008.

Lewis, Hywell D. *The Self and Immortality*. London: Macmillan, 1973.
Lindbeck, George A. "The Bible as Realistic Narrative." *Journal of Ecumenical Studies* 17.1 (1980) 81–85.
———. *The Church in a Post Liberal Age*. Edited by James J. Buckley. Radical Traditions: Theology in a Postcritical Key. London: SCM, 2002.
———. *The Nature of Doctrine: Religion and Theology in a Postliberal Age*. London: SPCK, 1984.
———. "The Search for Habitable Texts." *Daedalus* 117.2 (1988) 153–56.
———. "Toward a Postliberal Theology." In *The Return to Scripture in Judaism and Christianity: Essays in Postcritical Scriptural Interpretation*, edited by Peter Ochs, 83–106. Eugene, OR: Wipf and Stock, 1993.
Linke, Detlef B. "God Gives the Memory: Neuroscience and Resurrection." In *Resurrection: Theological and Scientific Assessments*, edited by Ted Peters, et al., 185–91. Grand Rapids: Eerdmans, 2002.
Lizza, John P. "Potentiality and Human Embryos." *Bioethics* 21.7 (2007) 379–85.
Lukes, Steven. *Individualism*. Oxford: Basil Blackwell, 1973.
Macmurray, John. *Persons in Relation*. Vol. 2. of *The Form of the Personal*. The Gifford Lectures 1954. London: Faber & Faber, 1995.
Macquarrie, John. *Principles of Christian Theology*. Revised Edition. London: SCM, 1977.
Marais, Nadia. "Eccentric Existence? Engaging David H. Kelsey's Theological Anthropology as a Basis for Ecological Theology." MA thesis, University of Stellenbosch, 2011. http://scholar.sun.ac.za/handle/10019.1/17934.
Marshall, I. Howard. "Being Human: Made in the Image of God." *Stone-Campbell Journal* 4.1 (2001) 47–67.
McAnnally-Linz, Ryan. "Extrinsic Grace and Eccentric Existence." *Modern Theology* 31.1 (2015) 179–94.
McCormack, Bruce L. *Orthodox and Modern: Studies in the Theology of Karl Barth*. Grand Rapids: Baker Academic, 2008.
McDougall, Joy Ann. "A Trinitarian Grammar of Sin." *Modern Theology* 27.1 (2011) 54–71.
McFadyen, Alistair I. *The Call to Personhood: A Christian Theory of the Individual in Social Relationships*. Cambridge: Cambridge University Press, 1990.
McFarland, Ian A. *Difference & Identity: A Theological Anthropology*. Cleveland: Pilgrim, 2001.
———. "Review of Eccentric Existence: A Theological Anthropology." *Interpretation* 64.4 (2010) 422–24.
Michener, Ronald T. *Postliberal Theology: A Guide for the Perplexed*. London: T & T Clark, 2013.
Middleton, J. Richard. *The Liberating Image: The Imago Dei in Genesis 1*. Grand Rapids: Brazos, 2005.
Mikhailovsky, Alexander. "The Anthropology of Hypostasis." *International Journal of Orthodox Theology* 2.3 (2011) 144–66.
Miller, J. Maxwell. "In the 'Image' and 'Likeness' of God." *Journal of Biblical Literature* 91.3 (1972) 289–304.
Molnar, Paul D. *Divine Freedom and the Doctrine of the Immanent Trinity: In Dialogue with Karl Barth and Contemporary Theology*. Edinburgh: T & T Clark, 2002.

Moltmann, Jürgen. *The Trinity and the Kingdom of God: The Doctrine of God*. London: SCM, 1981.
Moltmann-Wendel, Elisabeth, and Jürgen Moltmann. *Humanity in God*. London: SCM, 1983.
Moor, Andrew. *Realism and Christian Faith: God, Grammar, and Meaning*. Cambridge: Cambridge University Press, 2003.
Moran, C. A. "Review of Eccentric Existence: A Theological Anthropology." *Pro Ecclesia* 21.4 (2012) 457–61.
Morgan, Lynn M. "The Potentiality Principle from Aristotle to Abortion." *Current Anthropology* 54.7 (2013) 15–25.
Murphy, Nancy. "Nonreducive Physicalism: Philosophical Issues." In *Whatever Happened to the Soul*, edited by Warren S. Brown, et al., 127–48. Theology and the Sciences. Minneapolis: Fortress, 1998.
Musschenga, Albert W. "Personalized Identity in an Individualized Society." In *Creating Identity*, edited by Hermann Häring, et al., 23–30. London: SCM, 2000.
Neill, Stephen. *Man in God's Purpose*. New York: Association, 1961.
Neujahr, Philip J. "Hume on Identity." *Hume Studies* 4.1 (1978) 18–28.
Novakovic, Lidija. *Resurrection: A Guide for the Perplexed*. London: T & T Clark, 2016.
Ochs, Peter, ed. *The Return to Scripture in Judaism and Christianity: Essays in Postcritical Scriptural Interpretation*. New York: Paulist, 1993.
Outka, Gene, ed. *The Theological Anthropology of David Kelsey: Responses to Eccentric Existence*. Grand Rapids: Eerdmans, 2016.
Overstreet, R. Larry. "Man in the Image of God: A Reappraisal." *Criswell Theological Review* 3.1 (2005) 43–70.
Paasch, J. T. *Debates in Medieval Philosophy: Essential Readings and Contemporary Responses*. New York: Routledge, 2014.
———. "Scotus and Ockham on Universals and Individuation." 2012. http://www.academia.edu/2635780/Scotus_and_Ockham_on_Universals_and_Individuation.
———. "Scotus on Universals and Individuation." 2012. http://www.academia.edu/2046923/Scotus_on_Universals_and_Individuation.
Pannenberg, Wolfhart. *Anthropology in Theological Perspective*. Translated by Matthew J. O'Connell. Edinburgh: T & T Clark, 1985.
Parfit, Derek. *Reasons and Persons*. Oxford: Oxford University Press, 1986.
Parsons, Michael. "'In Christ' in Paul." *Vox Evangelica* 18 (1988) 25–44.
Pecknold, C. C. *Transforming Postliberal Theology: George Lindbeck, Pragmatism, and Scripture*. London: T & T Clark, 2005.
Penelhum, Terence. *Survival and Disembodied Existence*. London: Routledge & Kegan, 1970.
Peramatzis, Michail. *Priority in Aristotle's Metaphysics*. Oxford: Oxford University Press, 2011.
Phillips, D. Z. *Faith After Foundationalism: Plantinga-Rorty-Lindbeck-Berger: Critiques and Alternatives*. Oxford: Westview, 1995.
Pickstock, Catherine. "The One Story: A Critique of David Kelsey's Theological Robotics." *Modern Theology* 27.1 (2011) 26–40.
Pittenger, Norman W. *The Christian Understanding of Human Nature*. London: Nisbet & Co., 1964.

———. *The Word Incarnate: A Study of the Doctrine of the Person of Christ.* Digswell Place: Nisbet & Co., 1959.
Placher, William Carl. *The Triune God: An Essay in Postliberal Theology.* London: Westminster John Knox, 2007.
Pollard, Katherine S. "What Makes Us Human?" *Scientific American* 300.5 (2009) 44–49.
Ramsey, Paul. *Basic Christian Ethics.* New York: Scribner's Sons, 1950.
Ratzinger, Joseph. *Introduction to Christianity.* Translated by J. R. Foster. London: Burns & Oates, 1969.
Raynal, Charles. "Review of Eccentric Existence: A Theological Anthropology." *Journal for Preachers* 34.1 (2010) 37–41.
Reeling Brouwer, R. H. "(This One Is) One and Unique: On the Task of Respecting the Singularity of the Name." Paper presented at the Inaugural Speech, Protestant Theological University, October 5, 2012. https://www.pthu.nl/Over_PThU/Organisatie/Medewerkers/r.h.reelingbrouwer/english-text-of-the-inaugural-address.
Ricoeur, Paul. *Freedom and Nature: The Voluntary and the Involuntary.* Translated by Erazim V. Kohák. Evanston, IL: Northwestern University Press, 1966.
———. *Oneself as Other.* Translated by Kathleen Blamey. Chicago: University of Chicago Press, 1992.
———. *Time and Narrative.* Translated by Kathleen McLaughlin and David Pellauer. 3 vols. Chicago: University of Chicago Press, 1990.
Ritter, Wm. E. "Why Aristotle Invented the Word Entelecheia." *Quarterly Review of Biology* 7.4 (1932) 377–404.
———. "Why Aristotle Invented the Word Entelecheia (Continued)." *Quarterly Review of Biology* 9.1 (1934) 1–35.
Robison, Wade L. "Hume on Personal Identity." *Journal of the History of Philosophy* 12.2 (1974) 181–93.
Rogers, J. *Ecological Theology: The Search for an Appropriate Theological Model.* Reprinted from *Septuagesino Anno: Theologiche Opstellen Aangebsden Aan Prof. Dr. G. C. Berkouwer.* Netherlands: J. H. Kok, 1973.
Rohr, Richard. *Immortal Diamond: The Search for Our True Self.* London: SPCK, 2013.
Rudman, Stanley. *Concepts of Persons and Christian Ethics.* Cambridge: Cambridge University Press, 1997.
Sachs, Joe. "Aristotle: Motion and Its Place in Nature." *Internet Encyclopedia of Philosophy (IEP)*, 2005. http://www.iep.utm.edu/aris-mot.
———. *Aristotle's Physics: A Guided Study.* Masterworks of Discovery. New Brunswick, NJ: Rutgers University Press, 1995.
Schloss, Jeffrey P. "From Evolution to Eschatology." In *Resurrection: Theological and Scientific Assessments,* edited by Ted Peters, et al. Grand Rapids: Eerdmans, 2002.
Schönborn, Christoph von. *Man, the Image of God: The Creation of Man as Good News.* San Francisco: Ignatius, 2011.
Schwöbel, Christoph. "Human Being as Relational Being: Twelve Theses for a Christian Anthropology." In *Persons, Divine and Human: King's College Essays in Theological Anthropology,* edited by Christoph Schwöbel and Colin E. Gunton, 141–70. Edinburgh: T & T Clark, 1991.
Scorer, C. G. *Life in Our Hands: A Study in Human Values.* Leicester: InterVarsity, 1978.

Scott, Mark S. M. "God as Person: Karl Barth and Karl Rahner on Divine and Human Personhood." *Religious Studies and Theology* 25.2 (2006) 161–90.
Scotus, John Duns. *Early Oxford Lecture on Individuation*. Translated by Allan B. Wolter. St. Bonaventure: Franciscan Institute, 2005.
Shults, F. LeRon. "A Dubious Christological Formula: From Leontius of Byzantium to Karl Barth." *Theological Studies* 57.3 (1996) 431–46.
———. *Reforming Theological Anthropology: After the Philosophical Turn to Relationality*. Grand Rapids: Eerdmans, 2003.
Shutte, Augustine. "What Makes Us Person." *Modern Theology* 1.1 (1984) 67–79.
Spade, Paul Vincent. *Five Texts on the Medieval Problem of Universals: Porphyry, Boethius, Abelard, Duns Scotus, Ockham*. Cambridge: Hackett, 1994.
Spence, Alan. *Christology: A Guide for the Perplexed*. New York: T & T Clark, 2008.
Stout, Jeffrey. *The Flight from Authority: Religion, Morality, and the Quest for Autonomy*. London: Notre Dame, 1981.
Strawson, P. F. *Individuals: An Essay in Descriptive Metaphysics*. London: Methuen, 1959.
Swinburne, Richard. *The Christian God*. Oxford: Clarendon, 1994.
———. *The Coherence of Theism*. Oxford: Oxford University Press, 1977.
———. "The Structure of the Soul." In *Persons and Personality: A Contemporary Inquiry*, edited by Arthur Peacocke and Grant Gillett, 33–55. Oxford: Basil Blackwell, 1987.
Tanner, Kathryn. *Christ the Key*. Cambridge: Cambridge University Press, 2010.
———. *Jesus, Humanity, and the Trinity: A Brief Systematic Theology*. Minneapolis: Fortress, 2001.
Taylor, Charles. *Sources of the Self: The Making of the Modern Identity*. Cambridge: Cambridge University Press, 1989.
Tergel, Alf. "Human Rights and the Churches: Christian Conceptions of Human Rights." *Swedish Missiological Themes* 85.3 (1997) 309–24.
Thiel, John E. "Methodological Choices in Kelsey's Eccentric Existence." *Modern Theology* 27.1 (2011) 1–13.
———. "Methodological Choices in Kelsey's Eccentric Existence." In *The Theological Anthropology of David Kelsey: Responses to Eccentric Existence*, edited by Gene Outka, 1–15. Grand Rapids: Eerdmans, 2016.
Thiselton, Anthony C. *New Horizons in Hermeneutics*. London: Harper Collins, 1992.
Toren, Benno van den. *Christian Apologetics as Cross-Cultural Dialogue*. London: T & T Clark, 2011.
Torrance, Alan. *Persons in Communion: An Essay on Trinitarian Description and Human Participation with Special Reference to Volume One of Karl Barth's Church Dogmatics*. Edinburgh: T & T Clark, 1996.
Torrance, T. F. *Calvin's Doctrine of Man*. London: Lutterworth, 1949.
Tournier, Paul. *The Meaning of Persons*. Translated by Edwin Hudson. London: SCM, 1957.
Towner, W. Sibel. "Clones of God: Genesis 1:26–28 and the Image of God in the Hebrew Bible." *Interpretation* 59.4 (2005) 341–56.
Trueman, Robert. "Eliminating Identity: A Reply to Wehmeier." *Australasian Journal of Philosophy* 92.1 (2014) 165–72.
Tweedale, Martin M. *Scotus Vs. Ockham: A Medieval Dispute Over Universals*. Lewiston: Edwin Mellen, 1999.

Vidu, Adonis. *Postliberal Theological Method: A Critical Study*. Milton Keynes: Paternoster, 2005.

Visala, Aku. "Imago Dei, Dualism, and Evolution: A Philosophical Defense of the Structural Image of God." *Zygon* 49.1 (2014) 101–20.

Volf, Miroslav. *After Our Likeness: The Church as the Image of the Trinity*. Grand Rapids: Eerdmans, 1998.

———. *Exclusion and Embrace: A Theological Exploration of Identity, Otherness, and Reconciliation*. Nashville: Abingdon, 1996.

Waldrop, Charles T. *Karl Barth's Christology: Its Basic Alexandrian Character*. Berlin: Mouton, 1984.

Walker Bynum, Caroline. *The Resurrection of the Body in Western Christianity: 200–1336*. New York: Columbia University Press, 1995.

Wallace, Mark I. *The Second Naiveté: Barth, Ricoeur and the New Yale Theology*. Macoon: Mercer University Press, 1990.

Waltke, Bruce K. *Creation and Chaos: An Exegetical and Theological Study of Biblical Cosmogony*. Portland: Western Conservative Baptist Seminary, 1974.

Ward, Heather. *Giving Your Self Away*. Nottingham: Grove, 1988.

Wehmeier, Kai F. "How to Live Without Identity-And Why." *Australasian Journal of Philosophy* 90.4 (2012) 761–77.

Weiss, Paul. "On the Difference between Actuality and Possibility." *Review of Metaphysics* 10.1 (1956) 165–71.

Wells, Sam. "Review of Eccentric Existence: A Theological Anthropology." *Christian Century* 127.9 (2012) 35–37.

White, Lynn Jr. "The Historical Roots of Our Ecologic Crisis." *Science, New Series* 155.3767 (1967) 1203–7.

White, Roger. "Wittgenstein on Identity." *Proceedings of the Aristotelian Society* 78.1 (1977) 157–74.

White, Vernon. *Identity*. London: SCM, 2002.

Wildman, Wesley J. "A Theological Challenge: Coordinating Biological, Social, and Religious Visions of Humanity." *Zygon* 33.4 (1998) 571–97.

Williams, C. J. F. *What Is Identity?* Oxford: Clarendon, 1989.

Williams, Reginald. "Abortion, Potential, and Value." *Utilitas* 20.2 (2008) 169–86.

Williams, Thomas. "John Duns Scotus." *Stanford Encyclopedia of Philosophy*, January 12, 2015. http://plato.stanford.edu/entries/duns-scotus.

Witt, Charlotte. *Ways of Being: Potentiality and Actuality in Aristotle's Metaphysics*. New York: Cornell University Press, 2003.

Wittgenstein, Ludwig. *Philosophical Investigations*. Translated by G. E. M. Anscombe. 2nd ed. Oxford: Blackwell, 1958.

———. *Tractatus Logico-Philosophicus*. London: Routledge & Kegan, 1922.

Wood, Charles M. "A Response to Eccentric Existence." In *The Theological Anthropology of David Kelsey: Responses to Eccentric Existence*, edited by Gene Outka, 16–30. Grand Rapids: Eerdmans, 2016.

Wootten, Janet. "Yuri Milner and Stephen Hawking Announce $100 Million Breakthrough Initiative to Dramatically Accelerate Search for Intelligent Life in the Universe." *Break Through Initiatives*, July 20, 2015. http://www.breakthroughinitiatives.org/News/1.

Wright, John, ed. *Postliberal Theology and the Church Catholic: Conversations with George Lindbeck, David Burrell, and Stanley Hauerwas.* Grand Rapids: Baker Academic, 2012.

Zizioulas, John D. *Being as Communion: Studies in Personhood and the Church.* London: Darton, Longman & Todd, 1985.

———. "Human Capacity and Human Incapacity: A Theological Exploration of Personhood." *Scottish Journal of Theology* 28.5 (1975) 401–47.

———. "On Being a Person: Towards and Ontology of Personhood." In *Persons, Divine and Human: King's College Essays in Theological Anthropology*, edited by Christoph Schwöbel and Colin E. Gunton. Edinburgh: T & T Clark, 1991.

www.ingramcontent.com/pod-product-compliance
Lightning Source LLC
Chambersburg PA
CBHW050440240426
43661CB00055B/2455